Violent Delinquents

A Report to the Ford Foundation
From the Vera Institute of Justice

PAUL A. STRASBURG

MONARCH

Published by Monarch
A Simon & Schuster Division of
Gulf & Western Corporation
Simon & Schuster Building
1230 Avenue of the Americas
New York, New York 10020

Manufactured in the United States of America

1 2 3 4 5 6 7 8 9 10

Library of Congress Cataloging in Publication Data

Strasburg, Paul A.
  Violent delinquents.

  Bibliography: p.
  1.   Juvenile delinquency—United States.   2.   Violence
—United States.   I.   Title.
HV9104.S83   364.36′0973   77-17819
ISBN 0-671-18346-X

Contents

List of Tables and Figures

Foreword

JUVENILE VIOLENCE in this country has become a major concern of the mass media, of professionals in the juvenile justice system, and of ordinary citizens, who are often the victims of it and who even more often feel it as an oppressive fear in their daily lives. Paul Strasburg's *Violent Delinquents* is a thorough and illuminating examination of this problem that perplexes all of us.

Part of the problem is the question of whether today's juveniles are more violent than those of previous generations. Mr. Strasburg properly focusses on the conflicting evidence we have on this point. The available statistics do depict drastic increases in juvenile arrests—141 percent since 1960. The bulk of these, however, turn out to be for property crimes. His study also reveals that arrests for violent crimes committed by juveniles—homicide, forcible rape, robbery, and aggravated assault—have increased by 293 percent from 1960 to 1975 as compared to an increase of 130 percent for the same crimes committed by adults. But those juvenile arrests represented only 10 percent of the arrests for serious juvenile crime in 1975, and only 4 percent of all juvenile arrests. On the other hand, actual arrests may be only the tip of the iceberg; studies of anonymous "self reports" by large numbers of youngsters seem to show that they commit many more offenses than ever reach the juvenile courts.

Another part of the problem is that our juvenile courts and corrections institutions indiscriminately incarcerate non-violent status offenders with the more serious offenders. This approach has had negative effects on both groups of youngsters, as is shown by Mr. Strasburg's study and, time and time again, in testimony before the Senate Subcommittee to Investigate Juvenile Delinquency, which I chaired.

Thus, much of the information presented in Mr. Strasburg's report to the Ford Foundation reflects the need for a long-awaited reform of the juvenile justice system, which my Juvenile Justice and Delinquency Prevention Act has attempted to address. To assist state and local governments as well as individual and private organizations in their effort to provide an alternative, the Congress overwhelmingly approved and President Carter on October 3, 1977, signed into law my three-year extension of the Juvenile Justice and Delinquency Prevention Act of 1974. This legislation is designed to prevent young people from entering our failing juvenile justice system, to assist communities in developing more sensible and economic approaches for youngsters already in the juvenile justice system, and to provide $600 million through fiscal year 1980 to strengthen, continue and stabilize on a long-term basis the 1974 Congressional-citizen initiative which established juvenile crime prevention as *the* federal priority in the criminal justice area.

We still lack the funds and facilities necessary to provide an atmosphere where status offenders and delinquent youngsters—including the relatively few violent ones—can be given the necessary treatment, care, and counseling that they so desperately need in order to become more productive citizens. We have begun to provide alternatives, but much work is still needed to implement the Juvenile Justice Act satisfactorily.

As a legislator who is intensely concerned about the fate of our young people, I welcome contributions such as Paul Strasburg's *Violent Delinquents.* I believe his study will draw attention to and generate further discussions on the problems encountered by our juvenile justice system, which must handle not only our violent juvenile offenders, but also our non-violent status offenders. It is our responsibility to bring these matters to the attention of all our citizens so that together we can offer both our youngsters and our troubled communities a future worthy of anticipation.

Senator Birch Bayh
Chairman, Subcommittee on the Constitution,
Committee on the Judiciary

Preface

THIS BOOK presents the findings of a year-long study of the problem of juvenile violence, undertaken in my capacity as a staff member of the Vera Institute of Justice at the request of the Ford Foundation. At the time the study began, I knew little about this problem, although it had become such a prominent subject of media coverage and everyday conversation that a close look at the underlying facts seemed to be a worthwhile endeavor. Since then, I have received a considerable education, not only from the study itself but also from numerous discussions with colleagues at Vera and the Ford Foundation and with experts elsewhere, about what its results mean. I have discovered, above all, the impossibility of making a definitive statement about juvenile violence, especially within the framework of a single, limited study like this one. Nevertheless, in the end it seemed that the study had uncovered enough information of general interest to warrant release for wider examination.

Among many pressing issues of criminal justice, juvenile violence was selected for special study not because it is necessarily the most significant, but because of the controversy it has generated in recent years. That controversy threatens to engulf the entire juvenile justice system, producing demands for drastic changes that could reach well beyond the violent offender. The philosophy and rhetoric of juvenile courts have traditionally tended to blur the distinction between violence and other kinds of delinquency. The child, not the crime, has been the focus of policy. Now the pendulum is swinging to the other side, and the crime—the violent one, at least—is becoming more important than the child who commits it. In the process, subtler issues, important to all children brought before juvenile courts, are in danger of being slighted or disregarded altogether. To the extent that juvenile violence can be better understood, we felt that the chances for a calmer, more rational assessment of the entire system might be improved.

The study included a general literature search and discussions with judges, lawyers, probation officers, psychiatrists, researchers, administrators, and other professionals dealing with delinquents, as well as with a number of juveniles with violent histories. It included visits to programs and projects dealing with delinquents in a variety of ways. The study also involved analysis of over 500 court records of juveniles in three counties in the New York metropolitan region, in order to determine firsthand the extent and nature of violence among children seen by the courts and the courts' responses to them.

Although it covered a wide range of issues relating to juvenile violence, it would be misleading to call the study "comprehensive." One significant limitation is its concentration on delinquents apprehended by the police and subsequently caught up in the juvenile justice system. There were both substantive and procedural reasons for this choice, perhaps the most important was that data regarding apprehended delinquents are much easier to obtain than data on offenders and offenses that escape official detection. The practical consequence of the choice, however, is that the study concerns only a part (perhaps only a small part) of youth violence in our society (i.e., the violence committed by known juvenile delinquents). Many readers of preliminary versions of the study have found that to be a substantial shortcoming.

Another deficiency of the data collected by the criminal justice system is that they tell us almost nothing about causes, about why delinquents commit the crimes they do. Because this study is so largely based on these criminal justice data, it has nothing new to offer on that vital subject. Unfortunately, a review of available literature also indicates that this question has not yet been answered satisfactorily by other research approaches. Consequently, readers seeking to learn why some children become violent and others do not will find this study disappointing.

The strongest impression the study will leave on many readers is that the discussions of juvenile violence that dominate academic journals and the media today are grounded on a pitifully weak base of factual knowledge. This has been recognized by criminologists and other researchers in this field for some time. Nevertheless, I hoped to uncover at least a few solid pockets of information and a few promising ideas for dealing with juvenile violence that could be built on and tested systematically. Failing that, I hoped for some creative insight that would point the way to worthwhile experiments. Limited though they were, the study fell short of these hopes, but I did emerge convinced that this dark continent merits continued exploration, even if there is no immediate promise that definitive answers will be found.

Although I bear full responsibility for any errors, omissions, inconsistencies, and plain wrongheadedness that may be found in this book, I must share credit for anything of value with many people. My colleagues at the Vera Institute and the Ford Foundation provided counsel, criticism, and encouragement at every step. Special thanks go to Herb Sturz at Vera and Mike Sviridoff at Ford. Lucy Friedman at Vera and Peter Abrams at the Calculogic Corporation also provided valuable advice on research methodology. I am deeply indebted to the research assistants who helped me gather and analyze data for the study: Philip Barber, Patti Fager, Alan Heaps, Carolyn Kunin, David Prather, Carmen Rivera, and Mary Farrow, whose untimely death saddened all of us who worked with her. In addition, I want to thank Rosemary Johnston, whose extraordinary patience and skill were sorely tested in producing the manuscript of this study, and LaVerne Slade, who helped in that task. Last but not least, I must record my gratitude to my wife, Katherine, who cheerfully tolerated disorder and neglect while I struggled to make sense out of the piles of data and boxes of notes we had collected.

The list of people consulted in the course of this study—professionals working in or with the juvenile justice system as well as juveniles caught up in it—is too long for individual thanks. But it was their willingness to share their experiences and observations that turned what otherwise would have been a largely academic exercise into a rare and stimulating learning experience for me.

PAUL A. STRASBURG

1 Introduction

WHEN THE CONCEPT of a separate system of justice for juveniles took hold in the early part of the twentieth century, it was hailed as a major step toward enlightened treatment of children. No longer would the state react to delinquents as threats to society, with harsh punishments closely resembling those meted out to adults. Instead, delinquent children were seen as needing "parenting," which would be supplied by the state, acting through the juvenile courts in "the best interests of the child"—the *parens patriae* doctrine.

Juvenile courts have never fully worked out the philosophical conflict between their assigned role as guardians of children's interests and the traditional role of all courts as protectors of the social order. Three-quarters of the way through the century, the tension between those two roles has reached a point that threatens to destroy the foundation on which the juvenile justice system was built. Evidence is mounting that the courts' powers to serve the interests of children are limited. Some carry the argument further to say that court intervention into the lives of children, *parens patriae* notwithstanding, is more harmful than helpful. The evidence has been sufficiently persuasive to stimulate large-scale diversion of children away from juvenile court whenever possible.

1

The other side of the coin is equally tarnished. The juvenile justice system has been severely criticized for its seeming ineffectiveness in controlling the antisocial behavior of young people. In the face of soaring juvenile arrest rates over the past decade and longer, critics have sharpened their attack, accusing the courts of encouraging delinquent behavior with ambivalent, inconsistent treatment of young offenders.

The response of the juvenile justice system to this attack appears to be confusion. New approaches are proposed and tried with increasing frequency, often moving the system simultaneously in contradictory directions. Harsher penalties and more diversion are called for at the same time. California moves to transfer responsibility for juvenile corrections to local jurisdictions, while Florida moves to centralize its corrections system. The New York State legislature attempts to give judges more control over juvenile dispositions, as Kentucky passes a law to diminish judges' roles in that area. Alaska begins to embrace the rehabilitation model just as California is abandoning it. Everything seems to be going in circles. Nothing seems certain, proven, accepted.

In this confused atmosphere, public concern has focused on violent juvenile crime as a problem that stands out clearly, even if a solution does not. As we will see, arrests for violence have been growing at a faster pace than arrests for other kinds of juvenile crime for more than a decade. The character of juvenile violence also appears, in the public eye at least, to be changing for the worse. Media attention to murders, rapes, and other heinous crimes involving juveniles has created a belief, accurate or not, that today's delinquents are more ruthless, more dangerous than their predecessors in earlier years. Many people have thus come to associate a widely perceived increase in "urban terror" with the rise of a "new breed" of delinquents, and the conviction is spreading that current practices afford inadequate protection against them.

The truth behind this impression is not easy to capture. Isolated descriptions of violent acts by juveniles, no matter how frequently they appear, tell little about the scope of the problem or whether it is increasing or not. Nor do portraits of individual offenders, no matter how detailed and evocative, provide a valid description of juvenile delinquents as a group—if, indeed, such a description is possible at all. Similarly, it is impossible to discern from a few highly publicized cases the overall approach of the courts to the question of juvenile violence.

The study on which this book is based was an effort to dig below the surface of the problem of juvenile violence in several ways. It began with an extensive, although not exhaustive, search of the literature on juvenile violence, its causes and treatment, and official responses to it. When it became apparent that the literature contained little reliable information about the current magnitude of this particular problem, a decision was made to study juvenile court records in three counties of metropolitan New York to learn more about the crimes of violence committed by juveniles brought before the courts—the number of violent crimes, the number of delinquents committing them, and the seriousness of their consequences. In addition, interviews were conducted with sixty-nine judges, lawyers, prosecutors, psychiatrists, probation officers, program administrators, and researchers, and informal discussions were held with many others whose work is directly or indirectly concerned with this issue. Finally, visits were made to a number of programs that house, treat, or provide services to juveniles who are in trouble with the law.

One of the first and largest stumbling blocks encountered in this (or any) study of violence is the difficulty of defining the meaning of the term and sorting the violent from the nonviolent. The difficulty is illustrated by the two definitions of violence given in the *Random House Dictionary of the English Language:* "rough or immoderate vehemence, as of feeling or language," and "rough or injurious physical force, action or treatment." No one is immune to immoderate vehemence of feeling throughout life, and in that sense we are all violent sometimes. Yet, at the other extreme, no person who engages in rough or injurious physical force does so at all times, so neither is anyone totally violent. What point on the spectrum from feeling to action do we have in mind when we label a person violent?

Because the study dealt with criminal behavior of juveniles, the term "violence" is used generally to mean the illegal threat or use of force. But what acts does that encompass? Against whom or what? And how often must a person engage in such acts to warrant being identified as "violent"? It is important to be clear about these issues, but it is impossible to be precise without also being arbitrary.

We decided to focus on acts of physical force directed against people instead of property, although it is clear that some "property" crimes (arson, for example) can result in severe injury or death. In individual cases, it is useful to examine the details of serious property crimes to understand what they imply about the violence of the criminal, but in a broad survey it becomes unwieldy to include such ambiguous categories of behavior. Therefore, in this book the term "violence" refers to acts of homicide, forcible rape (or sodomy), robbery, assault, or attempts at any of these.

Homicide and sex offenses clearly fit within most definitions of violence. Robbery and assault present some problems, however. Robbery, unlike homicide, rape, or assault, may involve only the threat, but not the use of force. It thus encompasses situations in which violence may be more controlled in the actor and used with greater calculation. This raises the possibility that some robbers may be different from those who commit other kinds of violence. Moreover, because the objective of robbery is the taking of money or property, it might as legitimately be labeled a property crime as a violent crime.

Particularly with regard to juveniles, there is suspicion that offenses identified as robberies by police frequently involve little more than threats used to extort money or take a bicycle from another child, or a purse snatcher on the run. On the other hand, even for these crimes the fear created in the victim is real and cannot be disregarded. There is an intent to act in a way that produces fear, and that itself might legitimately be called violence. Consequently, to help distinguish acts according to the degree of violence employed, the analysis divides robberies into armed, injury, combination (armed and injury), and less serious robberies.

Assault creates similar problems. Although it accords with the general definition of a violent crime, it also covers a range of events that differ substantially with regard to seriousness, provocation, and other factors important in drawing inferences about violence.

Whenever possible, we attempted to exclude from the analysis minor assaults that by themselves say little about the violent or antisocial nature of the actor.

Possession of dangerous weapons, an increasing problem among juveniles, is another ambiguous category, like arson. The possession of weapons may be an index of premeditation in many cases; certainly it escalates the risk of serious consequences in a violent encounter. Possession, however, does not necessarily imply intent to use or threaten use of the weapon, especially in some ghetto areas where, it is said, many young people deem it necessary for self-defense or "status" reasons to be armed in some manner. Moreover, the definition of a "dangerous" weapon varies widely and is not infrequently arbitrary. Therefore, although possession of weapons is taken into account in some parts of the analysis, possession is not included within the definition of violent crimes.

In the course of this study I was impressed by the number of acts resulting in arrests of juveniles (even those labeled violent) that do not seem to fit the usual conception of what constitutes a crime. Schoolyard fights, children striking adults who threaten them, minor acts of extortion: all appear with high frequency in police and court records, particularly, it seems, with regard to poor and minority juveniles. The records may not present the whole picture, of course, but on the basis of the available evidence, I must agree with the conclusion of another study of assaultive boys.

> The forbidding legal names of their offenses (Armed Robbery, Assault and Battery with a Dangerous Weapon, Homicide) both represent these boys at their worst and may even over-represent that worst. . . . The minor-league quality of most of what pass for "assaults" is the most striking finding from the general point of view. . . .[1]

We took pains to include within our definition of violent offenses only those on which broad agreement could be expected, eliminating those of obvious "minor-league" quality, but it is also important to recognize that, from the point of view of the people in the street, "violence" probably means much more. Acts such as arson, vandal-

[1] D. H. Russell and G. P. Harper, "Who Are Our Assaultive Juveniles? A Study of 100 Cases," *Journal of Forensic Sciences* 18 (October 1973): 385–397.

ism, subway "marauding," disorderly conduct, and others create fear in residents of cities and contribute to the overall impression that violence is accelerating rapidly. This study does not pretend to be a thorough analysis of the problem of violence as perceived by the general public. Instead, it is an attempt to understand the relatively small part of the problem that is reflected in the most serious crimes of violence against persons.

Violent acts are identified in this study principally by arrests, which raises another troubling issue. The number of juvenile arrests that are never formally adjudicated is striking. Although diversion programs and high dismissal rates may be desirable, they leave many arrests without a clear resolution. Moreover, in many adjudicated cases, the record does not indicate the specific charge on which a finding is made. As a result, it is speculative to equate crimes charged with crimes committed. Maintaining the distinction throughout a study of this length becomes ponderous for the writer and tedious for the reader, and I will not attempt it. I do want to make clear, however, that I do not mean to imply that crimes attributed to juveniles in official records are in all cases crimes that they actually committed.

It would be somewhat artificial to consider the violent acts of juveniles without reference to other illegal behavior, even though violence is the subject of this study. Consequently, patterns of delinquent behavior, including concepts such as "recidivism," "chronic offending," and "seriousness," are frequently mentioned. But these terms, relating to the number of offenses and degree of damage or harm done, are not used as substitutes for the term "violence," which is reserved for the specific acts outlined.

Beyond classifying acts as violent or not, classifying offenders is even more complicated. Particularly when discussing adolescents, whose behavior is volatile and often tumultuous, and even more particularly when discussing adolescents subjected to the intense frustration and provocation faced by many living in inner-city ghettos, the line dividing an abnormally violent personality from a "normal" one is not always clear. To cope with this problem, we tried to draw boundaries around the group under consideration without adopting an inflexible standard. On the one hand, no delinquent was classified as violent unless he or she had been charged with one of the narrow range of designated offenses. On the other hand, individuals to whom this label applies are further described according to the frequency with which they commit violent offenses and the seriousness of the harm that they inflict. This approach strikes what I considered to be a reasonable balance between flexibility and precision, given the serious limitations of the data on which the study is based. Nevertheless, I am acutely aware that this classification scheme, however cautiously applied, remains an oversimplification that runs the risk of both overstating and understating the size of the violent subgroup of delinquents.

The term "dangerous" is not used as a substitute for the term "violent" in this study, because "dangerous" usually has a connotation of predictable future behavior that should be avoided. Virtually all studies of the prediction of violence agree that it cannot be done within tolerable limits of error.[2] Moreover, the most reliable index of dangerousness (although not very reliable itself) is the commission of a violent act.[3] Consequently, a violent act is a more useful guideline than a vague standard like "dangerousness."

Although the concept is also vague, pinpointing what is meant by "juvenile" is easier than defining violence. In the broadest sense, a juvenile is a person who is physically and mentally immature, but the age at which a person achieves maturity is obviously not uniform. Reason and self-control, the capacity to inflict harm on others, or the ability to understand consequences and change behavior patterns are not qualities that develop evenly in all children. In some of these respects a 15-year-old may resemble an 18-year-old, whereas in other respects he or she may be more like a 13-year-old. Nevertheless, an age limit on the population under study was obviously necessary.

[2] See, for example, Ernst Wenk, James O. Robison, and Gerald W. Smith, "Can Violence be Predicted?" *Crime and Delinquency* 18, no. 4 (October 1972): 393–402. The authors conclude that "the quest for an operationally practical predictor of violence from simple classification appears to be futile." Also see Norval Morris, *The Future of Imprisonment* (Chicago: University of Chicago Press, 1974) pp. 62–63; A. M. Dershowitz, "The Law of Dangerousness: Some Fictions About Predictions," *Journal of Legal Education* 23 (1970): 24–56; and J. J. Cocozza and H. J. Steadman, "Some Refinements in the Measurement and Prediction of Dangerous Behavior," *American Journal of Psychiatry* 131, no. 9 (1974): 1012–1014.

[3] See Harry L. Kozol, Richard J. Boucher, and Ralph Garofalo, "The Diagnosis and Treatment of Dangerousness," *Crime and Delinquency* 18, no. 4 (October 1972): 384.

For convenience, we opted to define a juvenile as a person under the jurisdiction of the juvenile court. The age of juvenile court jurisdiction varies throughout the country, however. In thirty-three states and the District of Columbia, juvenile status ceases at age 18. In twelve others it ceases at age 17, and in the remaining six (including New York) at age 16.[4] In spite of this complication, a legal definition of juvenile status is best suited to most of the purposes of this study. When the term "juvenile" is used, therefore, it generally means a person under the jurisdiction of the juvenile court by virtue of age. When this somewhat flexible legal definition is not appropriate (as it may not be, for example, in discussing national arrest data), we have drawn the upper limit at 18, simply because that is the most widely accepted standard.

To summarize, the terms on which this study centers have many denotations and connotations in their common usage. No definition imposed on them would satisfy everyone; any definition will include usages that are not liked by some and will exclude usages preferred by others. The best I can hope to do is be clear about what I mean. These terms, and the meanings attached to them, are as follows.

Violence (or violent crime): Any act of homicide, forcible rape, assault, or robbery, or any attempt at one of these acts.

Serious violence (or serious violent crimes): Acts of homicide; forcible rape; robbery in which a weapon is used or the victim is injured; and assaults in which more than minor injury is inflicted (i.e., the victim is at least treated by a physician). Attempted homicide and rape are included. Attempted robbery is included if a weapon is used or the victim is injured. Attempted assault is not included.

Serious crimes: Any of the seven major offenses listed in the FBI's Uniform Crime Reports: homicide, forcible rape, robbery, aggravated assault, larceny-theft, burglary, and auto theft.

[4] Mark M. Levin and Rosemary C. Sarri, *Juvenile Delinquency: A Study of Juvenile Codes in the U.S.*, National Assessment of Juvenile Corrections, 1974, p. 13. In two of the six states with an upper age limit of 15, the juvenile court can adjudicate 16- and 17-year-olds at the discretion of the prosecutor. In many states, moreover, juvenile court jurisdiction can vary with the category of crime charged.

Juvenile: A person under the jurisdiction of the juvenile or family court by virtue of age. (When no specific jurisdiction is referred to, a juvenile may be considered a person under the age of 18.)

Delinquent: A juvenile who has been charged by the police with an illegal act other than a status offense, whether or not the charge constitutes a formal arrest.

Violent delinquent: A juvenile charged at least once with any violent crime.

Seriously violent delinquent: A juvenile charged at least once with a serious violent crime.

Recidivist: A juvenile charged on two or more occasions with an offense, including at least one delinquent act.

Violent recidivist: A juvenile charged two or more times with any violent crime.

Seriously violent recidivist: A juvenile charged two or more times with any serious violent crime.

Chronic delinquent: A delinquent with five or more charges in his record.

Unless otherwise stated in the text, these are the definitions that we have in mind when these terms are used.

These definitions reflect the main focus of this study: youths who become known to the juvenile justice system as a result of being apprehended for criminal acts. Yet, there is considerable evidence (some of which will be discussed in subsequent chapters) that only a fraction of illegal acts result in arrest. Whether the arrest rate is higher or lower for violent crimes than for crimes in general, it seems clear that a substantial amount of violence cannot be dealt with by taking direct action against the offenders, because they are never caught. A comprehensive strategy for reducing violence must include both a plan for dealing with known violent offenders and a plan for preventing violent crimes in the first place.

Data relevant to prevention strategies are scarce. On the other hand, while great quantities of data on arrested delinquents exist (in the FBI's Uniform Crime Reports, in other research publications, and in court records), their quality and completeness are frequently in question. We are stuck, it seems, between a shortage of information needed to deal with half the problem and an abundance of information about the other half that is not wholly reliable.

In the face of this dilemma, I have chosen to lean more heavily toward the side of the abundant if not altogether reliable data, knowing their limitations and attempting to work around them. Most of the discussion, therefore, concerns youths arrested for violent crimes, and the principal recommendations arising from the study relate to improving the way they are handled. Because the other side of the equation is so important, however, the question of prevention is also discussed, less extensively, in Chapter 6.

2 The Scope of the Problem

THERE ARE MANY VIEWPOINTS but no clear perspectives on the significance of juvenile violence today. Definitional disputes are only partly responsible for the confusion. Even when there is agreement on what is to be measured, there is no agreement on the proper way to measure it or on what the yardstick says.

The most meaningful measure of the scope of the problem would be the number of violent acts by juveniles, whether or not the offender is caught. An obvious difficulty arises, however, in that unless the offender is identified, it is usually difficult to know whether the act was committed by a juvenile or not. Reported felonies, independent of arrests, have more than tripled in the past fifteen years. Violent crimes have grown slightly faster than non-violent crimes; robbery leads the list with a fourfold increase between 1960 and 1975. Yet not only do reported crimes say nothing about the age of the offender; they also understate the real magnitude of criminal activity generally, since many offenses are never reported to the police.

In an attempt to overcome this deficiency, surveys of the population have been employed in recent years to determine rates of victimization. These surveys indicate that about half of all felonies committed are reported to the police. In New York City, the figure

11

is somewhat higher for rape and robbery (about 60 percent) and somewhat lower for assault (about 40 percent). Again, however, the victimization surveys are unable to shed much light on the proportion of those crimes that are committed by juveniles.

A meaningful estimate of the number of children engaging in criminal violence, instead of the number of acts, and whether that number is increasing, is possible only by examining several different kinds of evidence, each deficient in some important way. Even this process does not yield a definitive answer, because the gaps separating the various ways of measuring the problem are wide and can be bridged only by guesswork.

Three common measures of the extent of juvenile violence will be analyzed briefly—arrest data, self-report studies, and cohort analyses. The results of these measures will be compared to each other and to the data we collected from court records in the New York metropolitan region. From those sources, an informed guess about the scope of the problem can be made.

Arrest Data

In 1975, police reported 2.1 million arrests of juveniles under the age of 18 for all categories of crime. Thus juveniles aged 7 to 18, who constituted 20 percent of the nation's population that year, accounted for 26 percent of all arrests.[1] Juveniles were heavily overrepresented in arrests for serious crimes. Approximately 43 percent of arrests for the seven serious offenses in the FBI's crime index involved juveniles.

Property crimes are the real specialty of juveniles, however. Juveniles accounted for slightly less than half of all arrests for serious property crimes and only 23 percent of all arrests for violent crimes. As Table 1 shows, 90 percent of all juvenile arrests for serious crimes in 1975 involved offenses against property; only 10 percent involved offenses against persons. Among violent crimes, juveniles were most often arrested for robbery (one-third of all arrests for that crime), followed by aggravated assault, rape, and homicide, in that order.

[1] Unless otherwise stated, arrest figures are taken from the FBI's 1975 Uniform Crime Reports.

Table 1 1975 Arrests for Serious Crimes, Nationally, by Age Group (in percent)

	Juveniles (under 18)	Adults (18 and over)
Property Crimes		
Larceny-Theft	52.7	48.7
Burglary	28.8	19.7
Auto Theft	8.0	5.1
	89.5	73.5
Violent Crimes		
Homicide	0.2	1.6
Forcible Rape	0.5	1.7
Robbery	5.4	7.9
Aggravated Assault	4.3	15.4
	10.4	26.6
	99.9[a]	100.1[a]
Total Arrests for Serious Crimes		
	819,561	1,082,250

SOURCE: 1975 FBI Uniform Crime Reports.

[a] Errors in percents are due to rounding.

The most criminally active juvenile ages are 13 through 17. That age group accounted for 92 percent of juvenile arrests for violent crimes in 1975. Although they make up only 10 percent of the total population, 13- through 17-year-olds were responsible for 21 percent of all arrests for violence in 1975—32 percent of robberies, 17 percent of rapes, 16 percent of aggravated assaults, and 9 percent of homicides.

These data indicate that violence, although not as extensive as property crime, is indeed a serious problem among juveniles age 13 or older. But is juvenile violence increasing?

As Table 2 shows, juvenile arrests for violent crimes have risen sharply, climbing 293 percent between 1960 and 1975. Robbery led the list, increasing 375 percent in the period, followed by aggravated assault (240 percent), homicide (211 percent), and rape (102 percent). Meanwhile, juvenile arrests for serious property crimes, much higher to begin with, rose by a smaller margin

(132 percent). The rate of increase in juvenile arrests for violence was more than twice the adult rate.

Table 2 Average Annual Increase in Juvenile and Adult Arrests, Nationally (in percent)

	1960–70	1970–75	1974–75	Total % Increase 1960–75
Juvenile Arrests				
Violent Crimes[a]	10.3	9.0	10.3	293.4
Property Crimes[b]	6.6	4.4	1.9	131.9
All Serious Crimes[c]	6.9	4.8	2.8	144.1
Adult Arrests				
Violent Crimes[a]	5.2	6.6	3.6	130.1
Property Crimes[b]	6.4	7.5	11.3	155.4
All Serious Crimes[c]	6.0	7.2	9.1	146.7

SOURCE: 1975 FBI Uniform Reports.

[a] Homicide, forcible rape, robbery, aggravated assault.
[b] Larceny, burglary, auto theft.
[c] Total of violent and property crimes.

Table 2 also shows that juvenile arrests grew faster in the 1960s than in the years since 1970. The annual average increase in arrests for all serious crimes was 6.9 percent between 1960 and 1970, dropping to 4.8 percent between 1970 and 1975. The decline in the latter years was largely attributable to a slowdown in the growth of property arrests, however. The average annual rate of increase in arrests for violence dipped only slightly from 10.3 percent before 1970 to 9.0 percent after 1970. (The increase was back up to 10.3 percent in the final year of the period.)

Adult arrest rates are moving in the opposite direction from juvenile rates for violence and property crime. Although the increase in juvenile property arrests is slowing down, adult property arrests are picking up at an increasingly rapid pace. On the other hand, increases in adult arrests for violent crimes are slowing, although juvenile violence arrests continue to increase steadily. Between 1974 and 1975, juvenile arrests for violence increased three times as much as adult arrests, while adult arrests for property crimes increased five times as much as juvenile property arrests.

Demographic changes were an important factor in these changing arrest rates. The baby boom of the post-World War II years produced, in the 1960s, an unprecedented 52 percent increase in the size of the adolescent population—five times the average increase of the previous seven decades. The social strain accompanying that explosion is a familiar, if not too pleasant, memory. Juvenile delinquency was one among many forms of alienation that seemed to come into their own. Toward the end of the decade, however, almost as quickly as it had come, the flood began to recede: the rate of growth in the adolescent population dropped back into the "normal" range and is expected to work out to about 11 percent for the 1970s.[2]

To get an accurate picture of changes in juvenile behavior, undistorted by changes in the juvenile population, it is necessary to take the demographic base into account by measuring the arrest rate per 100,000 children aged 7–17, the most common range of juvenile court jurisdiction. Table 3 summarizes arrest rates for violent crimes and property crimes between 1960 and 1975. Rates for violent crimes have tripled since 1960, and rates for property crimes have more than doubled. The arrest rate for violent crimes grew at a fairly steady pace throughout the period (except for a sharp decline in the final year, 1974–75, which may be an aberration), but the increase in the property crime arrest rate slowed noticeably after 1970. On the basis of these calculations, one must conclude that juvenile violence (but not property crime) has grown steadily since 1960, independent of the growth in the number of juveniles.

A comparision of arrest rates by age group is instructive. Table 4 shows rates for various violent crimes by three age groups: 11 through 14, 15 through 17, and 18 through 24. (Children under 10 are excluded because they represent a very small fraction of arrests

[2] Daniel P. Moynihan, "Peace—Some Thoughts on the 1960's and 1970's," *The Public Interest* no. 32 (Summer 1973): 3–12. The adolescent population measured in these calculations includes ages 14 to 24. According to the article, data were calculated by Professor Norman Ryder. Professor Ryder has characterized this phenomenon in even more colorful terms as " 'a perennial invasion of barbarians' who must somehow be civilized and made to contribute to society. In 1960 the 'defending army' of those between 25 and 64 was three times the size of the 'invading army' of youths aged 14 to 24. Now the defenders are only twice the number of the invaders and seem to be losing control of the battle to assimilate and socialize the young." (Quoted in *Time*, June 30, 1975, p. 17.)

Table 3 Arrests per 100,000 Population, Ages 7 through 17, Nationally

	Violent Crime[a]	Property Crime[b]	All Serious Crime[c]
Arrest Rates			
1960	78.0	811.0	889.0
1970	175.0	1644.6	1819.6
1974	256.4	2209.6	2466.0
1975	258.6	2148.7	2407.3
Average Annual Percentage Change			
1960–70	+8.4	+7.3	+7.4
1970–75	+8.1	+5.5	+5.8
1974–75	+0.9	−2.8	−2.4
Total Percentage Change			
1960–75	231.5%	164.9%	170.8%

SOURCE: 1975 FBI Uniform Crime Reports and Census Bureau data.

[a] Homicide, forcible rape, robbery, aggravated assault.
[b] Larceny, burglary, auto theft.
[c] Total of violent and property crimes.

for violent crimes.) In 1970, the young adult (18–24) group had the highest arrest rate, followed by older juveniles (15–17) and younger juveniles (11–14). Between 1970 and 1975, however, the arrest rate of older juveniles increased nearly three times as fast as the rate of young adults, so that by 1975, the overall violence arrest rate of older juveniles was higher than the young adult rate. Most of this difference was accounted for by robbery and aggravated assault: the older juveniles' robbery rate grew more than twice as fast as the young adults' robbery rate, and their arrest rate for aggravated assault increased at three times the young adults' rate. Younger juveniles also showed a sharp increase in the arrest rate for aggravated assault, which accounted for an overall increase in their violence arrest rate that was twice the young adults' increase.

Juvenile violence, like violence in general, has been more common in urban centers than in suburban and rural areas since national arrest statistics were first compiled. In 1975, the FBI's Uniform Crime Reports indicated that fifty-eight cities with over 250,000 inhabitants generated 51 percent of all reported major vio-

Table 4 Arrests Nationally per 100,000 by Age Group and Crime, 1970 and 1975

	Homicide	Forcible Rape	Robbery	Aggravated Assault	Total Violent Crime
1970					
Age 11–14	1.6	5.0	73.7	49.5	129.8
Age 15–17	15.5	29.4	224.2	160.0	429.1
Age 18–24	29.0	37.1	209.1	206.6	481.8
1975					
Age 11–14	1.7	5.9	85.4	69.4	162.4
Age 15–17	15.8	28.2	301.2	234.8	580.0
Age 18–24	33.6	38.2	238.5	237.2	547.5
Percentage Changes in Arrest Rates (1970–75)					
Age 11–14	+6.2	+18.0	+15.8	+40.2	+25.1
Age 15–17	+1.9	− 4.0	+34.3	+46.7	+35.1
Age 18–24	+15.8	+ 2.9	+14.0	ǀ 14.8	+13.4

SOURCE: 1970, 1975 FBI Uniform Crime Reports and Census Bureau data.

lent crimes, although they held only 23 percent of the reporting population.

Urban dominance in juvenile violence has been diminishing in recent years, however. Table 5 compares the growth in juvenile arrest rates in urban and nonurban areas between 1970 and 1974 and between 1974 and 1975.[3] With the exception of the final year, 1974–1975, arrests for serious crimes of all kinds have been increasing faster in nonurban areas than in urban areas since 1970 (and earlier), and the increase in nonurban arrest rates for violence has been the most dramatic of all. These changes cannot be attributed solely to demographic shifts, because arrests of nonurban juveniles have increased at a faster rate than the nonurban population. Nevertheless, arrest rates of urban juveniles for violent crimes were still about twice those of nonurban juveniles in 1975, suggesting

[3] It should be noted that the FBI Uniform Crime Reports, from which the data are taken, consider all areas with 2,500 or more residents to be urban.

Table 5 Average Annual Change in Arrest Rates per 100,000 Juveniles, Age 17 or Younger, Nationally

	Urban	Nonurban
Violent Crimes[a]		
1970–74	+7.6	+19.2
1974–75	+3.0	+ 0.9
Property Crimes[b]		
1970–74	+5.9	+12.1
1974–75	−3.0	− 5.1
All Serious Crimes[c]		
1970–74	+6.1	+12.5
1974–75	−2.5	− 4.7

SOURCE: 1970, 1974, and 1975 FBI Uniform Crime Reports and Census Bureau data.

NOTE: FBI Uniform Crime Reports define as "urban" areas of 2,500 or more in population.

[a] Homicide, forcible rape, robbery, aggravated assault.
[b] Larceny, burglary, auto theft.
[c] Total of violent and property crimes.

that the problem of juvenile violence will remain more serious in urban areas for years to come.

The following summarizes the conclusions suggested by arrest data. Juveniles have been arrested for all kinds of crime at increasing rates since 1960, but the increase has slowed considerably in the last half of the period. Rates of increase have been highest and steadiest for violent crimes, but violence is still only a small part (perhaps 10 percent) of the serious criminal activity of the young. Most of their antisocial behavior is concentrated on property. Among violent crimes, robbery is the most common and is increasing at a fast pace. Aggravated assault is close behind. Not surprisingly, older juveniles (15–17) are responsible for most of the violence, particularly the rapes and homicides, committed by persons under 18. And while nonurban violence is increasing much faster than urban violence, urban juveniles are still arrested for violent crimes about twice as often as nonurban juveniles.

Because arrest data have some well-known flaws, however, one should be cautious in drawing conclusions from them regarding juvenile violence or other kinds of delinquent behavior. Among their most important deficiencies are the following.

- Arrests describe only the apprehension of suspects. Without information regarding the outcomes of cases, the link between arrests and crimes is only speculative. Particularly with regard to juveniles, frequent diversions from court, dismissals, or withdrawals leave many crimes technically unsolved, even after arrest.
- Given low reporting rates (estimates of crimes known to the police range from 50 percent down to 10 percent) and low clearance rates (only 49 percent of all violent crimes are cleared by police, with rates running from 81 percent for murder down to 29 percent for robbery), arrest data give no more than a partial picture of criminal activity and criminals. Increases or decreases in arrests may reflect changes in reporting practices or police efficiency instead of real changes in criminal activity.
- Arrest figures may overrepresent younger offenders, since they are less experienced and thus may be easier to catch.
- Because they are based on broad penal code classifications, which mask complex differences in the nature and seriousness of offenses, arrest figures are not fully descriptive of criminal acts.
- Arrest data are concerned with single events. Standing alone, they tell little or nothing about patterns of criminal behavior, including recidivism, frequency of criminal activity, or group involvement.

Several kinds of research have been employed to avoid these pitfalls and give another perspective on the extent and growth of delinquency. Two of the more important kinds are self-report delinquency surveys and cohort studies.

Self-Report Surveys

Self-report surveys have been used since the 1930s to measure delinquency in Europe and the United States. The basic survey tool is either an anonymous, self-administered questionnaire or a confidential interview with a researcher. Each probes a child's delinquent acts, officially detected or not. Demographic characteristics of the respondent and other social and family data are also collected. Verification of the "confessed" information is a problem that has been managed in a variety of ways, including the use of informants and polygraphs. The problem has not been eliminated, but researchers have been able to determine the reliability of their samples reasonably well and at least understand the directions in which responses are likely to be biased.

One of the earliest American studies took place in Fort Worth, Texas, in 1943. A questionnaire listing offenses committed by children brought to juvenile court was administered to several hundred college students. Responses showed that all of the students had committed at least one of the acts listed. On the average, males had committed 17.6 offenses and females 4.7, although the "confessed" offenses were generally less serious than those committed by the court wards. None of the students had ever been detected by authorities—not even for serious offenses.[4]

A number of self-report surveys since then have yielded the same general conclusion, although not usually in such extreme terms. The rate of undetected delinquency is quite high, even for serious offenses. They have also shown, however, that the probability of being detected does increase with the frequency and seriousness of offenses.[5]

One of the most widely cited of recent self-report studies was done by Martin Gold in Flint, Michigan, in the mid-1960s. Gold conducted interviews with a sample of 600 boys and girls aged 13 through 16. Using data from informants, he tested the reliability of responses given by a subsample of 125. Seventy-two percent appeared to tell the "whole truth," 17 percent appeared to be concealers, and 11 percent were questionable. The study found that although only 16 percent of confessed delinquent boys were caught by the police at least once, official records did approximate

[4] Austin L. Porterfield, "Delinquency and Its Outcome in Court and College," *American Journal of Sociology* 49 (1943): 199–208. Cited in Eugene Doleschal, "Hidden Crime," *Crime and Delinquency Literature* 2, no. 5 (1970): 546–572.
[5] Doleschal, op. cit., pp. 551–557.

delinquent behavior in that the more delinquent boys were more likely to be caught by police. Compared to the least delinquent boys, police caught about four times as many of the most *serious* delinquents (measured on a scale of seriousness developed by Thorsten Sellin and Marvin Wolfgang).[6] Seventeen times as many of the most frequently delinquent as of the least delinquent were caught. Thus, Gold's study suggests that frequency of delinquency is a stronger determinant of apprehension than seriousness of offense. Even so, less than one-third of the most delinquent boys were caught by the police.[7]

Gold and his colleagues have since applied the self-report technique to a national survey that measures not only levels of self-confessed delinquency, but changes over time. The survey, first conducted in 1967 and then repeated in 1972, covered a stratified random sample of children throughout the country: 847 aged 13 through 16 in 1967, and 1,395 aged 11 through 18 in 1972. The 661 children in the 1972 survey who fell into the age 13 to 16 group were compared to the 1967 sample with regard to the frequency and seriousness of self-reported delinquent acts.

The results of that study are surprising and significant. Both frequency and seriousness of self-reported delinquent acts by boys declined over the five-year period, frequency by 9 percent per capita and seriousness by 14 percent. There was a marked decrease (ranging from 28–49 percent) in larceny, threatening assault, breaking and entering, and gang fighting. The only offenses that registered a significant increase over the period were fraud to obtain alcohol and use of marijuana and drugs. When these two categories are excluded, the decline in number of delinquent acts per capita was 20 percent. For the 13- through 16-year-old girls, the average number of incidents was 22 percent higher in 1972 than in 1967, although there was no difference in seriousness of offenses. Two offenses were entirely responsible for the increase in frequency among girls: drinking, which nearly doubled, and drug and

[6] See Thorsten Sellin and Marvin E. Wolfgang, *The Measurement of Delinquency* (New York: John Wiley and Sons, 1964). A summary of the scoring method is contained in Appendix C of this report.

[7] Martin Gold, "Undetected Delinquent Behavior," *Journal of Research in Crime and Delinquency* 3, no. 1 (1966): 27–46.

marijuana use, which increased ninefold. Excluding those two categories, there was no change in frequency of girls' offenses over the period.[8]

These findings run counter to the trend in FBI's Uniform Crime Reports for the same five-year period, which showed a 29 percent increase in arrests of juveniles under 18, including a 22 percent growth in arrests for serious property crimes and 6 percent for violent crimes. (Arrests for drug offenses increased 326 percent and for liquor violations, 10 percent.)[9]

Because of the great discrepancy between changes in · self-reported delinquency and changes in arrest rates, one is tempted to question the validity of the self-report mechanism. As the authors point out, however, even if the reliability of some individual responses can be doubted, there is no reason to believe that children in one year would be less truthful than children in another year. Since the Gold-Reimer study is concerned primarily with a comparison of reports at two different times, and not with absolute levels of delinquency, its conclusions must be given serious consideration.

Gold and Reimer address this conflict by asking "What happened to the teenage crime wave?" They answer their own question.

Journalistic accounts of the rise in youthful crime reflected official data such as the FBI Uniform Crime Reports and the records of metropolitan law enforcement agencies. Changes in rates might be accounted

---

[8] Martin Gold and David J. Reimer, "Changing Patterns of Delinquent Behavior among Americans 13 through 16 Years Old: 1967–1972," *Crime and Delinquency Literature* 7, no. 4 (December 1975): 453–517.

[9] The 1972 sample of Gold and Reimer reported the following offense rates per 100,000 children: larceny = 24,088; burglary = 3,467; assault = 34,672; robbery = 2,554. (Calculated from data given in Tables 3–6 in Gold and Reimer, op. cit.) According to the authors, 81 percent of the offenses reported were committed within the year prior to the interviews. Based on that average figure, a yearly self-confessed offense rate for each crime is given in the table below, in comparison to arrest rates of children aged 13 through 16 derived from the 1972 FBI Uniform Crime Reports. It seems that true offense rates surpass arrest rates by more than fifteen times for the crimes listed.

OFFENSES PER 100,000 CHILDREN AGED 13 THROUGH 16 (1972)

	Larceny	Burglary	Robbery	Assault	Total
Self-Reported	19,510	2,808	2,069	28,084	52,471
UCR Arrests	1,718	830	178	438	3,164

for by changes in record-keeping procedures, changes in definitions or policies relating to juvenile offenders, and other reasons, including even deliberate distortion of the data for political purposes. Official data on delinquency are tied so loosely to the actual behavior of youth that they are more sensitive to the changes in the measurement procedures than they are to the object of measurement. . . . It seems to us that the data we have reported here approximate as closely as any available the real levels and nature of delinquent behavior in the years under consideration. And they simply do not testify to rapidly rising rates of juvenile delinquency.[10]

This response contains elements of an explanation, but probably not the whole explanation. Changes in reporting procedures and policies probably did produce some increase in the numbers counted. Other factors might also have had some bearing, however. It is conceivable, for example, that police became somewhat more efficient in catching offenders (or at least young offenders) as a result of changes in technology, patrol deployment patterns, and the like, thus making more arrests, even though crimes were committed no more frequently. The huge gap between admitted offenses and arrests would certainly allow for that.

Another possible explanation, perhaps more likely, is an increase in police willingness to arrest and charge juveniles. The period covered by Gold and Reimer's study saw a proliferation in juvenile court diversion programs, whose intent was to provide less intrusive and less damaging responses to delinquent behavior. A frequently noted consequence of this expansion was an increase in the total number of juveniles sent to court, presumably because the new programs increased the total capacity of the system to control youth and offered a kind of control that was more appealing to those with the responsibility for making referrals. If this hypothesis is true, there is no reason to believe it did not also have an effect on the police. If police declined to arrest and charge youths in earlier years because they felt the consequences would be too damaging, the growth of alternative programs may have loosened the inhibition and made them more willing to initiate formal charges against juveniles. But this explanation, like others, is speculative.

[10] Gold and Reimer, op. cit., p. 514.

Regardless of their reliability vis-à-vis arrest data, self-report studies have a significant limitation for our purpose in that they do not normally cover serious violent offenses such as homicide and rape. The reasons seem apparent: either the numbers are too small to appear at a statistically significant level in a sample of 800 or less, or juveniles will not readily admit such offenses, or those who commit them are not at large in the population and thus do not get sampled.

Cohort Studies

Cohort studies of delinquency differ from existing self-report studies in several ways. First, they focus more sharply on a specific group of individuals born in the same period and passing through childhood and adolescence in the same place. Second, they gather information about the illegal activities of individuals throughout childhood and adolescence, or at least about some significant part of that period. (They may also continue beyond adolescence, of course.) Instead of a snapshot at one particular time, they thus provide a longitudinal history. Third, cohort studies usually rely heavily on official records, especially police arrest records, whereas self-reported data are sought as an alternative to official records. Cohort studies need not rely on police data alone, however. They may make use of information from the entire juvenile justice system (police, courts, probation, and corrections) as well as from schools and other agencies. Some also use personal interviews to verify or supplement data gathered from official sources. This extensive information base gives a more rounded picture of the individual offender (and nonoffender). Because it covers a broad time span, the information base also permits a richer analysis of patterns of criminal behavior, including age of onset, crime specialization, and recidivism. (Extensive long-term data also make cohort studies difficult and costly, which is the main reason they are so rare.)

Two recent cohort studies have been especially useful in illuminating the extent and pattern of juvenile delinquency. One was undertaken in Philadelphia by Marvin Wolfgang and his associates at the Center for Studies in Criminology and Criminal Law of the

University of Pennsylvania. The other is underway in nonmetropolitan Marion County, Oregon, under the direction of Kenneth Polk of the University of Oregon.

The Philadelphia cohort study contained data on 9,946 individuals—all those for whom records could be found—who were born in 1945 and lived in that city between the ages of 10 and 18. Data on delinquency were drawn from police records. "Delinquency" was defined as any police contact, including minor infractions and traffic offenses. Comparisons were made among those classified as delinquents, and between them and nondelinquent boys, on variables such as race, socioeconomic status, school performance, and the pattern and seriousness of offenses.[11]

The most impressive fact to emerge from this study was that 35 percent of the cohort (3,475 boys) had police records before they reached the age of 18. This was a far higher proportion than most experts had suspected, although not as high as the proportion actually engaging in delinquent acts according to self-report studies. Another impressive result was that slightly over half (50.2 percent) of nonwhite juveniles had police records, compared to 28.6 percent of white juveniles. Altogether, the delinquents in the cohort were detected in 10,214 illegal acts, an average of three per delinquent.

About one-fourth of the cohort's offenses were serious: 20.1 percent were serious property crimes (burglaries, larcenies, and auto thefts), and 4.6 were violent crimes (fourteen homicides, forty-four rapes, 193 robberies, and 220 aggravated assaults). In addition, there were 537 simple assaults constituting 5.3 percent of the cohort's offenses. One-fourth of the recorded delinquencies covered fourteen less serious offenses ranging from forgery through sex, drug, and liquor offenses to traffic violations. The largest category of all, 40 percent of offenses, was labeled "other" and included fifty-four kinds of minor crimes ranging down to keeping a vicious dog.

The proportion of delinquents in the cohort who committed violent offenses is not reported in the study. From available data,

---

[11] The data presented here are taken from Marvin E. Wolfgang, Robert M. Figlio, and Thorsten Sellin, *Delinquency in a Birth Cohort* (Chicago: University of Chicago Press, 1972).

however, it can be calculated that 31 percent of the delinquents committed at least one offense resulting in injury to the victim. Twenty-four percent committed only one injury offense, while 7 percent committed two or more. (Two percent—75 boys—committed three or more.)[12] Most of these offenses (72 percent) resulted in only minor injury. Only 7 percent resulted in hospitalization or death.

Extending these calculations to the entire cohort, it appears that 11 percent of all male youths in Philadelphia were arrested at least once for an injury offense, and 2.3 percent for two or more such offenses—strikingly high figures.

Not included in these calculations is robbery which, as noted, was the second most common serious violent crime in the cohort. Some robberies were undoubtedly committed by youths who also committed injury offenses, but most likely many were not. Thus, the proportion of Philadelphia delinquents committing violent acts including robbery may have been as high as 35 percent, or 12 percent of the entire cohort.

The Philadelphia study alone did not provide any insight regarding the rate of change in violence. That awaits another, later, cohort study to which it can be compared. Nevertheless, it did yield a rich lode of information that will be discussed further in other chapters.

One may be inclined to dismiss the significance of the Philadelphia study on the ground that it pertains to a large Eastern city with a decaying inner core and is therefore not generally descriptive of delinquency in America. That objection, however, was partially met by the Polk cohort study in Oregon.

Polk's cohort consisted of all sophomore boys in fourteen Marion County high schools who completed a questionnaire in the fall of 1964. The number of respondents (1,227) was more than 93 percent of the eligible population. Delinquency status was determined from court records and was defined as the appearance of a respondent's name at least once in connection with an offense other than a minor traffic violation. Other variables measured included socio-

[12] These figures are computed from data reported on page 78 and in Table 11.10 on page 190, ibid.

economic status, school grade point average and, for a subsample, interaction with peers.[13]

The results were as surprising as those of the Philadelphia study. One-fourth of the Oregon cohort had an official record of delinquency. Considering that this study excluded traffic offenses, which were included in the Philadelphia study, the difference in delinquency rates found by the two was small. Furthermore, when the Philadelphia data are controlled for race, to bring the two populations into alignment on that variable, differences between the city juveniles and the rural and small town juveniles all but disappear: 29 percent of the Philadelphians and 25 percent of the Oregonians were delinquent.

Unfortunately, the Oregon data have not been analyzed in a way that reveals useful information about violence by the cohort. Publications available from the project to date have concentrated mainly on the relationship between school performance and delinquency, dividing offenses simply into felonies and misdemeanors. Fifty-six percent of the delinquents were charged with one or more felonies. This figure indicates that a considerable amount of serious delinquency occurs among rural and small town youth including, no doubt, some serious violence. But from the evidence so far available, it is not possible to draw any clear crime-specific comparisons with urban youth in Philadelphia.

The Vera Institute Study

Self-report and cohort studies have added considerably to our understanding of delinquency. Yet large gaps remain, especially when the focus is on violence. Self-report studies do not cover some of the most serious violent crimes. Moreover, they rely on the candor of respondents, which may diminish as the seriousness of crimes goes up. The cohort studies currently available deal with a

---

[13] The data in this section are taken from "Teenage Delinquency in Small Town America." Research Report No. 5, National Institute of Mental Health, 1974; and Kenneth Polk, Dean Frease, and Lynn F. Richmond, "Social Class, School Experience, and Delinquency," *Criminology* 12, no. 1 (1974): 84–95.

period fast receding in history, and they tell us little about either old or new trends.

In an effort to develop more up-to-date information specifically about violent juvenile crime and the judicial responses to it, the Vera Institute undertook its own cross-sectional study of officially recorded delinquency in the New York metropolitan region.

A 10 percent random sample was drawn from delinquency petitions brought in 1974 in the juvenile (or family) courts of three metropolitan area counties: New York (Manhattan) and West-chester Counties in New York, and Mercer County in New Jersey.[14] These areas were chosen to provide a diversity of environments and approaches to juvenile justice. Westchester County has a suburban character for the most part, but also includes four urban centers (Yonkers, White Plains, New Rochelle, and Mount Vernon), where the majority of juvenile arrests take place. Mercer County contains the capital of New Jersey (Trenton), an old city of about 106,000 residents, as well as a substantial surburban and a smaller rural population. Manhattan, of course, is a densely populated urban center with a sizable minority population.

In Manhattan and Westchester, the age range of the sample was 7 through 15 (the upper limit for Family Court jurisdiction in New York State): the age range went from 8 through 17 in Mercer, because juveniles come under the Juvenile Court's jurisdiction until age 18 in New Jersey. Over half (52 percent) of the Mercer County sample fell into the 16- and 17-year-old groups.

Court and probation records were selected as the data source because they provided easier access to individual histories than police records, although they may occasionally be incomplete with regard to arrests that do not reach court. For each sampled case, 510 in all, detailed information was collected on the current offense and up to five prior offenses, together with less detailed summary information on the entire delinquency record of the individual. Insofar as it was available in court and probation records, demographic, family, school, medical, and psychiatric information was also taken.

This approach enabled us to examine the entire record of the

14 Further explanation of sampling procedures and additional data not presented in the text can be found in Appendix A.

juveniles in the sample as well as the disposition of each of their charges. It also provided more background on each juvenile than is available in most studies based on arrest data alone. However, a cross-sectional study such as this is inferior to a cohort study in that it includes only those offenses that occurred prior to the date the sample was drawn. For an unknown portion of the sample (one-time offenders and those who concluded more extensive delinquent "careers" with the sampled offense) our data are complete, but a relatively large number are caught by the study at the beginning or the middle of their delinquent careers. For that reason, the data tend to underrepresent the overall delinquent behavior of this group. To offset this drawback, however, cross-sectional data can be collected much more quickly and cheaply than longitudinal data.

In basing the sample on delinquency petitions filed in court, the study automatically excluded two important categories of arrested juveniles: status offenders, who are charged under a different kind of petition,[15] and delinquents who were not brought to court because their cases were disposed of in some other manner (i.e., they were "diverted"). (Roughly 45 percent of juveniles arrested on delinquency charges in the three counties in 1974 were diverted before petitions were drawn.) Together, diverted delinquents and status offenders constitute a majority of children who get into legal trouble, so their exclusion from the study requires that generalizations about juvenile offenders be carefully considered. On the other hand, status offenders and diverted delinquents usually do not include many charged with serious violent crimes, on the occasion in question at least. (Manhattan delinquents are an exception, as we will see.) The interplay between diversion, status offending, and violence could be examined to some extent by looking at the prior offense records of the children whose sampled offenses include violence, but who have previously also been charged with a status offense or diverted. Such an analysis has not been done, however.

The data available in court and probation records enabled us to classify children according to three separate measures of their delinquent behavior. The first is the number of offenses committed.

---

[15] Status offenses involve charges such as truancy or "incorrigibility," which cannot be applied to adults. Some status offenders were sampled in Mercer, but were excluded from the analysis presented here. See Appendix A for an explanation.

Following Wolfgang, we chose three groupings: first offenders, recidivists (two to four contacts), and chronics (five or more contacts).[16]

Second, we classified the sample according to whether a juvenile
had been charged with a violent or nonviolent crime, both in the
offense sampled and at any time in the six most recent offenses.[17]
Sampled offenses, also called "current" offenses, are arrests referred
for court processing in 1974,[18] the basis on which our sample was
drawn. Prior offenses are earlier police contacts, up to five before
the sampled offense, recorded in the delinquent's court file. These
include some that were not "official" arrests and, more frequently,
arrests that were not referred for judicial processing.[19] Delinquents for whom homicide, rape, robbery, or assault (or an attempt
at one of these) was the sampled offense are called "currently violent." Those charged with one of these offenses in any of the six
most recent contacts are called "ever violent," while those not
charged with these crimes are called "currently nonviolent" and
"never violent."[20]

Finally, we applied the seriousness scale developed by Sellin and
Wolfgang[21] to order offenses according to the severity of their
consequences for the victim or for society generally. Scores for all
offenses up to six committed by each child were calculated. Although crimes against persons and property crimes are lumped
together in this scale, the higher the seriousness score, the more
likely it is that violence against persons has occurred.[22]

Two points must be made at the outset regarding the data to be
presented. First, time limitations permitted us to analyze only the
most obvious and straightforward of relationships. Future analyses

[16] Wolfgang, Figlio, and Sellin, op. cit.

[17] Time and funding limitations made detailed analysis of all offenses committed
by the sample impossible. See footnote 23 in this chapter for a description of the
other offenses committed by the sampled delinquents.

[18] The offenses sampled in Mercer occurred in the period from September 1973
through August 1974, which is the official court year. Police data are from calendar
year 1974, however.

[19] The case for considering prior charges not referred to court is made by Wolfgang, Figlio, and Sellin, op. cit., pp. 13–15.

[20] "Never violent" may be a misnomer, since some youths in the sample might
have been charged with a violent crime in a contact that occurred prior to the six
most recent contacts. See footnote 23 in this chapter.

[21] Supra, footnote 7.

[22] See Appendix C for a list of crimes included in each seriousness grouping.

may reveal subtler and perhaps more meaningful descriptions of the behavior of these delinquents and the system's handling of them. Second, because of methodological differences between this study and others mentioned in this report, comparison of these results with those of other studies always involves a certain amount of risk. The most reliable conclusions are those based on comparisons among subgroups within the Vera study itself.

Offense frequency is a useful starting point for describing the sample, although by itself it tells nothing about violence. As seen in Table 6, 41 percent of the entire sample were first offenders, 36 percent were recidivists, and 23 percent were chronic offenders. Intercounty differences were noticeable, but they should not be taken too seriously, since they probably reflect the completeness of court and probation records in each county as much as they do actual police contacts. Mercer County records appeared to have the most complete data on prior arrests, so it is not surprising that the proportion of first offenders (34 percent) should be lowest there, and the proportion of chronics (29 percent) highest. Mercer figures are, in fact, probably a better reflection of offense frequency in the overall sample than figures from the other two counties. As a rough generalization, it can therefore be said that between one-quarter and one-third of the delinquents brought to these courts were chronic offenders, slightly over one-third were recidivists, and about one-third were first offenders.

In general, violent offenses are more likely than nonviolent offenses to be referred to court or otherwise noted in court and probation records. Table 7 shows the proportion of the sample in

Table 6 Distribution of Vera Sample Offenders by Number of Offenses and County

	First Offenders		Recidivists (2–4 offenses)		Chronics (5+ offenses)	
	N	%	N	%	N	%
Mercer	61	34.3	65	36.5	52	29.2
Westchester	53	48.2	33	30.0	24	21.8
Manhattan	95	43.2	84	38.2	41	18.6
Total Sample	209	41.1	182	35.9	117	23.0

SOURCE. Vera Institute Violent Delinquent Study.

each county charged with a violent crime (any robbery, assault, homicide, or forcible sex offense) in the petition sampled (currently violent), and the proportion that had ever been charged with one of these offenses. Overall, 29 percent were charged with violence in the sampled offense, but 44 percent had been charged with violence at some time in their recent record. Manhattan was far ahead of the other counties on both measures. In fact, more than half of the Manhattan sample (55 percent) had been charged on at least one occasion with a violent crime.

Table 7 Proportion of Vera Sample Population Currently Charged with Violence and Ever Charged with Violence, by County

	Currently Violent[a]	Ever Violent[b]
Mercer ($N = 178$)	16.9	33.7
Westchester ($N = 110$)	27.3	37.3
Manhattan ($N = 220$)	38.8	54.5
Total Sample ($N = 508$)	28.6	43.5

SOURCE: Vera Institute Violent Delinquent Study.

[a] Chi square = 23.3; $df = 2$; $p = 0.0000$.
[b] Chi square = 19.7; $df = 2$; $p = 0.0001$.

A description of the sample's violent offenses is given in Table 8. There were 510 current offenses, of which 145 (28 percent) fell into the violent category. Ninety-four of the current offenses (18 percent) resulted in known injury or death to the victim.

As noted, in addition to current offenses, details were gathered on all prior offenses up to a maximum of five.[23] The sample had

[23] Offenses beyond the fifth prior one (or six in total) are not included, because no details were collected on them. The line was drawn at five prior offenses simply to make the data collection manageable within the time and budget available. However, a check of all offenses listed in court and probation records (as thorough as time allowed) indicated that the entire sample of 510 delinquents had been charged with a total of 2,504 offenses. These were grouped according to the following general categories: 284 status offenses (11.3 percent), 406 victimless crimes (16.2 percent), 1,257 property crimes (50.2 percent), and 557 crimes against the person (22.2 percent). The 1,116 "excess" offenses (those for which details were not collected) appear to have been committed by about 17 percent of the sample, including nine delinquents each having twenty or more arrests. Approximately 75 percent of "excess" offenses were property crimes, and less than 10 percent were crimes against the person.

878 such prior offenses, bringing to 1,388 the total number of offenses committed by this group of delinquents for which details were obtained. In all, 326 of these crimes (24 percent) fell into the violent category, and 175 (13 percent) involved known injury or death to the victim.

Table 8 shows that assault was the most common of both current and all offenses, followed by robbery. However, twenty current assaults (22 percent of that category) and thirty-nine out of 178 total assaults (also 22 percent) included robbery as a component of the offense. If these acts had been coded as robbery instead of assault, robbery would have surpassed assault among all offenses, and it would have had a nearly equal position among current offenses.

Assaults are broken down into two categories, serious and minor. Minor assaults are those scoring less than 210 on the Sellin-Wolf-

Table 8 Violent Offenses Committed by Vera Sample

	Current Offenses		All Offenses[a]	
	N	%	N	%
Murder	3	0.6	3	0.2
Attempted Murder	2	0.4	5	0.4
Sex Offenses	8	1.6	13	0.9
Assault[b]	89	17.4	178	12.8
Serious	(66)	(12.9)	(89)	(6.4)
Minor	(23)	(4.5)	(89)	(6.4)
Robbery[c]	43	8.4	127	9.1
Armed	(7)	(1.4)	(28)	(2.0)
Injury	(8)	(1.6)	(17)	(1.2)
Combination	(2)	(0.4)	(3)	(0.2)
Other	(26)	(5.1)	(79)	(5.7)
Total Violent Offenses	145	28.4	326	23.5
Nonviolent Offenses	365	71.6	1062	76.5
All Offenses	510	100.0	1388	100.0

SOURCE: Vera Institute Violent Delinquent Study.

[a] Up to a maximum of six per offender. See footnote 23 in this chapter for an explanation.

[b] Includes charges of attempted assault and menacing, although these were a relatively small minority of all assault charges.

[c] Includes attempted robberies. Combination robberies involve both a weapon and injury to the victim.

gang scale. Essentially, this group includes all assaults in which
there was no injury or only minor injury. It also includes assaults
for which no details were available in the court and probation
records.[24] Serious assaults are those in which the victim's injuries
were known to require treatment by a doctor, at a minimum. The
commonly used categories of "aggravated" and "simple" assault
could not be used here, because they were not uniformly applied
in the jurisdictions studied. However, all "aggravated" assaults,
plus some that might not fit that legal terminology, are included
under serious assaults.[25]

Robberies were divided into four categories: armed robberies, in
which a weapon was present; injury robberies, in which an injury
occurred to the victim; combination robberies, in which both of
these conditions applied; and other robberies, in which neither
condition applied. "Other" is thus the least serious category of
robbery; it is typically an event in which property (e.g., a bicycle)
was taken from another person with a threat that did not involve a
weapon and was not actually carried out. The mean seriousness
scores for each category of robbery in the current offense were as
follows.

Armed robbery ($N = 7$)—614.
Injury robbery ($N = 8$)—500.
Combination robbery ($N = 2$)—793.
Other robberies ($N = 25$)—336.

Forty out of forty-eight serious (not "other") robberies ever committed by the sample occurred in Manhattan.

If minor assaults and "other" robberies are disregarded, there
remain ninety-six crimes among the current offenses (19 percent)

[24] Offenses for which no details were available were scored 209, the mean score
for nonaggravated assaults in the Philadelphia cohort. This score automatically placed
such offenses in the minor assault category. Absence of details was much more likely
with regard to prior offenses than current offenses, which may explain why serious
assaults outweighed minor assaults among current offenses, but not among all
offenses.

[25] If the arrest charge was aggravated assault, but no details were available, a
score of 601 was assigned—the mean score for aggravated assaults in the Philadelphia
cohort. Thus all aggravated assaults are included in serious assaults, even though
details might be missing in some cases.

and 158 crimes among all offenses committed by the sample (11 percent) that can be labeled serious violent crimes.

Table 9 shows the distribution of offenders committing any violent offense and any serious violent offense, by frequency of com-

Table 9 Distribution of Vera Sample Offenders by Frequency of Violent Offenses, by County (in percent)

	Number of Violent Offenses				
	0	1	2	3+	Total
All Violent Offenses[a]					
Mercer ($N = 178$)	66.3	24.7	6.2	2.8	100.0
Westchester ($N = 110$)	62.7	30.0	5.5	1.8	100.0
Manhattan ($N = 220$)	45.5	33.6	12.7	8.2	100.0
Total Sample ($N = 508$)	56.5	29.7	8.9	4.9	100.0
Serious Violent Offenses[bc]					
Mercer ($N = 178$)	81.5	17.4	1.1	—	100.0
Westchester ($N = 110$)	80.0	18.2	1.8	—	100.0
Manhattan ($N = 220$)	57.7	30.0	9.5	2.8	100.0
Total Sample ($N - 508$)	70.9	23.0	4.9	1.2	100.0

SOURCE: Vera Institute Violent Delinquent Study.

[a] Chi square = 26.3; $df = 6$; $p < 0.005$. Two missing observations in Manhattan.

[b] Chi square = 50.9; $df = 6$; $p < 0.001$. Two missing observations in Manhattan.

[c] Includes all violent offenses except robberies in which there was neither a weapon nor a resulting injury and assaults with a seriousness score less than 210 (in effect, assaults in which there was no injury or only minor injury).

mission. Two facts stand out in the table. First, although 29 percent of the sample was charged at least once with a serious violent crime, the proportion charged on more than one occasion with serious violence is much smaller (6 percent).[26] (These figures parallel data in the Philadelphia cohort study: 31 percent of those delinquents were arrested at least once for an injury offense, 7 percent twice or more.) This lends support to the contention that

[26] The information available on all offenses of the sample, including those for which details were not collected (see footnote 23, supra) shows that 133 juveniles (26 percent of the sample) were charged with two or more crimes against the person, but these were not necessarily violent crimes.

delinquents who engage in violent crime do not usually do so repeatedly. The second apparent fact is that Manhattan is again far ahead of the other two counties in the proportion of delinquents having multiple charges of serious violence (12 percent compared to less than 2 percent in the other two counties). The Manhattan sample included six delinquents charged with three or more serious violent crimes (3 percent of the sample), whereas in Mercer and Westchester there were none. Projecting the figures for the sample onto the entire delinquent population before the Manhattan Family Court in 1974, there were perhaps 250 children who had been charged on two or more occasions with a serious violent crime, including perhaps sixty with three or more such charges.[27]

The two halves of Table 9, read together, also make clear that the Manhattan Family Court hears fewer cases of minor robberies and assaults compared to the two other counties. When minor offenses are subtracted from violent offenses, the proportion of nonviolent offenders in Mercer and Westchester increases more than the figure in Manhattan. Most likely, minor assault and robbery charges are diverted at intake in Manhattan more frequently than they are in the other two counties.

Differences between Manhattan and the other two counties with regard to juvenile violence were suggested by other variables measured in the study. For example, the proportion of violent crimes in which the victim was a stranger to the defendant varied significantly. In Manhattan, 63 percent of current petitions involving violence were brought by complainants who were strangers to the offender, whereas in Westchester the figure was 37 percent and in Mercer 25 percent. Conversely, 22 percent of the Manhattan petitions, compared to 33 percent in Westchester and 54 percent in Mercer, were brought by relatives or acquaintances. (The balance in each county was made up of police, school authorities, or others.)

When the Sellin-Wolfgang seriousness scale, based on the facts

[27] A study by the Juvenile Justice Institute of the New York State Division of Criminal Justice Services shows that 624 children in all of New York City (Manhattan plus four other counties) charged with one of eleven categories of violent crimes against the person in a twelve-month period of 1973–1974 had been charged with one of those crimes on at least one prior occasion in the *same* year. (Juvenile Justice Institute, New York State Division of Criminal Justice Services. "Juvenile Violence." May 1976. Mimeo.)

of the crimes, was applied to the sample's offenses to help smooth out differences that might have been introduced by variations in crime codes or in police charging practices, a sharp divergence between Manhattan and the other two counties appeared again. Mean seriousness scores by county are summarized in Table 10. On each measure, and particularly for violent offenses, Manhattan delinquents surpassed the others in the seriousness of their acts.

Table 10 Mean Seriousness Scores in Vera Sample, by County

	Mercer	West-chester	Manhattan	Total Sample
Total Score of All Offenses up to 6	611.0	525.1	843.6	692.9 ($N = 505$)
Average Score of All Offenses up to 6[a]	208.4	241.4	343.5	273.8 ($N = 505$)
All Current Offenses[b]	238.2	286.4	415.7	325.1 ($N = 504$)
Violent Current Offenses[b]	291.7	380.1	673.9	533.1 ($N = 144$)

SOURCE: Vera Institute Violent Delinquent Study.

[a] The lower score for the average of all offenses than for current offenses may be due to the fact that court records had details for a smaller percentage of prior offenses than current offenses. The scoring method used when details were absent resulted in slightly lower scores. See Appendix C for details.
[b] Current offenses are the most recent ones committed.

Mean seriousness scores for each type of violent offense are given in Table 11. For both robberies and assaults, Manhattan delinquents registered significantly higher seriousness scores than delinquents in the other two counties. (There were no murders or rapes in the Mercer and Westchester samples.) The average robbery score of 300 in Mercer County, for example, suggests that the typical event would involve no weapon and either minor injury coupled with loss of property valued at $10–$250, or no injury coupled with loss of property valued at more than $250. In other words, a purse snatch would be typical. In contrast, the average score of 516 in Manhattan suggests that the typical event involved a weapon coupled with minor loss of property; no weapon but injuries requiring treatment by a doctor and minor loss of property; or perhaps no weapon, minor injury, but loss of property valued at more than $2,000. Similarly, the average assault score of 293 in Mercer County implies no weapon and minor injury, whereas the average score of 592 in Manhattan implies use of a weapon and minor injury, or no weapon but injury requiring treatment by a doctor.

Table 11 Mean Seriousness Scores of Vera and Philadelphia Samples for Current Violent Offenses, by County[a]

	Murder (N = 3)		**Rape (N = 5)**		**Robbery (N = 34)**		**Assault (N = 78)**	
	$\bar{X}$	Stand-ard Devia-tion	$\bar{X}$	Stand-ard Devia-tion	$\bar{X}$	Stand-ard Devia-tion	$\bar{X}$	Stand-ard Devia-tion
Mercer	——	——	——	——	300.0	100.0	293.3	189.5
Westchester	——	——	——	——	431.2	147.7	387.7	298.1
Manhattan	3000.0	360.6	940.0	194.9	516.3	215.3	592.4	290.3
Total Sample	3000.0	360.6	940.0	194.9	482.2	205.0	452.9	295.5
Philadelphia Cohort[b]	2635.7	74.5	895.7	511.3	315.9	188.5	209.0[c]	169.6

SOURCE: Vera Institute Violent Delinquent Study.

[a] The following offenses are omitted from this table: attempted murder (two), sodomy (three), attempted robbery (nine) and attempted assault or menacing (eleven).

[b] Personal communication from Professor Marvin E. Wolfgang. N = 10,214.

[c] The score used here is for "other assaults," of which there were 537 in the cohort. The mean score for aggravated assaults in the cohort (N = 220) was 601.4. Because of crime code differences, aggravated assaults and other assaults were not separated in the Vera sample. Averaging both categories together for the cohort gives a mean score for all assaults of 323.0.

There are two possible explanations for this disparity between Manhattan and the other counties. The first is that the Manhattan court population is more heavily weighted toward the seriously violent, either because Manhattan diverts a larger proportion of nonviolent or less seriously violent cases away from court than the other counties, or because it catches and processes a greater proportion of its violent delinquents. The evidence available appears not to support this explanation, however. Mercer County probation staffs say that it is official policy never to divert a juvenile charged with violence, although 60 percent of all police "contacts" never reach court, and 13 percent of those that do are diverted to non-judicial processing. Consequently, a juvenile charged with violence in Mercer has a much greater chance of appearing in court than a juvenile charged with a nonviolent crime. In Manhattan, on the other hand, the odds that a juvenile charged with violence will be petitioned for court appearance are about the same as the odds facing a juvenile charged with a nonviolent crime. In 1974, 51 percent of all arrested children were diverted at court intake whereas, according to a study by the Juvenile Justice Institute of the New York State Division of Criminal Justice Services, 54 percent of juveniles arrested for violent crimes between July 1, 1973 and June 30, 1974 were diverted at court intake.[28] Complete information on diversion policies in Westchester County could not be obtained, because there are more than thirty police departments and three family courts. It appears, however, that Westchester falls between Mercer and Manhattan, diverting some juveniles charged with violence (but not so many as half) and a large number charged with nonviolent crimes.

This evidence speaks only to the category of crime committed, not to the seriousness of the crime, nor to the prior record of the juvenile. Both factors undoubtedly play a role in the decision to divert in all three counties, but that role is impossible to determine from the evidence available in our study or elsewhere. The most that can be said is that diversion policies do not seem to load the Manhattan court population disproportionately with violent juveniles, as defined by the category of the charge, in comparison to the other counties.

The second possible explanation, which seems more likely, is simply that Manhattan delinquents are more violent than delinquents in the other counties. In any case, the incontestable fact is that the Family Court in Manhattan is faced with more frequently and more seriously violent delinquents than the courts in Mercer and Westchester are.

Table 11 also contains a comparison of seriousness scores for violent offenses between our sample and the Philadelphia cohort, which passed out of its juvenile era more than a dozen years ago. For each violent crime in each county (except robbery in Mercer),

28 Juvenile Justice Institute, op. cit.

our sample registered higher seriousness scores than the Philadelphia cohort. This implies that the consequences of juvenile violence have increased in seriousness in the time since the Philadelphia study or, more precisely, that violent delinquent acts were more serious in 1974 in the three counties studied than they were in Philadelphia eleven years before.

Comparisons of other data in the two studies are more difficult. Excluding only minor assaults, the proportion of violent crimes in the six most recent offenses of the Vera sample (17 percent) was considerably higher than the proportion of violent offenses in the Philadelphia cohort's crimes (4.6 percent). On the other hand, the proportion of *offenders* in the two studies committing at least one violent offense (again excluding only minor assaults) was similar: 37 percent in the Vera sample, 30–35 percent in the Philadelphia cohort. The proportion committing two or more such offenses was 12 percent in the Vera study and about 7 percent in the Philadelphia cohort.

On the surface, these results taken together suggest that the proportions of arrested delinquents charged with violent crimes today and ten to fifteen years ago are about the same, but the violent group commits violent offenses somewhat more frequently now than then. Unfortunately, however, vast methodological differences in these two studies make direct comparison between the two periods impossible. For example, the exclusion of status offenses and diverted delinquents undoubtedly raises the violence quotient of the Vera sample. It is also probable that inclusion of more than six offenses in the analysis of the Vera sample would have reduced its proportion of violent crimes and brought the two groups somewhat closer together on this measure (see footnote 23 in this chapter). Therefore, we cannot say for certain whether delinquents' propensities to commit violent crimes have increased, decreased, or stayed the same.

Summary

All this evidence together points to the following general conclusions regarding the scope of juvenile violence today.

1. *Delinquent behavior is a widespread phenomenon, however one chooses to measure it.* Self-report studies show that most if not all juveniles commit illegal acts. Thirty-five percent of the boys in the Philadelphia cohort were detected at least once in a delinquency, and in small town and rural Oregon, the figure was 25 percent.

2. *Violent acts by juveniles are much less frequent.* Only 10 percent of all juvenile arrests in 1975 were for serious violent crimes. In the Philadelphia cohort, only 4.6 percent of delinquent acts were of a serious violent nature, and an additional 5.3 percent were simple assaults. In the 1974 sample studied by the Vera Institute, 11 percent of all offenses examined (up to six per offender) were of a serious violent nature, and an additional 12 percent were assaults and robberies of a relatively nonserious nature.

3. *Although other forms of delinquent behavior are much more frequent than violence, a surprisingly high proportion of arrested delinquents engage in violent acts at least once.* In the Philadelphia study, 31 percent of all delinquents (or 11 percent of all boys) were charged with an injury offense at least once. With robbery included, the proportion charged with violent offenses might have reached 35 percent of all delinquents. In the Vera sample, 44 percent of delinquents brought to court had been charged at least once with a violent crime, although only 29 percent had been charged with serious violence.

4. *Repeated violence is not a common phenomenon, however.* Only 7 percent of the Philadelphia delinquents (or 2.3 percent of all boys) were charged twice or more with injury offenses. In the Vera sample, 6 percent had been charged more than once with a serious violent crime. When projected to all youths arrested in 1974 in the three jurisdictions studied, this figure suggests that only 3–5 percent had shown a pattern of two or more violent offenses.

5. *The most common violent crime committed by juveniles is simple assault, but the most common serious violent crime is robbery, followed by serious assault.* On this point, arrest data and the Vera sample agree, but this rank ordering was

reversed in the Philadelphia study. Self-report studies indicate that assaults are much more common than robberies, but these data include many "assaults" (more aptly, fights) in which an arrest would not be considered appropriate. Murder and sex attacks are a small fraction of crimes committed by juveniles: 0.6 percent in the Philadelphia cohort, 0.7 in 1975 arrest data, and 1.2 percent in the Vera court sample.

6. *Juvenile violence does appear to be increasing.* Arrest rates are clearly on the rise, and have been for more than a decade. The greatest increase has occurred in robbery and assault. A comparison between the Philadelphia cohort and the Vera sample also suggests that the violent acts of today's delinquents have more serious consequences than those of a decade or more ago. Data in one self-report study contradict these findings, however, indicating no increase in either the frequency or the seriousness of delinquent acts, including robbery and assault, between 1967 and 1972. The explanation for this discrepancy offered by the author of the study, Martin Gold, traces it to changes in reporting procedures that are not related to changes in the behavior of youth. This may well be true in general, but it is probably less true for the most violent kinds of delinquency.

7. *The most serious problem of juvenile violence is still found in the large urban centers, even though suburban rates have increased faster than urban rates in recent years.* Arrest data show this, and it is dramatically apparent in the Vera study. In Manhattan, 42.3 percent of the children brought to court had been arrested on a serious violent charge at least once, 12.3 percent on two or more occasions, and 2.8 percent on three or more occasions. Projected to the entire population before the Manhattan Family Court, these figures imply that there are several hundred repeatedly violent children to contend with in that borough each year. Although the dimensions of this problem fall short of the extreme estimates of alarmists, they are impressive enough. And although New York may be *sui generis* in many respects, there is reason to believe that, in this respect at least, it is representative of other large metropolitan centers.

3 Characteristics of Violent Delinquents

WE TURN NOW to a general summary of what is known about demographic and personal characteristics of violent delinquents. It is worth reemphasizing here that the main sources of data from which this description is drawn (arrest reports, cohort studies, and the court records studied by Vera) all relate to juveniles apprehended by the police. Self-report data are also available, but they are more limited and do not always agree with arrest based data. The resulting picture, therefore, portrays mainly delinquents who get caught. It may be that delinquents who never get caught are different from those described here. However, given that police are more likely to arrest juveniles who are more frequently and more seriously delinquent, according to self-report studies discussed in the previous chapter, the description provided by arrest-based data is likely to be most reliable with regard to the most violent offenders.

We will open this examination by extending the line of inquiry begun in the previous chapter. We saw there that although a rather high proportion of delinquents had committed at least one violent offense, relatively few had committed more than one. This raises some questions: Are there delinquents who "specialize" in violence? Or are there, at least, clear patterns of delinquent behavior that make the occurrence of violence predictable? And even if there are no such patterns, are there at least some characteristics that clearly distinguish juveniles who commit violent acts from those who do not? These are the issues that will be addressed in this chapter.

Patterns of Delinquency and Violence

The best available evidence regarding the pattern of delinquent behavior and the place of violence in that pattern comes, once again, from the Philadelphia cohort study. A little over half (54 percent) of the delinquents in the cohort were recidivists; the remainder were one-time offenders. Recidivists were responsible for 84 percent of the cohort's offenses, including more than 90 percent of those resulting in physical injury. Within the recidivist group, a subgroup of 627 chronic offenders (18 percent of the delinquents, 6 percent of the entire cohort) committed 52 percent of all offenses, including 53 percent of all personal attacks and 71 percent of all robberies.

Possibly the most significant finding in this part of the study was the absence of any clear pattern in the offenses of the recidivist group. Most important, the probability of committing more serious offenses did not increase as offense number went up. Only a weak tendency to "specialize" in any serious crime appeared, principally with respect to theft. With regard to violence, delinquents rarely repeated (or, more accurately, got caught repeating) a homicide, rape, or aggravated assault. They were more likely to repeat a robbery, but even this pattern was weak. Neither did the seriousness score of offenses, regardless of type, increase significantly as more were committed by an individual. The one exception to this latter observation was injury offenses by nonwhites, which showed a strong tendency to grow more serious as more were committed.

Data in the Vera study presented a similar picture for the most part. In the sample as a whole, there was a moderate tendency for the seriousness of the most recent offense committed to increase with the number of prior offenses. One-time offenders had a mean score of 293 on the sampled offense, recidivists 339, and chronics 361. This relationship was strong only in Manhattan, however. In Mercer and Westchester, there was no clear relationship between offense number and seriousness of the last offense. Nor was there any clear pattern in any of the counties with regard to offense number and average seriousness per offense of all offenses. Moreover, recidivists and chronic offenders appeared to be no more likely than first offenders to commit a violent act in the sampled offense. In the sample as a whole, 28 percent of both one-time offenders and recidivists were charged with a violent offense in their last petition, as compared with 31 percent of chronic offenders. That offense was seriously violent (i.e., more than a minor assault or petty strong-arm robbery) for 18 percent of first offenders, 19 percent of recidivists, and 24 percent of chronic offenders—a modest increase that is not statistically significant.

These results indicate that the number of offenses a delinquent has already committed has little to do with the likelihood of that delinquent committing a violent offense at any given time. Nor does it have much to do with the seriousness of the next offense committed, violent or not (except in Manhattan, where the seriousness of the most recent offense tends to increase according to the number of prior offenses the delinquent has committed). Thus a juvenile's prior record is of little use in predicting whether the delinquent will act violently next time or in predicting how serious the next offense will be.

Recidivism is not altogether irrelevant to violence, however. Recidivists (including chronics) in the Vera sample, as in the Philadelphia cohort, were responsible for most of the harm done by the group: they were charged with 85 percent of all offenses committed by the sample on which data were collected, including 82 percent of all violent offenses. The number of violent crimes per recidivist (0.90) was nearly four times as high as the rate for one-time offenders (0.28). This same phenomenon was observed by the Task Force on Crime of the 1969 Violence Commission.

By far the greatest proportion of all serious violence is committed by repeaters, not by one time offenders. When all offenders are compared, the number of hardcore offenders is small relative to the number of one-time offenders, yet the former group has a much higher rate of violence and inflicts considerably more serious injury.[1]

Thus the more often a juvenile commits delinquent acts, the greater the probability that a violent act will eventually be committed. If a way could be found to stop recidivists from committing further offenses after the first or second, most criminal violence would be stopped, as would most crime in general. But the fact remains that with the exception of a small handful of hardcore delinquents committed to violent crime, delinquents engage in violence only occasionally as part of an apparently random pattern of illegal behavior.

Sex

Juvenile violence is predominantly a masculine phenomenon, even more so than delinquency in general. Girls are involved in 22 percent of all juvenile arrests, but only 8 percent of arrests for major violent crimes. In 1975, the female juvenile arrest rate for serious violence was thirty-seven per 100,000, compared to male rate of 296 per 100,000. The male rate surpassed the female rate by 9:1 for homicide, 12:1 for robbery, and 5:1 for aggravated assault.[2]

Many observers have noted that girls have become more frequently and more seriously violent in recent years.[3] UCR data support this observation, showing an overall increase in arrests of juvenile females for violent offenses of 74 percent between 1970 and 1975. Arrests for the most common violent female offense, aggravated assault, rose 80 percent in the period. On the other hand, Gold and Reimer's self-report survey showed a decline in most kinds of delinquency by females between 1967 and 1972, including assaults, gang fights, and robberies.[4]

[1] Donald J. Mulvihill, Melvin M. Tumin, and Lynn A. Curtis, *Crimes of Violence: A Staff Report Submitted to the National Commission on the Causes and Prevention of Violence* (Washington, D.C.: U.S. Government Printing Office, 1969), p. XXIX.
[2] Rates are calculated from 1975 FBI Uniform Crime Reports and Census Bureau data.
[3] See, for example, Donald Hayes Russell, "Juvenile Delinquency," *Psychiatric Annals* 5, no. 1 (January 1975): 10.
[4] Gold and Reimer, op. cit., Table 4, p. 498.

In the Vera sample, 15 percent of juveniles facing the court were girls.[5] In all three counties, a significantly larger proportion of girls than boys were first offenders (56 percent to 38 percent), and a significantly smaller proportion were chronic offenders with five or more offenses (7 percent to 26 percent). The proportion of girls and boys who were recidivists (two to four offenses) was about equal (37 percent to 36 percent). There was no significant difference between boys and girls in the percentage ever charged with a violent crime—41 percent of the girls and 44 percent of the boys. But boys were more likely to be seriously violent than girls: 29 percent of the girls and 38 percent of the boys had been arrested at least once for a violent crime, not counting minor assaults. Among the girls' 74 current offenses, there were twenty assaults, three robberies, and one rape.

Table 12 summarizes seriousness scores for offenses by males and females. The mean score for all current offenses was about the same for males and females, except in Manhattan, where the girls' score was higher than the boys'. Violent offenses by females were, on the average, less serious than violent offenses by males.

Table 12 Mean Seriousness Scores of Current Offenses in Vera Sample, by Sex and County

	Mercer	Westchester	Manhattan	Total Sample
All Offenses				
Male (N = 429)	238.0	291.6	408.4	325.1
Female (N = 74)	239.5	259.4	471.7	323.6
Violent Offenses				
Male (N = 119)	305.4	434.1	687.3	552.7
Female (N = 24)	100.0	235.6	607.1[a]	441.0

SOURCE: Vera Institute Violent Delinquent Study.

[a] The one female involved in a rape in Manhattan raised the seriousness score of female violent offenses considerably. When that case is removed, the female violent offense score decreases to 408.

[5] The gap between this figure and the nationwide arrest figure (22 percent female) is probably due to the exclusion of status offenses from the Vera sample (girls are more heavily represented in status offenses than in other kinds of offenses) and to the fact that girls are diverted from court at higher rates than boys.

The difference between girls in Manhattan and in the other two counties is as striking as that for the boys. Seriousness scores were three and six times higher for violent crimes by Manhattan girls than by the others (or two and four times higher, if the one Manhattan rape involving a female is not considered). More impressive yet is that 61.5 percent of delinquent girls before the Manhattan court had been charged at least once with violence other than minor assault. In Mercer and Westchester, only 14.3 percent and 9.5 percent of the girls, respectively, had ever been charged with similar offenses. Moreover, only 50.5 percent of Manhattan boys had ever been so charged. (It should be noted that the number of females in the sample who were charged with serious violence was small ($N = 22$), so these comparisons may not be reliable.)

In summary, female delinquents brought to court seem to be about as likely to be violent as male delinquents, but generally with less serious consequences. Females in the Manhattan court, however, appear to be somewhat more violence-prone than their male counterparts and with consequences nearly as serious. Nevertheless, in Manhattan and elsewhere, the number of females committing violent acts and other kinds of delinquency remains small relative to the number of males.

Age

Of all age groups, 16-year-olds have the highest arrest rate for serious crimes, according to the FBI's Uniform Crime Reports. The Philadelphia cohort study[6] and Gold's self-report study in Flint[7] also showed 16 years to be the peak age for both number and seriousness of delinquent acts. But for *violent* crimes specifically, UCR data indicate that 18 is the peak age. Figure 1 plots combined arrest rates for homicide, rape, aggravated assault, and robbery in 1975. In each of these four crime categories, arrest rates increase relatively smoothly as age increases, up to 18. Thereafter, the rates decline. Although 18 is the peak age for violent crimes,

[6] Wolfgang, Figlio, and Sellin, op. cit., p. 112.
[7] Martin Gold, *Delinquent Behavior in an American City* (Belmont, Calif.: Brooks-Cole, 1970), pp. 66–72.

Figure 1 Arrest Rates Nationally per 1,000 for Homicide, Rape, Assault, and Robbery, by Age Group (1975)

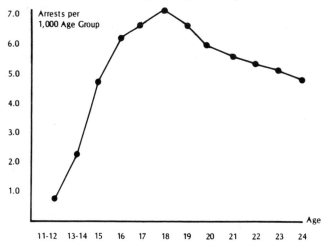

Source: 1975 FBI Uniform Crime Reports and Census Bureau Data.

Note: Population figures, calculated from U.S. Census Bureau projections for each age group In 1975, are adjusted to reflect the proportion of the population covered by FBI Uniform Crime Reports data.

Figure 1 also shows clearly that 16 through 24 are all high risk ages. We saw in Chapter 2 (Table 4), however, that arrests for violence are rising faster among juveniles than among the young adults. Older juveniles (15- to 17-year-olds) show the fastest growth in arrests for robbery and aggravated assault, followed by 11- to 14-year-olds.[8]

Criminological research has frequently shown the age of onset of delinquent behavior to be strongly related to the level of subsequent delinquent activity. The younger a child is when first arrested, the more seriously delinquent he or she is likely to be.[9] Russell has explained this phenomenon in psychological terms.

[8] In comparison, Gold and Reimer's trend analysis of self-reported delinquency indicated that within the juvenile group, 15-year-old males committed more crimes in 1972 than in 1967, whereas 16-year-olds (and all younger groups) reported committing fewer. (Gold and Reimer, op. cit., pp. 501–502.)

[9] See, for example, Task Force on Juvenile Delinquency, President's Commission on Law Enforcement and the Administration of Justice. *Task Force Report: Juvenile Delinquency and Youth Crime*, 1967, p. 122.

The age at which an adolescent becomes manifestly in trouble with the law can often be seen as an index of the strength or weakness of his personality structure. The boy or girl who stays out of trouble until the age of 16 or so is usually in better shape psychologically than the child whose problems emerge in full force at age 13. Also, it is axiomatic that a child of 12 or younger who is a source of severe trouble in the community either is a seriously neglected child or is seriously emotionally disturbed.[10]

In a sophisticated analysis of the relationship between age and seriousness of delinquency in the Philadelphia cohort, Wolfgang and his colleagues concluded that the effects of age vary with the kind of crime. Violence against persons (homicide, rape, and assault) increased with age, but robbery, property crimes, and other serious offenses either decreased with or were unaffected by age. The effects of age also appeared to vary with race. Nonwhites' offenses at younger ages were more serious than those of whites at older ages. For example, the weighted rate (accounting for frequency and seriousness together) of nonwhites aged 7 to 10 was higher than the rate of whites aged 14 and 15. As nonwhites grew older, they were involved in more violent crimes, but fewer property and other offenses; whites also became slightly more violent as they got older, but otherwise showed no clear age-related pattern.[11]

Because the data in the Vera study are cross-sectional, they are of limited use in furthering our understanding of patterns of criminal behavior by age. Nevertheless, they are of some interest. Table 13 shows the distribution by age of both the entire sample and the subsample charged with violent crimes in the most recent offense. Each age group contributes a roughly proportionate share to the violent subgroup, suggesting that among delinquents brought to court, no age group is significantly more likely than any other to be charged with a violent offense.

With regard to the seriousness of delinquent acts, a surprising

10 Russell, op. cit., p. 101.
11 Wolfgang, Figlio, and Sellin, op. cit., p. 122.

Table 13 Age Distribution of Vera Sample and of a Subsample Currently Charged With Violence (in percent)

	10 and Under	11–12	13	14	15	16 and Over[a]	Total
Total Sample (N = 494)	2.6	9.1	9.5	25.7	34.2	18.8	99.9
Currently Violent (N = 141)	2.8	7.8	12.1	29.1	34.0	14.2	100.0

SOURCE: Vera Institute Violent Delinquent Study.

[a] All Mercer County observations. Five Manhattan delinquents whose age was coded as 16 were dropped from this table because of doubts about the validity of the given age (15 is the maximum age of jurisdiction of the Family Court except in special cases).

and potentially significant age-group difference did appear. Even though the maximum age of the sample was 17 in Mercer and 15 in Manhattan and Westchester, in each county the age with the highest mean seriousness score for current offenses was 13. And the 13-year-olds' mean scores were well above those of the next age group in each county.[12] Moreover, when only violent current offenses are considered, age 13 again had the highest mean score, taking the sample as a whole. (County by county, however, 13 always followed one of the older age groups in mean score for violent offenses.) Finally, in Manhattan, a higher proportion of 13-year-olds (54 percent) than any other age group were charged with violence in the most recent offense, although in the overall sample there was no clear pattern by age. Although these data must be treated cautiously, since they cover only part of the "careers" of many delinquents in the sample, the dominance of 13-year-olds lends some support to the argument that violence is growing more serious among younger juveniles, particularly in Manhattan.

[12] In Manhattan, five delinquents aged 16 entered the sample for one reason or another, although normally the maximum age of Family Court jurisdiction is 15. This group of five registered a higher mean seriousness score than the 13-year-olds, but their number is too small and their circumstances too unusual to regard them as representative.

Race

One of the most common findings in criminological research is a strong correlation between race and violence. In 1975, blacks were 14 percent of the population under 18, but they accounted for 22 percent of all juvenile arrests and 52 percent of juvenile arrests for violence; 56 percent of arrests for homicide; 51 percent for rape; 63 percent for robbery; and 40 percent for aggravated assault. Table 14 shows arrest rates of black and white juveniles for violent

Table 14 1975 Arrests Nationally per 100,000 Juveniles, Ages 7–17, by Race

	Homicide	Rape	Robbery	Aggravated Assault	Total
White	2.1	5.6	43.8	62.7	114.2
Black	16.3	36.2	467.6	259.1	779.2

SOURCE: 1975 FBI Uniform Crime Reports and Census Bureau data.

NOTE: Population figures, calculated from Census Bureau projections for race and age groups for 1975, are adjusted to reflect the proportion of the population covered by FBI Uniform Crime Reports data.

crimes in 1975. The overall arrest rate of black juveniles for violent crimes is seven times the white rate, with the black rate for robbery surpassing the white rate by 11:1.

In the Philadelphia cohort study, nonwhites committed all the homicides, 86 percent of the rapes, 82 percent of the aggravated assaults, 89 percent of the robberies, and 63 percent of all offenses resulting in physical injury; yet they comprised only 29 percent of the cohort. Differences between white and nonwhite offense rates were highest for assaultive crimes: nonwhites had ten times the white rate for aggravated assault, fifteen times for rape, and twenty times for robbery. Overall, the nonwhite crude offense rate (considering only the frequency of offenses) was 3.1 times as great as the white rate, and the weighted rate, taking seriousness into account as well, was 4.4 times higher for nonwhites than for whites. For injury offenses, nonwhites' seriousness scores were 15 percent higher than whites' scores.

Some important racial differences were also evident with regard to offense patterns. Whites were about twice as likely as nonwhites to cease further offending after each offense. In addition, nonwhite delinquents began serious acts at younger ages than whites and were more likely to follow an offense with an act of physical violence.

Arrest figures show that rates of violence among black juveniles increased faster than among whites over the past fifteen years, although in the last several years that trend has been reversed. Between 1973 and 1975 the white juvenile arrest rate for violent offenses grew by 67 percent, while the black rate increased only 15 percent. In Gold and Reimer's self-report study, black males reported more assaults and significantly more robberies in 1972 than in 1967, while white males reported fewer.[13]

Data from the Vera sample conform to this picture in general. Blacks were overrepresented both in the delinquent sample as a whole and in the violent subgroup. Forty-nine percent of the sample was black, 22 percent was Spanish-speaking, and 29 percent was white.[14] Blacks were charged with 56 percent of all offenses, Spanish-speaking delinquents with 17 percent, and whites with 27 percent. But 62 percent of all violent offenses was charged to blacks, 21 percent to Spanish-speaking delinquents, and 17 percent to whites. Overall, 51 percent of black delinquents had been charged with violence at least once, compared to 47 percent of Spanish-speaking delinquents and 28 percent of white delinquents. When only serious violent acts are considered, there is a shift in the relative positions of black and Spanish-speaking delinquents: 32 percent of the black delinquents and 39 percent of Spanish-speaking delinquents committed at least one serious violent offense.

Table 15 provides additional data on the three racial groups. It can be seen that a higher proportion of black delinquents than of the other groups were chronic offenders and committed two, three, or more serious violent offenses and reached the highest level in total seriousness of their offenses. However, blacks were surpassed

[13] Gold and Reimer, op. cit., Table 3.
[14] Data on race were available for 87.1 percent of the sample: 99.5 percent in Mercer, 82.6 percent in Westchester, and 79.7 percent in Manhattan.

Table 15 Comparison of Racial Groups in Vera Sample on Frequency and Seriousness of Offenses (percent in each category)

	Number of Offenses			Number of Serious Violent Offenses[a]			
	One-time	Recidivist (2-4)	Chronic (5+)	0	1	2	3+
White	43.8	32.8	23.5	82.8	14.1	2.3	0.8
Black	27.5	38.5	34.0	68.6	22.9	6.9	1.9
Spanish Surname[b]	47.5	40.4	12.1	60.6	32.3	6.1	1.0

Chi square = 23.9; $df = 4$; $p < 0.005$.　　Chi square = 110.1; $df = 6$; $p < 0.005$.

	Seriousness Level, Most Recent Offense[c]				Total Seriousness Level, Up to Six Offenses[d]				
	I	II	III	IV	I	II	III	IV	V
White	16.4	57.0	20.3	6.3	23.4	22.7	18.8	13.3	21.9
Black	6.9	58.8	22.2	12.0	13.4	20.3	18.9	13.4	34.1
Spanish Surname[b]	7.1	50.0	25.5	17.3	9.2	27.6	25.5	16.3	21.4

Chi square = 15.9; $df = 6$; $p < 0.05$.　　Chi square = 18.3; $df = 8$; $p < 0.05$.

SOURCE: Vera Institute Violent Delinquent Study.

[a]Excluding robberies in which no weapon was used and no injury resulted, and minor assaults (seriousness score less than 210).

[b]81.8 percent of the Spanish-speaking sample members were located in Manhattan, where scores on all indexes of seriousness and frequency were higher than in the other counties.

[c]I = least serious, IV = most serious. See Appendix C for description of offenses in each level.

[d]I = least serious. V = most serious. Total serious scores fell into groups approximately equal to quintiles for the entire sample.

by Spanish-speaking delinquents in the seriousness of the most recent offense.[15]

[15] Racial data in Manhattan were most complete for the Spanish-speaking group. Since Manhattan delinquents recorded higher scores than those in other counties, and most Spanish-speaking delinquents were in Manhattan, the overall Spanish-speaking

At the county level, these results tended to be most significant in Manhattan (where there were many more minority youths in the sample than whites) and significant to a lesser degree in Mercer (where the disparity in numbers was less). But in the Westchester sample, where minorities and whites were about equal in number, differences among racial groups were insignificant on all of these measures.

The county-level differences underscore a crucial point: although race and violence are associated, the strength of that association varies from place to place, and it comes close to disappearing altogether in Westchester County. Consequently, the correlation by itself tells us little, if anything at all, about causality. Being black does not make a person violent any more than being white makes a person violent, certainly not in Westchester and most likely not anywhere else. The geographic variation in the association between race and violence implies instead that some other factor (or fac-·tors) in the environment, linked to race through circumstance perhaps, contributes to the violence of these youth. It is no secret that socioeconomic status, residential location, education, health services, and other amenities are generally distributed in a way that disfavors minorities. But the pattern of distribution is not the same from one location to another. It is conceivable, when one takes into account superficial social and economic differences between Manhattan and Westchester, that minorities in Westchester have access to higher social status, better education and health services, and more desirable residences, and in general lead more secure lives than minorities in Manhattan. And it is a reasonable hypothesis, at least, that the variation in the distribution of these amenities (not race) accounts for the observed variation in rates of violence. Before reaching any conclusions, therefore, it is necessary to examine

---

score was high. If more blacks had been identifiable in Manhattan, the overall black score theoretically could have risen to or above the Spanish-speaking level. However, the mean seriousness score on the most recent offense of the forty-three Manhattan delinquents whose race was unknown (338) was well below the mean for both Manhattan black (487) and Spanish-speaking (406) delinquents, and close to the mean score for the entire sample (325). Consequently, it is highly unlikely that more complete racial data would have changed the relative position of the black and Spanish-speaking delinquents with regard to the seriousness of the most recent offense.

what is known about the impact of these and other variables on violent behavior.

Family Structure

The "failure" of family life has always been given a central place in analyses of delinquency. Quoting Professor Urie Bronfenbrenner, James Q. Wilson reports that "thousands" of studies have shown family disorganization to be an " 'omnipresent, overriding factor' in behavior disorders and social pathology. And," he writes, "disorganization is increasing."[16] The data Wilson cites on this point are impressive. One-third of all black children and one-fourteenth of all white children currently live in single-parent, usually female-headed, households. This amounts to more than 2 million children under 6, and 6 million children under 16, twice the numbers of ten years ago. These children are deprived of one parent, and they are often also deprived of a decent standard of living. The average income for a single-parent family with children under 6 years of age in 1970 was $3,100—"well below the official poverty line."[17]

Other equally compelling facts support Wilson's argument. A study of juveniles before New York City's family courts in 1973 showed that only 21 percent came from intact families, and 59 percent came from families on welfare.[18] At "The Door," a drop-in center serving more than 600 runaway, homeless, alienated, or simply bored and curious adolescents in New York City, half of the children in the program have no functioning family at all; they either never had one or have severed all ties. Half of the remainder are in touch with their families, but find the relationship essentially destructive. Only 10 to 15 percent find their families' involvement to be helpful, according to directors of the program.[19] In

[16] James Q. Wilson, "Lock 'em Up," *New York Times Magazine*, March 9, 1975, pp. 11, 44–48.
[17] Ibid.
[18] Office of Children's Services, New York State Office of Court Administration. "Juvenile Injustice," October 1973, pp. 23–28. (Mimeo.)
[19] Interview with Lorraine Henricks, M.D., and Charles Terry, June 6, 1975.

Massachusetts, a recent analysis of 700 children examined in court clinics showed "a considerable incidence of family losses and deficiencies during developmental years": 46 percent of the children's parents were divorced or permanently separated; another 14 percent had lost a parent by death; 21.5 percent had parents with chronic illnesses, and 18 percent had parents suffering from severe alcoholism.[20]

The delinquent population sampled in the Vera study also contained a large proportion from broken homes: 39 percent had parents who were separated, 11 percent divorced, and 16 percent widowed, a total of two-thirds from broken homes.[21] Available data permitted analysis of the relationship between family structure and both violence and delinquency generally. Family structure appeared to have some influence on the number of crimes charged to a youth, but not on the propensity to be violent. In the sample as a whole, a significantly larger proportion of youths from broken homes than from intact homes were recidivists, having two to four offenses (41 percent to 32 percent), and chronic offenders, having five or more offenses (30 percent to 24 percent). There was no significant difference, however, between children of intact and broken families in any of the counties with regard to the probability of committing a violent offense, either in the most recent petition or ever. While children from broken homes had significantly higher total seriousness scores for all offenses up to 6 than children from intact homes, that was due to their tendency to commit more crimes instead of more serious crimes. There was no difference between the two groups in the mean seriousness score per offense.

These data, taken together, imply that the presence of two parents may reduce a child's chances of becoming delinquent and may play some role in limiting the number of offenses committed if the child does become delinquent. But it has little impact on whether the child will become violent. Other factors appear to outweigh family structure in that regard.

Among those other factors, an important one may be the strength of the relationship between the parent (or parents) and

[20] Russell, op. cit., p. 17.
[21] Data on family structure were available for 81 percent of the sample.

the child. Studies have shown that a single-parent home in which the child and parent have a good relationship may offer more protection against delinquency than a two-parent family in which relationships are strained.[22] If so, it may also offer more protection against violent behavior.

Defective parent-child relationships are, in fact, among the most frequently cited explanations for juvenile (and adult) violence. The Fortune Society, a voluntary organization for ex-offenders in New York City, estimates that half of its members were seriously abused or neglected by their parents when they were children.[23] A study by Dr. Jay Katz of ghetto boys removed from the community and placed at the Wiltwyck School in New York found three common, interrelated factors underlying their problems.

> . . . A massive lack of early mothering; chronic and serious child-hood problems left without help until the boy reached adolescence and engaged in aggressive behavior; and extreme disorganization of family life, within cramped quarters. Violence and sexuality were seen as the aggressive responses of these boys to the overwhelming agony resulting from maternal rejection or inadequacies which the boys could not and would not admit. Aggressive behavior had become the defense against a sense of despair and depression that was all but overwhelming.[24]

Other studies have found inadequate maternal care and affection to have a significant impact on delinquent behavior, but there is also evidence to suggest that "when father-son and mother-son relationships are compared, the father-son relationships appear more determinative in whether or not delinquent behavior develops."[25] Regardless of which relationship is the more critical, the association between the quality of parent-child relationships and delinquency is by now well established.

[22] Daniel Glaser, *Strategic Criminal Justice Planning,* Center for Studies of Crime and Delinquency, National Institute of Mental Health, 1975, p. 50.

[23] *Time,* June 30, 1975.

[24] As cited in Justine Wise Polier, "Keynote Address: The Juvenile Delinquent: To Bestow or to Withhold Resources—The Power and the Duty," in *Summary Report: Conference on New York City Juvenile Justice Resources,* Institute of Judicial Administration, Inc., May 28, 1974, p. D-7. (Mimeo.)

[25] President's Commission on Law Enforcement and the Administration of Justice, op. cit., p. 46.

Socioeconomic Status and Social Environment

An enormous volume of research has identified the strong relationship between delinquent behavior and social class. The Philadelphia cohort study, for example, revealed that both the number and kind of offenses were influenced by social class standing. Among lower-class boys, 27 percent were recidivists, including 11 percent who were chronic offenders. Among higher-class boys, in comparison, the figures were 11 percent recidivists and 3 percent chronics. Lower-class boys had an offense rate that was nearly five times greater than higher-class boys for assault, six times higher for robbery, and 3.5 times higher for property offenses.[26] The strength of the relationship between socioeconomic status and delinquency in the Philadelphia study was, in fact, surpassed only by the association of race to delinquency.

There is a significant divergence, however, between the findings of studies based on arrest figures and studies based on self-report data. A number of self-report studies have shown that socioeconomic status has slight effect, if any, on delinquency rates, at least in America; some British studies have reported higher delinquency rates among lower classes, but Scandinavian and Canadian studies show no special class differences.[27] Gold's study in Flint, Michigan, reported some relationship between delinquency and socioeconomic status, but not nearly so strong as official figures suggested. Flint's official statistics put the ratio of lower-class to middle-class delinquency at about 8:1, whereas Gold's data showed that among the 20 percent most delinquent, the ratio was actually 3:2.[28]

Daniel Glaser has identified a feature of self-report studies which may partly (but not fully) explain their conflict with arrest data. Most self-report studies are confined to single schools or neighborhoods, drawing social class distinctions among the students or residents in the chosen area. When self-reporting is com-

[26] Wolfgang et al., op. cit., pp. 72–73, 91.
[27] Doleschal, op. cit., pp. 546–568.
[28] Gold, *Delinquent Behavior*, p. 150.

pared among different kinds of neighborhoods and communities (as was done by Clark and Wenninger in 1962),[29] substantial differences in the type and number of delinquencies appear— much greater than differences among social classes within the same neighborhood. There is more delinquency generally in slum areas, with the greatest contrasts in theft, violence, truancy, vandalism, and disorderly conduct. Unfortunately, the Clark and Wenninger study did not cover a wide range of felonies and has not been repeated, so it tells us less than it might have about violence and socioeconomic status and leaves us in the dark about changes over time. But Glaser was able to draw an important conclusion from this and similar studies.

> Delinquency is apparently more a function of the average social class level of a neighborhood or school district than of the contrast within the area. . . . The predominant class in a neighborhood determines its subculture. . . . The social and cultural conditions of urban slums may have a different significance for delinquency than conditions elsewhere.[30]

This formulation takes the focus off individual economic and class differences and shifts it to broader environmental conditions.

Glaser does agree, however, that the variation in admitted delinquency from one neighborhood or community to another is far less than the variation in arrest and adjudication rates. Consequently, the argument that police and court records (and practices) overstate the relative importance of juveniles from lower socioeconomic status retains some validity. But slum children do commit more (and more serious) delinquencies,[31] not so much because they have less money or a less desirable social position as because something in their environment encourages such behavior. Police may thus be justified in concentrating their attention on

[29] J. P. Clark and E. P. Wenninger, "Socioeconomic Class and Area as Correlates of Illegal Behavior Among Juveniles," *American Sociological Review* 27, no. 6 (December 1962): 826–843.

[30] Glaser, op. cit., pp. 64–67.

[31] The Task Force on Crime of the 1969 Violence Commission cited studies in Minneapolis, Cleveland, St. Louis, Boston, and Harlem, all of which showed delinquency differentials between the ghetto and the rest of the city ranging between two and four times—high enough to override doubts based on statistical biases in arrest figures. (Mulvihill, Tumin, and Curtis, op. cit., p. 607.)

children from the slums, but not, apparently, to the extent they have.

Glaser's hypothesis that neighborhood or community environment has a more significant impact on delinquency than individual socioeconomic differences within communities seems to be borne out by data from the Vera sample.[32] In total seriousness of offenses and average seriousness per offense, lower-class delinquents had a higher mean score than middle-class delinquents in the sample as a whole. When the sample was broken down by county, however, middle-class delinquents had higher scores than lower-class delinquents in both Mercer and Manhattan (but not in Westchester). With regard to violent offenses, lower-class delinquents' mean seriousness scores again surpassed those of middle-class delinquents in the sample as a whole, although middle-class delinquents had higher scores than lower-class delinquents in Westchester and Manhattan (but not Mercer this time). The reason for these "reversals" at the county level is that Manhattan, which had the highest seriousness scores overall, had many more lower-class than middle-class delinquents, so the weight of their influence in the overall sample gave the lower class high scores.[33]

On other measures, including the number of offenses and the probability of a violent charge, there was no significant difference between lower-class and middle-class delinquents, either in the sample as a whole or on the county level.

Over 80 percent of black and Spanish-speaking delinquents in the sample lived in lower-class neighborhoods, whereas only 41 percent of whites lived in lower-class neighborhoods. (These figures correspond closely to those in the Philadelphia cohort study: 89 percent of nonwhite and 38 percent of white delinquents

[32] Socioeconomic status (SES) was measured using census tract income data. Although this is not an altogether satisfactory measure for many reasons, it was easiest to work with. In any case, it is more appropriate when examining the influence of neighborhood environment (which is the focus here) than measuring income levels of individual families. In the sample, 72 percent were from lower SES neighborhoods, and 28 percent were from middle or upper SES neighborhoods.

[33] Middle-class delinquents were less than 10 percent of the Manhattan sample, making class comparisons within that county almost meaningless. (Middle-class delinquents were 63.7 percent of the delinquents in Westchester and 30.5 percent in Mercer.) The most reasonable explanation for the low figure in Manhattan is that middle-class delinquents are usually diverted from juvenile court in Manhattan and thus appear infrequently in a sample drawn from court petitions.

were from lower-class homes.) Lower-class black and Spanish-speaking delinquents had slightly higher mean seriousness scores for the average of all offenses than middle-class black and Spanish-speaking delinquents. On the same measure, middle-class white delinquents outscored lower-class whites. On mean score for violent offenses, lower-class blacks outscored middle-class blacks, but middle-class white delinquents again outscored lower-class white delinquents. The same held true with regard to serious violence. In both Mercer and Westchester, where middle-class delinquents were numerous, lower-class minority delinquents were more likely than middle-class minority delinquents to commit serious violence in the most recent offense, but lower-class whites were less likely than middle-class white delinquents to do so.[34] These results add weight to the argument that social class per se is inadequate to explain delinquent behavior.

Data were available on the source of family income for 70 percent of the sample. Overall, 43 percent of the sample were children of families receiving welfare, the balance were supported by a working parent or parents or by income from some other source. In Manhattan, 70 percent of the delinquents were from welfare families, compared to 26 percent in Mercer and 25 percent in Westchester.

For the sample as a whole, there was virtually no difference between welfare delinquents and nonwelfare delinquents with regard to frequency and seriousness of offenses. For example, the mean seriousness score for the average of all offenses was 268 for both welfare delinquents and nonwelfare delinquents. The mean score of violent offenses was 404 for welfare delinquents and 408 for nonwelfare delinquents. Welfare delinquents averaged 3.28 offenses per offender and 1.65 violent offenses per violent offender, compared to 3.01 and 1.47, respectively, for nonwelfare delinquents. Finally, 49 percent of welfare delinquents were charged at least once with a violent crime, compared to 42 percent of the nonwelfare delinquents—not a statistically significant difference.

---

[34] The number of middle-class Spanish-speaking delinquents committing violent offenses was only six, so comparisons for Spanish-speaking delinquents as a separate group are not reliable.

At the county level, when differences between welfare and non-welfare delinquents emerged, more often than not they favored the welfare delinquents. In Manhattan, where the majority of delinquents came from welfare families, nonwelfare delinquents scored higher on every measure of frequency, seriousness, and violence of offenses. And in Westchester, which had the fewest delinquents from welfare families, nonwelfare delinquents scored higher on most of the indices. Thus, just as individual socioeconomic status is inadequate to explain delinquent behavior, so too is dependence on public assistance.

Education and Learning

Hearings held in 1975 by the U.S. Senate Subcommittee to Investigate Juvenile Delinquency on the question of violence in schools made it plain that schools are primary settings for the hostility and aggression of children. The Subcommittee reported an increase of 19 percent in school homicides, 40 percent in rapes, 85 percent in assaults on students and 77 percent in assaults on teachers between 1970 and 1973.[35] According to the National Association of School Security Directors, there were an estimated 12,000 armed robberies, 9,000 forcible rapes, and 204,000 aggravated assaults in schools in 1974;[36] the Senate Subcommittee, however, put the figure for assaults on teachers at 70,000 per year.

But schools are more than settings for violence. There is much evidence that the educational system and educational processes may be significant contributors to the problem. The Task Force on Juvenile Delinquency of the President's Commission on Law Enforcement and Administration of Justice came to the conclusion that some schools contribute to delinquency both by being passive in the face of a child's problems and by actively encouraging delinquent behavior "by the use of methods that create the conditions

[35] *New York Times,* June 14, 1975, p. 57.

[36] Ibid. The School Security Directors' figures must be viewed with skepticism, for they exceed the total number of arrests of persons under 18 by two-and-one-half times for rape and eight times for aggravated assault.

of failure for certain students."[37] Florida's former Director of Youth Services, Joseph Rowan, says, "I used to blame delinquency on parents and schools about fifty-fifty. Now I blame the schools for 85 percent of it."[38]

In a review of research on this subject, Daniel Glaser found considerable evidence of strong associations between conflict with school authorities, poor performance on aptitude tests, poor grades, and student dislike of school, on the one hand, and delinquency on the other.[39] In the Philadelphia cohort study, more than half (55 percent) of the delinquents were below average in school achievement, compared to only 27 percent of nondelinquents.[40]

Many programs working with delinguent youth report that reading and other educational deficiencies are commonplace. The Neighborhood Youth Diversion Program, which attempts to develop nonjudicial solutions to problems of delinquent youth in one of New York City's highest crime areas, has found that approximately 60 percent of its clients have school problems, and these are among the most serious of all problems confronting the children.

Precisely how and why schools fail children is less clear. Does the problem lie with the school, in the way it is organized and carries out its mandate to educate children? Or does the problem begin with the child, in what he or she brings to the classroom by way of abilities and disabilities that either contribute to or detract from the school's capacity to educate the child?

Those who locate the problem essentially with the schools have many explanations. Some single out the inability of teachers who work in crowded, resource-poor, inner-city schools to devote adequate personal attention to students, particularly slow learners and troubled children. Others point to the seeming irrelevance of school to the lives and futures of these children, resulting in a

---

[37] President's Commission on Law Enforcement and the Administration of Justice, op. cit., p. 49. For a thorough discussion of school failure and delinquency, see also Walter E. Schaefer and Kenneth Polk, "Delinquency and the Schools," Appendix M in that report.

[38] *Corrections Magazine* 1, no. 1 (September 1974): 74.

[39] Glaser, op. cit., pp. 43–47.

[40] Wolfgang, Figlio, and Sellin, p. 63.

situation that is little more than enforced boredom and frustration. Some support for this explanation (and an economic corollary to it) is found in arrest data, which show a significant decline in property crime, especially among lower-income youth, once they pass their sixteenth birthdays and become eligible to leave school and search for jobs.[41]

A study by Elliot and Voss, published in 1974, explored in depth the relationship between leaving school and delinquent behavior in a cohort of 2,617 California students beginning the ninth grade. It concluded that school is the critical social context for the generation of delinquent behavior. Delinquent behavior increased the probability of dropping out in the population studied; in turn, dropping out decreased the probability of further delinquency. While in school, delinquents who subsequently dropped out had much higher police contact rates than students who remained in school. Once they had left school, however, the dropouts' contact rates declined sharply, while the students who continued in school registered increases in police contacts. The association between dropping out and reduced delinquency was especially strong with regard to delinquents who had been serious offenders: their involvement with serious offenses declined sharply after leaving school. The authors found that this relationship between delinquency and dropping out could not be explained by class, sex, "differential visibility," or the deterrent effect of adjudication.[42]

Countless times during the course of our study, we heard of schools that promote bored, undereducated children who cannot read or write, advancing them on schedule through the system until they reach the tenth or eleventh grade, at which point they are stopped and subjected to pressure to drop out so that no diploma need be awarded. At a minimum, such a process constitutes a failure to act responsibly and professionally to identify pupils' problems, even if they cannot be dealt with adequately within the system. Students handled in this manner realize that they are being ignored and misled, which can only increase their frustration and disdain for the society around them.

[41] Glaser, op. cit., p. 46.
[42] Delbert S. Elliot and Harwin L. Voss, *Delinquency and Dropout* (Lexington, Mass.: D.C. Heath and Co., 1974).

It is probably inaccurate and unfair, however, to put the full blame on the schools for student failure and associated delinquency. Some children's learning problems have their source outside the school, in the child's psychological or intellectual makeup.

A specific link between learning problems, educational failure, and delinquency that is now receiving considerable attention is the question of learning disabilities. The term refers to a variety of perceptual problems, such as the tendency to read letters backward or inverted, that hamper a child's ability to learn to read and write. The causes of learning disabilities and the neurological mechanisms behind them are not well understood. The problem is not always readily spotted and frequently goes undetected altogether, although estimates of the afflicted school population run as high as 20 percent, or about 10 million children across the country.[43]

In the past several years, research claiming to have found evidence that learning disabilities lead to delinquency has generated widespread publicity of this issue. On close examination, however, these studies almost invariably fail to demonstrate any causal relationship. While they do show a statistical correlation between delinquency and learning disability, methodological shortcomings in the studies frequently impair the strength of that conclusion. A recent major review of the literature on the link between learning disability and delinquency concluded that although "the evidence for a causal link is feeble," owing largely to the fact that "the quantitative work to date has been so poorly designed and presented," there is such a vast amount of qualitative data from observational studies by professionals who work with delinquents pointing to the existence of a link that further systematic exploration is warranted.[44]

Although the causal relationships are not well understood, it is not hard to imagine that the frustration of having to cope with a subtle learning deficiency that may not even be detected, much less understood, could be an important factor leading a child to antisocial behavior and even violence. Inability to acquire reading

[43] "The Strange Malady Called Learning Disability," *New York Times Magazine*, March 3, 1975, p. 16.

[44] Charles A. Murray, *The Link Between Learning Disabilities and Juvenile Delinquency* (Washington, D.C.: American Institutes for Research, 1976), pp. 65–68.

and writing skills retards the development of verbal skill, which in turn retards the development of other social skills. The Task Force on Crime of the 1969 Violence Commission concluded that children with limited verbal ability may find "homicide or assault . . . the easiest ways to terminate altercations."[45] Charles King, former Deputy Director of the New York State Division for Youth and a psychiatric social worker by training, spelled out this connection in some detail in a study of nine children who had committed homicide.

> Among our youth, a most disabling deficit in their development was . . . their inability or disinclination to master the prevailing language. They had not learned to read well or to deal effectively with symbols. Those who had mastered elementary symbols or, in some rare instances, beyond, did not make a conscious connection between this mastery and positive social adjustment. . . . Thus, at the very entry level into mastery these youths were handicapped. Unable to fathom the language cues of the prevailing society, they could only cope by responding to what must have been inner cues. This created an unproductive, further isolating adjustment, eventuating in a "familiar" omnipotence: I know it all. To sustain that omnipotence and to meet the reality that there is another, more powerful world than theirs, they strove to reduce the symbols of communication between these two worlds to the primitive expedients of terse speech, and, ultimately, action. Terseness and action warded off talk and the cognitive challenge of reason, so difficult for them to deal with. They attempted to make action the language of communication. By limiting the responses of others to reactions to their *behavior,* the youths also reduced the potential of possible interchange concerning the act to a comfortable and comprehensible level.[46]

Even when learning problems clearly originate in the child, schools are frequently remiss in diagnosing the problem and in providing remedial programs to help overcome or compensate for such deficiencies. For example, New York State law requires that special classes be developed to serve children who, "because of mental, physical or emotional reasons, cannot be educated in reg-

[45] Mulvihill, Tumin, and Curtis, op. cit., p. 231.

[46] Charles H. King, "The Ego and the Integration of Violence in Homicidal Youth," *American Journal of Orthopsychiatry* 45, no. 1 (January 1975): 138. Emphasis in the original.

ular classes but can benefit by special services and programs."[47] Yet an authoritative report on the education of emotionally handicapped children in New York City indicates that there are programs for only 7,000 out of 20,000 such children. The shortage is particularly acute at the high school level and affects poor minority children with behavioral problems most severely of all.[48]

School records and IQ scores for children in the Vera sample were too infrequently and too incompletely available in the court files to offer any meaningful clues regarding the role of education and learning in their delinquency or, more specifically, in their violence. There is, however, no reason to doubt that the educational and learning problems outlined here apply to this particular sample.

Psychiatric Characteristics

To begin with an oversimplification, delinquents who commit violent acts may be considered to fall into three psychiatric categories: those who occasionally act out in an assaultive but not seriously violent manner, and who are for the most part not seriously disturbed; the more frequently or more seriously violent, who are more likely to be disturbed but not psychotic; and, finally, psychotic delinquents.

The third group, psychotic delinquents, is by almost all accounts the smallest in number. One expert estimates that less than 1 percent of all delinquents are psychotic.[49] Only two out of 143 delinquents (1.4 percent) in the Vera sample for whom psychiatric diagnoses were available were diagnosed as psychotic. The term "psychotic" denotes persons with a marked degree of disorganization of mental processes. Schizophrenia is the most common manifestation of psychosis. It is important to note that few schizophrenics have histories of violence, although the presence of violent

---

[47] N.Y. Education Sec. 4401 (1).
[48] William J. Jesinkey and Jane R. Stein, *Lost Children* (Long Island City, N.Y.: Alternative Solutions for Exceptional Children, Inc., 1974).
[49] Donald H. Russell, Interview, July 14, 1975.

tendencies in a schizophrenic individual "immeasurably compounds the risk that he will do terrible harm."[50]

The middle group, disturbed delinquents who commit frequent or serious violent acts but are not psychotic, is a larger, although still relatively small, category.[51] The most seriously disturbed among this group are frequently diagnosed as antisocial psychopathic personalities, a term synonymous with several other labels, including sociopath, character disorder, or antisocial personality. Although a psychopath is not psychotic (or neurotic), neither is he or she "normal," as that term is applied to the majority of members of a community. One analysis equates psychopathology with "dangerousness," which is defined as follows.

> The essence of dangerousness appears to be a paucity of feeling concern for others. The potential for injuring another is compounded when this lack of concern is coupled with anger. . . . When the patient commits the assaultive act, he appears as a social isolate who has remained at or regressed to an infantile level of emotional prematurity where his primary concern is to satisfy primitive needs immediately.[52]

The authors go on to say that "increasing evidence suggests that the psychopath is made, not born, and that his attitudes and distortions are the result of conditioning relationships. It follows that he should be modifiable, and in some cases we have demonstrated that he is."[53]

Only fourteen out of the 143 delinquents (9.8 percent) in the Vera sample with psychiatric diagnoses in their records were labeled psychopathic or one of its equivalents. This accords with prevailing opinion that such seriously disturbed children are only a small part of the delinquent population. Even so, they can be severely destructive and may be responsible for a disproportionate share of the serious violence committed by delinquents.

[50] Kozol, Boucher, and Garofalo, op. cit., p. 383.

[51] A 1975 survey of detention facilities found that staff regarded 18 percent of delinquents detained to be "severely disturbed," although 79 percent were regarded as having some emotional disturbance or behavioral problems. (Rosemary Sarri, *Under Lock and Key*. National Assessment of Juvenile Corrections, University of Michigan, Ann Arbor, December 1974, p. 56.)

[52] Kozol, Boucher, and Garofalo, op. cit., p. 379.

[53] Ibid., p. 381.

The largest category of all, undoubtedly a sizable majority, consists of juveniles who only occasionally commit violent acts and are not seriously disturbed. Many psychiatric labels commonly used to describe youths in this category are merely elaborations of symptoms, and vague ones at that: adjustment reaction of adolescence or childhood, acting-out behavior, unsocialized aggressive reaction, and so forth. In the words of one psychiatrist, these labels simply mean that "we don't know what is wrong."

Dr. Donald Russell and Dr. G. P. Harper of the Judge Baker Guidance Center in Boston report that a number of delinquents in this group have neurotic character disorders and fall mainly into two categories: those whose delinquencies they call "sociosyntonic"—juveniles "who do not appear to show any appreciable defects of impulse control, but whose particular cultural status, environment, and social milieu seem to enable or influence certain kinds of antisocial (assaultive) activity in expression of their inner neurotic conflicts"; and those whose assaults occur in panic states— juveniles "who have imperfect and precarious impulse controls and certain brittle ego defenses and can consequently become involved in, or react with, assaultive behavior or acts when they perceive their defenses to be acutely threatened."[54]

Regardless of the particular classification scheme employed, a small number of characteristics appear regularly in most psychiatric descriptions of violent delinquents. These include strong repressed feelings of rage, low self-esteem, inability to form bonds of feeling (or empathy) with other persons, limited control over impulses, and low thresholds of frustration. Other frequently mentioned characteristics are an inability to communicate verbally with ease and, in the most serious cases, a sense of omnipotence, which may be terrifying to the delinquent. These personality disturbances are the usual targets of therapeutic intervention based on the psychiatric model.

In addition to personality defects, however, throughtful analyses often point out the importance of environmental influences and situational pressures in triggering the expression of violence in the vast majority of cases. The psychology of violence appears to involve a complex interaction between internal impulses and con-

[54] Russell and Harper, op. cit., p. 387.

trols, on the one hand, and external factors on the other. Some personality types are thus more likely than others to engage in violent behavior or to do more serious damage when violent, but the conjunction of heightened violent impulses, lowered internal controls, and violence-inducing stimuli in the environment (or the absence of inhibiting external circumstances) is so chancy that predicting violent behavior in an individual involves a high probability of error.

Physical Health

In contrast to the relationship between mental health and delinquency, the subject of a vast amount of research, relatively little attention has been paid to the relationship of physical health to delinquency, violent or otherwise. Studies focusing specifically on the connection between health and delinquency are scarce. Even in studies oriented to broad descriptions of the social problems of delinquents, health is infrequently mentioned and then only in passing.

In one broad study, data on the health status of a delinquent sample are reported: of 700 children examined, 5 percent reported significant illnesses during the year preceding the examination, 8 percent had suffered a significant illness in the past, 2 percent had neurological defects, 3 percent reported recent injuries from accidents, and 11 percent had suffered broken bones or severe lacerations from accidents during childhood. Dental problems were the most common deficiency. These results led the author to conclude that the delinquents were "by and large a healthy lot."[55] The clinical procedures used in these diagnoses are not reported, however, so their reliability cannot be determined.

The most commonly studied physical problem of delinquents is neurological impairment. Some researchers have found a higher incidence of minor neurological problems and sensorimotor malfunctioning in delinquent youths than in nondelinquent youths.[56]

[55] Russell, op. cit., p. 17.
[56] See, for example, I. Hurwitz et al., "Neurological Function of Normal Boys, Delinquent Boys, and Boys with Learning Problems," *Perceptual Motor Skills* 25 (1972): 387–394.

A number of studies have also noted an association between psychomotor epilepsy and delinquency, although others have failed to find such an association. In one recent study, eighteen out of 285 delinquents referred to a court clinic were found to have symptoms of psychomotor epilepsy. This incidence (6 percent) is about fifteen times higher than the incidence of all forms of epilepsy in the general population.[57]

Another health problem currently receiving some attention as a possible factor in antisocial behavior is malnutrition. Several laboratory studies with rats have demonstrated nutritional deficiencies (or excesses) to be associated with aggressive behavior.[58] Practitioners are now treating children with learning and behavior problems by altering their diets to counteract food allergies, hypoglycemia, and vitamin deficiencies. For example, studies of the effects of diet therapy on behavior disorders in juvenile delinquents have been undertaken at the Full Circle Residential Research and Treatment Center in Bolinas, California. In a preliminary research period, seven delinquents were selected for evidence of learning disabilities and for behavioral problems that precluded referral to other therapeutic programs. Extensive diagnoses revealed six of the seven to have evidence of hypoglycemia and all seven to have food allergies that produced severe behavioral reactions. After six months of diet therapy, six of the delinquents responded with noticeable improvement in behavior.[59] Full Circle hopes eventually to develop procedures that can reduce the cost of diagnosing dietary allergies and deficiencies from the current level of about $5,000 per child to about $500. If that can be accomplished, wider testing of delinquents (and nondelinquents) for dietary problems will become feasible, permitting controlled research with much larger numbers.

Health and nutrition are also being studied in another context that bears indirectly on delinquent behavior—the influence of these variables on learning disabilities. If learning disabilities have

[57] Dorothy Otnow Lewis, "Delinquency, Psychomotor Epileptic Symptomatology and Paranoid Symptomatology: A Triad," *American Journal of Psychiatry* 133 no. 12 (1976):1395–1398.

[58] For example, research by Dr. John Calhoun at the National Institute of Mental Health has shown that high doses of vitamin A reduce aggression in rats.

[59] Personal communication from Dr. Michael Lerner, Research Director, Full Circle Residential Treatment and Research Center, January 1975.

a physical basis, it is reasoned, then perhaps poor health and malnutrition might be doing damage that results in learning disabilities. And since learning difficulties have been observed in a high proportion of delinquents, another possible link to delinquency (and violence) might someday be established.

Given the fundamental importance of health and nutrition to growth and development, the idea that health and nutritional deficiencies might contribute to delinquent violence has intuitive appeal, not only to professional researchers, but also to practitioners on the front lines. Delinquents in one community-based program told staff that they would have no trouble with a new enrollee charged with various violent acts as long as they "keep him fed." Teachers in an alternative school for delinquent dropouts observed that if the school did not provide lunches, the children would be "tearing the place apart." Nevertheless, the empirical basis for establishing an association between health and nutrition, on the one hand, and violence, on the other, is exceptionally thin. Formulation of theories of causality is in a primitive state, and research to establish causal linkages is even further behind. Consequently, although this is a field that should be, and no doubt will be, investigated much more intensively, it is premature to draw any practical conclusions about a relationship between violence and physical well-being.

Other Characteristics

Several other factors associated with juvenile violence must be mentioned, although they cannot be discussed at length.

Weapons. Weapons were present in 14 percent of the most recent charges brought against the juveniles in the Vera sample. Assuming that up to half of all arrests are diverted from court, some of which may also have involved weapons, we can conclude that in 7 to 14 percent of these offenses, weapons were present. In comparison, in the Philadelphia cohort of ten years ago, weapons were present in only 2.6 percent of offenses.

The presence of weapons ranged from 10 percent of cases in

Mercer County to 17 percent in Manhattan. Spanish-speaking delinquents were most likely to have weapons (18 percent), followed by blacks (14 percent) and then whites (11 percent). Overall, there was no significant difference between one-time offenders, recidivists, and chronic offenders in the propensity to have weapons, but Manhattan recidivists and chronics were about twice as likely as one-time offenders to have weapons.

It is the impression of many people who deal directly with delinquents that guns, in particular, are increasingly available to the young and increasingly a factor in their delinquencies. Guns were present in 5 percent of the most recent offenses of the Vera sample. Guns are the dominant weapon in homicides and armed robberies, according to national data,[60] and often the only difference between an aggravated assault and a homicide is in the nature of the weapon and the skill (or luck) with which it is used. Thus, if it is true that the consequences of juvenile violence are growing more serious (as a comparison between the Vera and Philadelphia data suggests), the increased availability of guns may, to some degree, be responsible.

Gangs. There is a great deal of contradiction in research literature and among professionals who deal with delinquents regarding the role of gangs in promoting violence. In reviewing literature on the peer relationships of delinquents, Glaser found that "most adolescent offenders are more markedly and consistently differentiated from nonoffenders by their conflict with the school, the family, and other agencies normally presumed to be crime prevention influences, than by their rapport with the presumed crime-promoting persons or groups in their neighborhoods."[61]

While it is true that most adolescent felonies are committed by two or more youths acting together,[62] it is doubtful that that alone constitutes evidence of formal gang activity. The Task Force on Crime of the Violence Commission found the weight of research evidence to be against gang violence. Its own survey of victims and offenders revealed "gangs and groups" (three or more people) to

[60] Mulvihill, Tumin, and Curtis, op. cit., pp. 234–238.
[61] Glaser, op. cit., p. 43.
[62] Ibid., p. 53.

be involved in 25 percent of armed and unarmed robberies and 10 percent of rapes, but only 5 percent of homicides and aggravated assaults.[63]

Vera's research data agree that most violence (most delinquency, in fact) involves more than one person. Sixty-four percent of the most recent petitions sampled involved acts committed by two or more people, while 69 percent of violent crimes charged involved two or more people. As the size of the group increased, so did the likelihood that the act was violent. This, too, falls far short of demonstrating that formal gangs are a factor in violent delinquencies. But it does point out the communal nature of violence among the young and requires attention in the formulation of policies to deal with the problem.

Alcohol and Drugs. Research on alcohol and drugs, two other factors commonly assumed to be associated with delinquency and violence, has not yielded definitive results. On balance, available research suggests a positive correlation between alcohol and violence, but no correlation between drugs and violence. In the Vera sample, data on these factors were inadequate for reliable conclusions.

Media Violence. In recent years, more and more concern has been expressed about the amount and manner of violence portrayed in the media, especially by television, and the role this might play in promoting violent behavior on the part of susceptible individuals.

The issue was featured in the recent trial of a Florida youth charged with robbing and fatally shooting an eighty-two-year-old female neighbor. Ronny Zamora, the fifteen-year-old defendant, pled not guilty by reason of "television intoxication"; he claimed that he had seen so much violence on television that he had "lost the ability to distinguish right from wrong."[64] The jury rejected the defense, convicting Zamora of premeditated murder.

Although research has identified television as an important means by which children acquire both information about societal

[63] Mulvihill, Tumin, and Curtis, op. cit., pp. 608–610.
[64] "TV is on Trial, and at Trial, in Miami," *New York Times*, October 7, 1977, page 18.

values and models for interaction,[65] the precise impact of long-term exposure to media violence on adolescent delinquency remains an unresolved question. Expert testimony in the Zamora trial differed on this issue, and none of the experts could cite a "scientific study that linked a specific crime with a specific television show or television viewing in general."[66]

Two recent studies by British researchers have turned up conflicting answers. One, a six-year study of 1565 London boys by William Belson, a professor at North East London Polytechnic, found that "those who watch screen violence for long periods commit 50 percent more rape and other mayhem than those whose viewing is limited." Belson admitted, however, that his research could not resolve the chicken-egg question: Are those who watch more violent television more violence-prone to begin with?[67]

The second study, a literature review by Stephen Brody of the Home Office, found some evidence to support the theory that television violence may even be cathartic, "serving as a vehicle for the absorption and harmless amelioration of fears, anxieties and hostilities." On balance, however, Brody concluded that the direct impact of television violence on delinquent behavior—whether negative or positive—remains unproven. "The mass media," in his words, "are no different than other forms of cultural expression, which, though they reveal the state of a society or civilization, cannot be said to determine its development."[68]

Juvenile Violence and Adult Violence

In addition to the extent of juvenile violence and the characteristics of violent offenders, the relationship between juvenile violence and subsequent adult criminality is also of interest. The limited

[65] For example, Bandura, Ross and Ross concluded that under some circumstances, television may become as influential as parents in shaping children's behavior. Albert Bandura, Dorothea Ross, and Sheila A. Ross, "Imitations of Film-Mediated Aggressive Models," *"Journal of Abnormal and Social Psychology* 66 (1963): 3–11.

[66] "Despite Conviction of Youth, Debate over TV Violence Continues," *New York Times,* October 8, 1977, page 10.

[67] "Violence and TV: A Split Decision," *International Herald Tribune,* September 19, 1977, page 16.

[68] Ibid.

information available on this point, from the two cohort studies by Wolfgang and Polk, is still tentative. Moreover, the conclusions drawn by these two researchers are contradictory.

Wolfgang and his colleagues have undertaken a follow-up study of 10 percent of their cohort through age twenty-seven. They found that of 226 adult offenders in this subsample, 66 percent had also been arrested as juveniles, while 34 percent had not. The proportion of the entire cohort with a police record, projecting from the subsample data, increased from 35 percent at age 18 to 43 percent at age twenty-seven. Based on this additional information, Wolfgang concludes that "the chances of becoming an adult offender are much higher for persons who had a delinquency record than for those who did not. The probability of being arrested between eighteen and twenty-six years of age, having had at least one arrest under age eighteen, is 0.4357, which is three-and-one-half times higher than the probability (0.1218) of being arrested as an adult, having had no record as a juvenile."[69] Furthermore, Wolfgang has commented that "youth violence does seem to predict adult violence. If there is any pattern at all in the less-than 18 group, it is in violence. And the best predictor of adult violence is youth violence."[70]

Polk's study in Oregon, however, has tentatively reached the opposite conclusion. Examining the arrest records of that cohort between the ages of 18 and 23, he found just over half (51 percent) of those with records as young adults had *no* records as juveniles. Furthermore, he discovered that the most serious juvenile offenders (those with felonies) were only slightly more likely to commit adult offenses (58 percent) than those with only misdemeanors on their juvenile records (51 percent). Only 28 percent of delinquent felons committed felonies as adults. "Thus," Polk concludes, "not only have our data called into question the common notion of problematic histories evaporating with the onset of adulthood, but also the common assumption that adult deviance is largely the outgrowth of juvenile misbehavior."[71]

Since both conclusions rest on preliminary data about criminal

[69] Marvin E. Wolfgang, "Crime in a Birth Cohort," *Proceedings of the American Philosophical Society* 117 no. 5 (October 1973): p. 410.
[70] Marvin E. Wolfgang, Interview, June 20, 1975.
[71] "Teenage Delinquency in Small Town America," p. 5.

careers, it is necessary to be tentative on this issue. However, because Wolfgang's data reach further into the adult years and deal more explicitly with violence and seriousness of crimes, perhaps a slight edge should go toward his interpretation that juvenile violence is a strong predictor of adult violence.

Summary

This brief review of literature dealing with the characteristics of violent delinquents, although by no means complete, highlights how little is really known. For the most part, the focus has been on descriptive statistics dealing with the characteristics commonly addressed in the literature. Even at this relatively rudimentary level, clear consensus supported by consistent data is hard to find. When one searches further for viable theories as to why individuals become violent, the intellectual landscape is bleaker yet. We seem to be at a standstill with regard to causality. The only accepted fact is that violent behavior is highly complex and multiply determined. Even the most sophisticated studies available are constrained by the quality of their data and the limitations of their methods, unable to examine more than a few possible explanations for the occurrence of violent behavior in some youth but not in others, and unable to demonstrate conclusively the power of any single explanation.

We are therefore driven back to a few basic, frequently observed facts as the building blocks from which to begin construction of an explanation for juvenile violence. These may be summarized as follows.

1. Violent acts appear, for the most part, to be occasional occurrences within a random pattern of delinquent behavior, rather than a "specialty" of juveniles. The number of delinquents who are chronically violent is quite small. Recidivists are responsible for the large majority of violent offenses by juveniles, but it is not possible to predict violence simply on the basis of prior offense records. On the other hand, the best among many unreliable predictors of future violence is a prior record of violence.

2. When committing a violent act, a delinquent is more likely to do so in company with at least one other juvenile than alone.
3. Boys are more delinquent than girls, but female delinquents are as likely to commit a violent act as male delinquents. Female violence tends to have somewhat less serious consequences, however.
4. Older juveniles tend to be more seriously violent than younger juveniles, but there is growing evidence, including data in the Vera study, that the younger age groups (13 to 15) are catching up.
5. Minority youths (and especially black youths) tend to be both more delinquent and more violent than white youths.
6. The great majority of violent delinquents are not psychotic or otherwise seriously disturbed emotionally, although many are neurotic and characterized by poor impulse controls. Psychopathic or sociopathic delinquents are relatively few in number, but are responsible for considerable violence and damage. Rage, low self-esteem, lack of empathy, and limited frustration tolerance are typical of violent youths. Environmental factors play an important role both in developing these traits and in facilitating their expression through violence.
7. Many if not most delinquents have learning problems, but the causes of those problems and their relationship to delinquency and violence are not easy to establish. Specific learning disabilities may be an important factor, although existing research is inadequate to prove a causal connection.
8. A two-parent family seems to offer some protection against delinquent behavior, but the presence of both parents has little to do with whether a delinquent becomes violent. Other factors, probably including the quality instead of the quantity of familial relationships, seem to be more influential in this regard.
9. Within community boundaries, differences in socioeconomic status appear to be weakly correlated with juvenile violence, although children from poor communities (particularly from ghettos in large metropolitan centers) are more likely to become delinquent and violent than children living in more affluent communities. Whether a child comes from a welfare

family or not appears to bear little relationship to his or her chances of becoming violent.

In this list of characteristics, only three stand out as being truly useful in separating violent from nonviolent delinquents: race, recidivism, and location. Of the three, location is the most powerful. This is evident in Table 16, which shows the proportion of delinquents who become violent and the mean seriousness scores of their violent offenses, by race, offense number, and location.

Table 16 The Relationship of Violence to Race, Number of Offenses, and Location, in Vera Sample

	Race			Offense Number		
	Black	Spanish Surname	White	One Time	Recidivists (2–4)	Chronics (5+)
Percent Ever Violent						
Mercer	43.8%	20.0%	19.4%	14.8%	30.8%	59.6%
Westchester	43.8	30.8	37.0	34.0	39.4	41.7
Manhattan	62.5	50.6	40.0	33.7	61.9	87.8
Mean Seriousness Score, Violent Offenses						
Mercer	272.9	400.0[a]	287.5	214.4	297.7	489.0
Westchester	352.8	714.0[a]	420.1	401.5	248.3	285.3
Manhattan	541.6	605.7[a]	491.0	477.8	621.1	562.7

SOURCE: Vera Institute Violent Delinquent Study.

[a] $N = 1$ in Mercer, $N = 4$ in Westchester, $N = 40$ in Manhattan.

In each county, black delinquents are more likely to be violent than whites, although the difference is insignificant in Westchester County. Whites are more likely to be violent than Spanish-surname delinquents in Westchester; the converse is true in Manhattan; and the two are about equal in Mercer. Yet a greater percentage of each racial group is violent in Manhattan than in the other counties. With regard to the seriousness of violent offenses, there is no clear pattern by race among the three counties. But, again, the offenses of Manhattan delinquents are more serious than those of their racial counterparts in the other counties.[72]

Similarly, in each county the probability of ever committing a violent offense increases significantly with offense number (except in Westchester, where chronics are only slightly more likely than recidivists to commit a violent crime). But recidivists and chronics are far and away more likely to commit a violent act in Manhattan than they are in the other counties. The seriousness of violent acts also tends to increase with offense number in each county. (Again, Westchester is an exception in that one-time offenders have higher seriousness scores than recidivists or chronics.) But the most significant difference is the high seriousness score of Manhattan's violent delinquents compared to their counterparts in the same group in the other counties.[73]

How is one to explain this powerful association between location and violence? And how can the widely noted association between race and violence—or the other frequently observed relationships between socioeconomic status or family instability and delinquency—be accounted for? Two theoretical frameworks applied to these phenomena provide at least a starting point for analysis.

One is the now familiar delineation of a "subculture" of violence. A subculture is a collection of values, norms, and behavior patterns that are different, but not wholly different, from those of the dominant culture in a society, which in America is middle-class adult white culture. The subculture is distinguishable by the differences it manifests from the dominant culture, but it persists

[72] Spanish-surname delinquents in Westchester are an exception to the pattern. This may be a statistical contrivance traceable to the small number of observations in Westchester and Mercer.

[73] These results were confirmed in regression analyses taking the number of arrests, age, socioeconomic level, parents' marital status, race, and location as the independent variables, and number of arrests for serious violence and a charge of serious violence (or not) in the most recent offense as the dependent variables. With regard to violence in the most recent offense, the only significant independent variable was location (beta = 0.2036). Race followed location, but at an insignificant level (beta = .0623). With regard to the number of serious violent offenses, the significant independent variables were number of all offenses (beta = 0.3937) and location (beta = 0.3200). Race followed these two, but again at an insignificant level (beta = 0.0438).

and continues to function because of its similarities with that culture. A number of subcultures have been identified within American society (poverty subcultures, ethnic subcultures, age subcultures, etc.). In addition to sharing some characteristics of the dominant culture, these subcultures overlap each other.

A "violent" subculture is one in which violent behavior has a different (or at least partially different) meaning and place than it does in the dominant culture. It is not age or race or class standing alone that imbues violence with a different cultural meaning. Instead, it is a complex interaction of certain attributes associated with age, race, and class, combined with inputs from and interaction with the dominant culture. For example, the need of young males to assert their masculinity, the prevalence of female-headed households in black communities, lower-class frustration in the search for jobs and the material fruits of middle-class life, as well as for less tangible benefits such as dignity and self-esteem, and role models provided by television or other media may all play a part in the formation and expression of a ghetto youth's self-image.[74]

From this theory is derived one hypothesis as to how race and other variables can have a different relationship to violence in different places. Changes in location, even within geographic boundaries, bring small but important changes in age, race, and socioeconomic composition, in economic opportunity, in family structure, and in other variables. These changes, in turn, produce a somewhat different subcultural environment, in which violence takes on a somewhat different meaning. Outside the urban ghetto, a black subcutlure may still predominate, but it may be more middle class in its values or less dominated by youth. Although the impact of these different subcultural blends is hard to quantify, it is at least reasonable that changes in one or more key elements could result in a variation in the extent of violence in the com-

[74] For a full discussion of the subcultural theory of violence, see Marvin E. Wolfgang and Franco Ferracuti, *The Subculture of Violence* (London: Tavistock Publications, 1967). A shorter discussion is available in Marvin E. Wolfgang, "The Culture of Youth," Appendix I of the Task Force Report on Juvenile Delinquency and Youth Crime of the President's Commission of Law Enforcement and the Administration of Justice.

munity.[75] The limitation of this theoretical approach is its inability to explain variations in violent behavior that occur within a given subcultural milieu: why, for example, one child becomes violent while a sibling does not.

An alternative framework for approaching the issue of causality might be called the "stress" model. In this model, the violent delinquent is regarded as a person subjected to high levels of stress whose natural defenses against its effects are inadequate. In such a person, violent behavior may develop as an alternate means of coping with intolerable stress.

Tolerable stress levels may be exceeded by pressure from a single trauma (severe abuse or neglect, a physical injury, etc.) or by the gradual accumulation of pressure from many sources (multiple traumas, inadequate or inappropriate nutrition, learning disability, social and economic discrimination, etc.). Most individuals are able to withstand normal amounts of stress throughout their lives and abnormal amounts on occasion. But high levels of stress throughout life, and particularly in infancy, childhood, and adolescence, put human beings to a severe test. Stress is usually combatted by defense mechanisms such as normal health, strength, body chemistry, and neurological functioning; a protective family; and nurturing relationships with other human beings. When these are diminished by genetic damage, disease, family breakdown, or other causes, the individual becomes much more vulnerable.

A tentative hypothesis as to how these factors might lead to violent behavior has been suggested by Dr. Michael Lerner.

As weakened organisms, [some individuals] are subjected to exceedingly high levels of environmental stress, to which they are extraordinarily sensitive. This precipitates the onset of degenerative processes which many of their parents clearly manifest. The degenerative processes vary according to the biochemical individuality of the child. The pituitary, adrenals, kidney, liver, lymph system, brain are dif-

[75] Lynn Curtis has taken a step toward quantification with a preliminary hypothesis that relates disproportionate violence by poor blacks to a very large black population, "say in excess of 500,000," which is consistent with another hypothesis that "intervening cultural variables related to violence committed by poor blacks require a critical black population mass before their effect is felt." Lynn A. Curtis, *Criminal Violence* (Lexington, Mass.: D.C. Heath and Co., 1974), p. 151.

ferentially affected depending on the child and the specific stressors. . . . These degenerative processes further weaken the child. *Apparently* the inhibitory processes of the brain are interfered with. The child is flooded with sensory and movement impulses. Amphetamines (or danger or excitement) may temporarily stimulate the brain enough to reinforce the inhibitory processes; this would explain the "paradoxical" effect of amphetamines in calming these children. It would also explain why these children court danger and excitement so assiduously: it helps them integrate.[76]

While this particular hypothesis may or may not stand up under further testing, the concept of total stress acting on "weakened organisms" with inadequate defense systems to produce violent (or other deviant) behavior is provocative. It is consistent with the observed fact that many violent delinquents suffer from multiple problems and deficiencies. It might explain why large cities, and particularly ghetto areas in those cities, produce more juvenile violence than other areas: urban ghettos are filled with social and environmental stress. The concept might also explain some of the reasons why low-income families tend to produce more delinquents than higher-income families: they have fewer resources with which to protect their children, including not only the money to purchase adequate food, clothing, and shelter, but also access to health care, education, and basic information about child care. Low-income parents may themselves suffer the effects of childhood stress and resulting physical and emotional damage, and thus be less able to offer the nurturing care needed to protect their children from further damage. Finally, this framework may help to explain why some children become violent delinquents while others from the same environment (often from the same family) do not. Individual histories undoubtedly show important differences in the amount, nature, and timing of stress, while defense mechanisms (genetically acquired or socially provided) also vary in strength and viability.

For the moment, neither of these theoretical models—the subculture of violence model and the stress model—has been devel-

[76] Personal communication (January 1976) from Dr. Michael Lerner, Research Director of the Full Circle Residential Research and Treatment Center in Bolinas, California, to whom I am indebted for first suggesting this general framework of analysis. Emphasis in the original.

oped or tested sufficiently. An enormous amount of work remains to be done on both. In the end, it is possible that they may turn out to be compatible explanations of the causes of violent delinquency. The subcultural theory, for example, may be more relevant to the large numbers of poor, inner-city children who commit isolated violent acts as part of a random pattern of delinquent behavior, while the stress theory may be most useful in explaining the behavior of the small group of hard-core delinquents who habitually commit violent acts. In its final report, in fact, the Task Force on Crime of the 1969 National Commission on the Causes and Prevention of Violence seemed to accept implicitly both theories.

> Combine poverty, deteriorated and inadequate housing, lack of good employment opportunities, economic dependency, poor education and anonymous living with population density, social and spatial mobility, ethnic and class heterogeneity, reduced family functions, and broken homes—and an interrelated complex of powerful criminogenic forces is produced by the ghetto environment. . . . The urban ghetto produces a subculture within the dominant American middle class culture in which aggressive violence is accepted as normative and natural in everyday life, not necessarily illicit. . . . To be young, poor, male, and Negro; to want what the open society claims is available, but mostly to others; to see illegitimate and often violent methods of obtaining material success; and to observe others using these means successfully and with impunity—is to be burdened with an enormous set of influences that pull many toward crime and delinquency.[77]

[77] Mulvihill, Tumin, and Curtis, op. cit., pp. xxxiii–xxxv.

4 Official Responses to Juvenile Violence

THROUGHOUT THE COUNTRY there are 2,974 juvenile courts with 3,202 judges who hear approximately 1 million delinquency and status offense cases each year.[1] It has been estimated that one of every nine juveniles (and one out of every six boys) will be referred to juvenile court before reaching the age of 18.[2] The annual cost to the nation of dealing with these juveniles is about $1 billion.

Juvenile courts are the central, but by no means the only, official agency dealing with delinquents. The network is complex. Each of its primary elements—police, courts, probation, and corrections—has its own objectives and standards and responds to its own internal and external incentives. Moreover, these agencies frequently report to separate administrative and political authorities: police to local governments, courts to county or district governments, and corrections to state government, for example. Numerous other institutions that relate to these primary agencies and profoundly affect their work are usually even less well integrated into and coordinated with the juvenile justice system. Among the most im-

[1] *Time*, June 30, 1975, p. 24.
[2] President's Commission on Law Enforcement and Administration of Justice, op. cit., p. 1.

portant of these other institutional actors are child welfare and social service agencies, the education system, and the mental health establishment.

This chapter will include a description of the process by which delinquents move through the juvenile justice system, an analysis of outcomes it produces for violent delinquents (drawn primarily from data in Vera's three-county study), and a discussion of the treatment and correctional remedies usually applied to violent delinquents.

Police and Court Processing

A delinquent's first contact with the juvenile justice system is usually with the police.[3] It may also be the last contact, because police are given discretion in deciding whether to press charges further. A child may be warned and released without being officially charged with a crime; referred for special handling (usually counseling) either within or outside the police department, again without being officially charged; or charged and referred to juvenile court for further processing.

Nationally, about half the children apprehended by the police (53 percent in 1975) are referred to court. In cities over 100,000, the proportion is greater (61 percent), and in the suburbs it is less (45 percent).[4] Less often do police divert a child who is charged with a serious violent crime or who has a substantial record. In some jurisdictions, in fact, legislation prohibits police diversion of such cases.

Once in court, a child has a second chance to be diverted. Diversion decisions at court intake are made by court or probation officers assigned to screen incoming cases. Decisions are based on varied considerations such as the seriousness of the charge; the child's prior record; the intake officer's judgment as to whether the facts of the case will support a finding of delinquency; whether the

---

[3] If the offense is a status offense, one that would not be a crime if committed by an adult (such as truancy), a parent, school official, or other person can bring the charge directly to court without involving the police.

[4] 1975 FBI Uniform Crime Reports.

police or complainants insist on pressing charges; the parents' willingness and ability to assume responsibility for the child's future behavior; or whether, in the intake officer's judgment, the child's problems could be dealt with better by some social agency outside the judicial context.

In many instances, court diversion (or "adjustment," as it is often called) entails no further responsibility on the part of the child. In other instances, there may be a waiting period before adjustment becomes final, during which the child must demonstrate a willingness to stay out of trouble or perhaps make restitution for his or her misdeeds. In still others, the intake officer may request that the child take part in some form of treatment or counsel. Conditions imposed by intake officers generally cannot be enforced, however, since technically the child has not yet been found guilty of a crime. The only sanction available to encourage compliance with a condition of diversion is the threat of referral to the next stage of court processing. Often that is not much of a sanction.

With encouragement from state and federal governments, court diversion programs have expanded steadily if slowly in the last decade. In 1960 an estimated 50 percent of juvenile cases reaching court were diverted before adjudication. In 1972 the figure reached 59 percent, but then dropped back to 54 percent in 1973 The reasons for this decline are not readily apparent, and no subsequent figures are available to indicate whether it is an aberration or the beginning of a trend reversal. In any event, diversions in 1973 were more common in "semiurban" areas (66 percent of cases) than in urban areas (50 percent of cases).[5]

The violent offender is generally less likely to have his or her case adjusted than the nonviolent offender, although laws and policies on this point vary. In Trenton, New Jersey, for example, it is the policy of court intake officers never to divert a child charged with a violent offense. In New York City, on the other hand, 54 percent of arrests for violent crimes between July 1973 and June

[5] "Juvenile Court Statistics, 1973." U.S. Department of Health, Education and Welfare, Office of Youth Development.

1974 were adjusted at intake, slightly higher than the percentage of diversions for nonviolent arrests.[6]

Even if diversion is denied at the intake stage, a child may yet avoid adjudication. Judges in many states have access to a diversion mechanism of their own, known as "adjournment in comtemplation of dismissal," or ACD. ACD means, simply, that a judge can postpone hearing a case for a period of time (usually six months) and, if the child stays out of trouble, close the case without reaching a decision as to guilt or innocence. ACD implies no special supervision of the child by the court during the waiting period. No national figures are available regarding the extent to which this device is used, but in New York State in 1974, 6 percent of juvenile cases involving serious violent crimes (homicide, arson, rape, other sex offenses, robbery, assault, and possession of dangerous weapons) were settled with an ACD.[7] Judges also have the option of dismissing a case outright if it can be shown that the child is not in need of supervision, treatment, or confinement, even though the child may be guilty of the act for which he or she has been petitioned.

Apart from diversion, a large proportion of cases are dropped for lack of prosecution or failure of witnesses to cooperate, as they are in adult courts. Particularly since the Supreme Court's ruling in the Gault case,[8] which provided juveniles with many of the due process rights accorded adult defendants (but not the right to trial by jury), prosecutors in many cases have found it difficult to obtain convictions, or "findings," as they are called in the gentle parlance of the juvenile court. In New York State in 1974, 59 percent of juvenile cases involving the serious violent crimes listed above were dismissed for lack of sufficient proof or were withdrawn.[9] Plea bargaining, however, is not the common feature of defense and prosecution behavior in juvenile courts that it is in criminal courts because, with some exceptions, sentencing depends not on the

[6] This figure is from *Juvenile Violence,* Juvenile Justice Institute, New York State Division of Criminal Justice Services, May 1976. A law subsequently passed by the state legislature, which requires that adjustments of serious felonies be approved by the Director of Probation, may well reduce the extent to which serious and violent offenders are diverted.

[7] Figures supplied by the New York State Office of Court Administration.

[8] In re Gault, 387 U.S. 1 (1967).

[9] Figures supplied by the New York State Office of Court Administration.

severity of the crime proved but on the needs or "best interests" of the child.

The residue of diversion and dismissal are the children who are adjudicated and found to be delinquent. In dealing with this group, judges have three basic options. They can decide to do nothing at all and release a child. If supervision and control seem to be required, they can put a child on probation, perhaps with the condition that he or she attend school, participate in treatment, or avail himself or herself of some social service. Or they can place a child in foster care or an institutional setting, to assure that he or she receives the kind of treatment required and to protect the public against the child's further misbehavior. In keeping with the philosophy that the juvenile court should act "in the best interests of the child," decisions on which course to follow are based, at least in some measure, on an investigative report covering the child's prior record, family and school circumstances, mental condition, and the availability of the requisite social services.

The most common sanction applied by juvenile courts is probation. Approximately five delinquent children are put on probation for every one placed in an institutional setting.[10] In theory, probation is a form of official control over the lives of delinquents, a restriction of their liberty. In practice, it often amounts to little or no control. A partial explanation, as a number of studies have shown, is that probation staffs are overworked. The Task Force on Crime of the Violence Commission, for example, noted that the national average workload was seventy-one to eighty cases per probation officer per month, far in excess of the maximum standard (fifty per officer per month) established by the National Council on Crime and Delinquency, and far too many to permit close supervision and control.[11] Caseload size is not the whole problem, however. Experiments with reduced caseloads have generally shown no improvement in recidivism rates over those of normal caseloads, although there is some evidence that increased time de-

---

[10] Even among delinquents adjudicated of serious crimes against persons (again using New York State figures), probation exceeds placement as a disposition by nearly two to one. Figures supplied by the New York State Office of Court Administration.

[11] Mulvihill, Tumin, and Curtis, op. cit., p. 624.

voted to supervision has a positive effect.[12] It is widely believed that many probation officers, perhaps the majority, are inadequately trained to deal with the complex problems of today's delinquents. Subjective observation does suggest, however, that probation may be somewhat more effective in suburban and small town environments, where social control is generally easier to exercise, than in large cities.

Probation is sometimes offered to a delinquent "with conditions." This means that probation will be ordered instead of residential placement if the delinquent agrees to comply with other orders of the court. Sometimes the condition may simply be that the delinquent attend school or observe a curfew. It may also require participation in remedial or therapeutic programs that the court thinks will help to solve some of the problems underlying a delinquent's behavior. Nonresidential (or day treatment) programs in the community have become increasingly available, both as an outgrowth of the movement toward more diversion and as a recognition that traditional probation is frequently inadequate by itself as a treatment for delinquency.

The other option, placement, comes in many forms. Institutions accepting placement of court-referred children include private profit and nonprofit agencies, religious organizations, and state or local child welfare and correctional agencies. Two crucial distinguishing characteristics of placement programs are their size and setting. Size and setting range from individual foster care in a family within the community to isolation in large, prisonlike training schools far from the community. A consensus is emerging within the child welfare and juvenile justice establishments that, from a humanitarian perspective and possibly from a treatment perspective as well, small group environments close to the child's home community are superior to other placements.[13] They also tend to cost about half as much per child as large institutional settings.

Group homes for between five and twenty delinquents are beginning to appear in larger numbers around the country. Approxi-

[12] James Robison and Gerald Smith, "The Effectiveness of Correctional Programs," *Crime and Delinquency* 17, no. 1 (January 1971): 76–78.

[13] See, for example, Rosemary Sarri, *Under Lock and Key*, National Assessment of Juvenile Corrections, University of Michigan, Ann Arbor, December 1974.

mately 1,600 detained and adjudicated juveniles were housed in 149 group homes and halfway houses operated by state and local agencies in 1973, compared to only 1,000 in seventy-eight such institutions two years earlier.[14] Another placement mode of growing importance is the open institution housing twenty-five to fifty children and offering remedial education, group therapy, and other forms of treatment.

As options like these have expanded and the use of diversion has increased, populations in training schools and other traditional correctional institutions have begun to drop. In 1971 there were 192 training schools and 114 public ranches, forestry camps, and farms for juveniles; in 1973 the numbers had declined to 187 and 103, respectively. In the same period, the populations of these kinds of institutions declined 16 percent nationally. Only nine states, mostly in the South and Far West, increased the number of juvenile inmates in traditional institutions during those years.[15] Nevertheless, about 100,000 juveniles were incarcerated in 1975, either in pretrial detention or in correctional institutions. Half of these were status offenders.[16]

Despite the breadth of the trend toward smaller, community-based facilities, many observers believe that it is proceeding too slowly and that the range of alternatives for placement and supervision of children available to most judges is still too limited. Community-based placements remain a small minority of all placements: only 17.7 percent of placed delinquents are sent to community pro grams, while the rest go to training schools, camps, and ranches.[17] Furthermore, the community-based programs now available often do not accept children found guilty of serious or violent offenses or children with special emotional or physical problems.[18] In this field,

[14] "Children in Custody: A Report on the Juvenile Detention and Correctional Facility Census of 1971," and "Children in Custody: Advance Report on the Juvenile Detention and Correctional Facility Census of 1972–1973," U.S. Department of Justice, Law Enforcement Assistance Administration.

[15] Ibid.

[16] *Time,* June 30, 1975, p. 24.

[17] Robert D. Vinter, George Downs, and John Hall, *Juvenile Corrections in the States: Residential Programs and Deinstitutionalization,* National Assessment of Juvenile Corrections, University of Michigan, November 1975.

[18] *Juvenile Justice Confounded: Pretensions and Realities of Treatment Services.* Report of the Committee on Mental Health Services Inside and Outside the Family Court in the City of New York, National Council on Crime and Delinquency, Paramus, New Jersey, 1972.

as in many others, scarcity has induced the practice of "creaming."

This, in brief, is the system that deals with juvenile delinquents. To summarize, a number of factors, including growth of diversion programs, increased attention to the procedural rights of children, and a movement toward private and voluntary placements, have contributed to a reduction in the proportion of arrested children who are subjected to the full judicial process and to its harsher consequences. Between 80 and 90 percent of arrested children are diverted or dropped from the judicial process with little or no mandatory control or supervision. Half are diverted by the police themselves. Half of the remainder are diverted at court intake. And up to two-thirds of the cases left (based on selected data from New York State) may be withdrawn, dismissed, or adjourned in contemplation of dismissal. Among the approximately fifteen children in one hundred arrested who are adjudicated, perhaps eight will be put on probation, five released without supervision, and only one or two placed in some residential program including, with decreasing frequency, traditional training schools and camps.

By themselves, these figures have limited meaning. They can be, and often are, used to prove that the system is both working well and failing miserably. Those who feel that contact with court is bound to have a negative effect on a child may applaud the fact that 85 percent of those arrested escape adjudication; or they may lament that half still have some kind of court contact. Those who argue, on the other side, that permissiveness or inefficiency on the part of the courts is a prime factor in encouraging juvenile crime could find ready support for their position in these calculations. Further analysis is clearly required.

Since we are concerned essentially with the system's handling of violent delinquents, as contrasted with its handling of nonviolent delinquents, that is the framework within which we will examine how well it works. We will first consider two fairly concrete questions. How successful are the courts in adjudicating violent delinquents compared to nonviolent delinquents? What consequences do they produce for violent delinquents compared to nonviolent delinquents? On the basis of the answers to those questions, drawn principally from data in Vera's three-county study, we will then be in a better position to judge less concrete features of the system's functioning.

Court Outcome and Disposition in the Vera Study

The three counties included in the Vera study have substantially different juvenile court structures. Manhattan, with a population of about 1.5 million, has one family court with eleven judges. These judges, however, rotate with twenty-eight other judges among the family courts of all five counties of New York City, sitting for varying durations in each county. In addition to delinquency cases which include children up to age 16, they hear status offense, neglect, dependency, and other kinds of family cases. In 1974, 4,313 juvenile arrests were made in Manhattan, fifteen per thousand children under age 16. (Approximately twice as many police contacts *not* resulting in arrest, many of them trivial, also occurred, which makes the total police "contact" rate about forty-four per thousand.) Of the arrests, 2,124, or 49 percent, became petitions in family court. In other words, 51 percent of arrested children were diverted, virtually all at the court intake stage instead of by police. Approximately 84 percent of all contacted children never reached court.

Westchester County, with a total population of about 900,000, has three branches of family court. They are located in the county's urban centers: White Plains, where three judges sit; Yonkers, with one judge; and New Rochelle, with one judge. Westchester courts hear the same range of cases as the Manhattan court. Jurisdiction over delinquents stops at age 16, as in Manhattan. In 1974, Westchester county police had at least 6,000 "contacts" with juveniles, including 2,293 reported arrests, for a rate of twenty-four contacts and nine arrests per thousand children under 16.[19] From these contacts, 636 delinquency petitions were filed, a much smaller number than in either of the other counties. The diversion rate, therefore, was 90 percent of contacted juve-

[19] There is reason to suspect that the reported arrest figure for Westchester may understate actual arrests somewhat. No juvenile arrests were reported by several localities in which actual arrests seem likely.

niles—75 percent at the police level and 15 percent more at probation intake. Diversion of arrested juveniles totaled 72 percent, with police and probation intake playing approximately equal roles.

Mercer County (population 315,000) has one juvenile court with one judge, who has presided for over seventeen years. In Mercer, as in the rest of New Jersey, juvenile court jurisdiction extends up to age 18. In 1974, Mercer police had 6,717 contacts with juveniles under the age of 18, a rate of seventy contacts per thousand. In court-year 1974 (September 1973 through August 1974) the court received 2,720 complaints from police (a rate of 28 per thousand juveniles), drew 2,363 petitions, and referred 357 cases back to local Juvenile Conference Committees for nonjudicial handling. Thus, approximately 60 percent of contacted juveniles were diverted by the police themselves, and about 5 percent more by court personnel.

Even before petitions are drawn, therefore, differences in the three counties' handling of delinquents are apparent. (These differences are summarized in Table 17.) Mercer police arrest or in

Table 17 Juvenile Contacts, Arrests, and Petitions in Three Counties (1974)

	Mercer	Westchester	Manhattan	Total
Police Contacts	6,717	6,000[a]	13,000[a]	25,717
Arrests	2,720	2,293	4,313	9,326
Petitions	2,363[b]	636	2,124	5,123
Vera Sample	178	111	221	510
Population of Age Group Under Juvenile or Family Court Jurisdiction	96,000	249,000	295,000	640,000
Contacts/1000 Juveniles	70.0	24.0	44.0	40.2
Arrests/1000 Juveniles	28.3	9.2	14.6	14.6
Petitions/1000 Juveniles	24.6	2.6	7.2	8.0

SOURCE: Various county police and court records.

[a] Estimate.

[b] Figures from court year 1974 (September 1973 through August 1974).

other ways "have contact with" a substantially larger proportion of the juvenile population than Manhattan and Westchester police.[20] More contacted juveniles are diverted from judicial processing in Manhattan and Westchester than in Mercer. Diversion of juveniles who are formally arrested is done mainly by the police in Mercer, is shared by police and probation intake personnel in Westchester and is handled almost exclusively by probation intake in Manhattan.

The results of postintake processing are shown in Table 18. Overall, the manner in which the 510 sampled petitions were resolved conforms to the national picture outlined in the first part of this chapter. Exactly half were dismissed, withdrawn, or adjourned in contemplation of dismissal. Seven percent had reached no outcome by the time the data were collected (a minimum of seven months after the petition was filed), and 5 percent were transferred to different petitions or different jurisdictions. The balance, 38 percent, were adjudicated delinquent.

To be "adjudicated" means, in a juvenile proceeding, roughly the same thing as "found guilty" in an adult criminal proceeding. But this niceness of language in the juvenile courts can obscure the courts' findings; an adult is found guilty of violating specific penal law sections, but the specific crime or crimes underlying an adjudication of delinquency may not be shown on the record. This is a significant deficiency in the data analyzed below, and it should be constantly borne in mind in interpreting the findings in this chapter. Court records, especially in Manhattan, frequently do not indicate the specific crime for which a juvenile is adjudicated delinquent. It may be the crime originally charged in the petition, or it may be a lesser crime. Because the focus in juvenile courts is traditionally on the child instead of on the crime, many judges do

20 The fact that jurisdiction over juveniles in New Jersey extends up to age 18, whereas the limit is 16 in New York, is a factor in Mercer's comparatively high contact rate. The older age group, the higher the rate. Nevertheless, even if arrests through age 19 in Manhattan are added to contacts of persons 15 or younger, the rate per 1,000 persons is only 52.4, compared to a rate of 70 per 1,000 persons under 18 in Mercer. Thus it is fair to conclude that Mercer County police are more active in contacting juveniles than police in Manhattan and Westchester. Arrest rates for the entire adult and juvenile population vary less among the three areas: 77.3 per 1,000 in Manhattan, 50.4 per 1,000 in Westchester, and 51.3 per 1,000 in Mercer.

Table 18 Judicial Outcome and Disposition of Cases in Vera Sample, by County

	Mercer		Westchester		Manhattan		Total	
	N	%	N	%	N	%	N	%
Outcome								
Adjudicated ("Guilty")	114	64.0	47	42.3	30	13.6	191	37.5
Not Adjudicated	57	32.1	46	41.4	152	68.8	255	50.0
Dismissed	(51)	(28.7)	(15)	(13.5)	(110)	(49.8)	(176)	(34.5)
Withdrawn	(1)	(0.6)	(13)	(11.7)	(28)	(12.7)	(52)	(10.2)
ACD	(5)	(2.8)	(18)	(16.2)	(14)	(6.3)	(27)	(5.3)
Transferred to Another Petition or Jurisdiction[a]	4	2.2	14	12.6	8	3.6	26	5.1
Pending	3	1.7	4	3.6	31	14.0	38	7.4
Total	178	100.0	111	100.0	221	100.0	510	100.0
Disposition[b]								
Placed	5	4.4	6	12.8	6	20.0	17	8.9
Probation	59	51.8	19	40.4	11	36.7	89	46.6
Released	37	32.4	11	23.4	7	23.3	55	28.8
ACD	(36)	(31.6)	(8)	(17.0)	(–)	(–)	(44)	(23.0)
Dismissed/Withdrawn	(1)	(0.9)	(3)	(6.4)	(7)	(23.3)	(11)	(5.8)
Suspended Sentence	12	10.5	–	–			12	6.3
Transferred to Another Petition or Jurisdiction[a]	1	0.9	7	14.9	1	3.3	9	4.7
Pending	–	–	4	8.5	5	16.7	9	4.7
Total	114	100.0	47	100.0	30	100.0	191	100.0

SOURCE: Vera Institute Violent Delinquent Study.

[a] Case to be heard simultaneously with another charge against same child, or moved to another jurisdiction. Can occur at either the adjudication or disposition stage.

[b] Adjudicated cases only.

not consider it essential to state the specific finding for the record. Hence my analysis of the seriousness of the delinquent acts is based on the allegations of the petitions and not on facts proven or admitted in court.

Only 62 percent of the adjudicated delinquents (those found "guilty") were placed under official control: 47 percent put on probation, 9 percent placed in institutions, and 6 percent given suspended sentences involving threat of future incarceration. Among the remaining "guilties," 29 percent were dismissed or released under ACDs, 5 percent were transferred to other petitions or jurisdictions for final disposition, and 5 percent were still awaiting dispositional decisions. In short, most of the delinquents petitioned were never adjudicated, and only about two-thirds of those who were, were put under official control. Three in 100 (or about one in 100 arrested) were placed.[21]

Among the three counties, however, clear differences are evident. Mercer adjudicated most of its delinquents (64 percent), but sent less than 5 percent of the "guilty" to institutions. At the other extreme, Manhattan adjudicated a small proportion (14 percent), but placed 20 percent of the "guilty" in institutions. In between was Westchester, adjudicating less than half (42 percent) and placing 13 percent of those. Westchester placed a higher percentage of all petitioned delinquents (5.4 percent) than either Manhattan (2.7 percent) or Mercer (2.8 percent).[22] As a form of social control, probation was favored most in the smallest jurisdiction (Mercer) and least in the largest (Manhattan). The proportion of "guilty" delinquents put under no social control at all (ACD, dismissed, or withdrawn) differed only moderately among the three jurisdictions: 23 percent in Manhattan and Westchester, and 32 percent in Mercer.

We saw in preceding chapters that Manhattan's delinquents were significantly more serious than delinquents in Mercer or

[21] In comparison, 6.4 percent of arrests in the Philadelphia cohort resulted in institutionalization. (Wolfgang, Figlio, and Sellin, op. cit., p. 219.)

[22] Thoroughout this analysis, no distinction is made among kinds of placements (training schools, group homes, etc.), although such distinctions are quite important. The reason for this omission is that the court records, from which data were drawn, contained inadequate information on the kind of placement ordered.

Westchester, both in terms of the frequency and harm of their offenses and in terms of their propensity to commit violent crimes against the person. Is this difference related to the low rate of adjudication or the relatively high rate of placement in the Manhattan court? More generally, is offender type related to outcome and disposition in all these courts?

To answer these questions, we again divided the sample according to the three classifications outlined in Chapter 3: number of offenses; violence or nonviolence of offenses; and seriousness of offenses according to the Sellin-Wolfgang scale. Each of the dependent variables, outcome and disposition, was analyzed in terms of these classifications.

In describing the results, three shorthand terms are employed to characterize the behavior of the judicial system: "proportional" when the system holds on to serious or violent offenders more frequently than it does nonserious or nonviolent offenders, and when it exercises more control over the more serious and violent among the guilty; "disproportional" when it behaves in the opposite way; and "random" when there is no meaningful difference between its handling of serious, violent offenders and nonserious, nonviolent offenders. It is perhaps unnecessary (but advisable, nonetheless) to point out that these terms are not applied to specific decisions of identifiable individuals, but refer to the overall results of the judicial process. In using these terms, we also mean (for the moment) to beg the question of whether it is good or bad for juveniles to be involved with the court. We are assuming only that if the court should be involved with juveniles at all, it should be more so with the serious and violent cases.

These classifications and descriptive terms, of course, obscure innumerable differences among the cases in any particular grouping, and they create the false impression of a neat distinction between serious and less serious delinquents. They also fail to take account of the many factors that influence the workings of the system that have little or nothing to do with "proportionality." Despite these inevitable problems, however, they make the presentation of the material a simpler task and are useful for gaining some initial insight into the performance of the system.

Outcome. The three court systems, taken together, appear to have behaved with some proportionality in processing cases according to the number of offenses in a delinquent's record. Table 19 shows the distribution of outcomes of the most recent petitions

Table 19 Case Outcomes in Vera Sample, by Number of Offenses[a]

Outcome	One-time Offenders		Recidivists		Chronic Offenders	
	N	%	N	%	N	%
Adjudicated	74	35.6	62	34.1	55	46.6
Not Adjudicated	114	54.8	93	51.1	45	38.1
Dismissed	(71)	(34.1)	(62)	(34.1)	(39)	(33.1)
Withdrawn	(23)	(11.1)	(15)	(8.2)	(4)	(3.4)
ACD	(20)	(9.6)	(16)	(8.8)	(2)	(1.7)
Transferred	6	2.9	10	5.5	10	8.5
Pending	14	6.9	17	9.3	8	6.8
Total	208	100.0	182	100.0	118	100.0

SOURCE: Vera Institute Violent Delinquent Study.

NOTE: Chi square = 18.51; $df = 8$; $p < 0.05$.

[a] Two missing observations.

according to offense number. There was virtually no difference between outcomes for one-time offenders and for recidivists. But chronic offenders were more frequently adjudicated (found "guilty") than either of the other groups, and less frequently dropped from the system. Cases of chronic offenders were dismissed at the same rate as recidivists' and one-time offenders' cases, but chronics were granted ACDs by judges less frequently and had petitions withdrawn (usually at the initiative of the complainant) at a lower rate.

The only court in which proportionality (defined in this way) did not prevail is the Mercer County Court. One-time offenders in Mercer were adjudicated more frequently (72 percent of such cases) than either recidivists (57 percent) or chronic offenders (62 percent). Correspondingly, one-time offenders were dropped from the system less frequently than recidivists or chronics. This may seem odd, since only in Mercer does the judge have access to the defendant's prior record before reaching a verdict on "guilt" or "innocence."[23]

It must be noted, however, that a comparatively large number of *all* juvenile offenders were adjudicated in the Mercer court. Manhattan's court, in contrast, while proportionally selective in "deciding" who gets adjudicated, nonetheless adjudicated only a small fraction of all delinquents.

With regard to violence, court outcomes appeared to be less proportional. Overall, violent offenders (whether defined as those ever committing a violent crime, those violent in the petitioned offense, or those with two or more violent offenses on their records) were adjudicated less frequently than nonviolent or less violent offenders. (See Tables 2-A and 3-A, Appendix A.) In Mercer, the court behaved disproportionally, adjudicating more nonviolent than violent delinquents. The Westchester and Manhattan courts behaved randomly; there was no significant difference in outcomes for violent and nonviolent delinquents in those counties.

The term "violent," as used above, refers of course to the nature of the crime as defined in the penal code. Generally, it means a nontrivial crime against the person. Using the Sellin-Wolfgang scale as a measure of the seriousness of offenses committed, however, proportionality once again appears to reign. Mean seriousness scores in each county and for the entire sample are given in Table 20 according to the outcome of the case. It can be seen that, on average, the adjudicated cases were more serious than the unadjudicated cases in each county (although not for the sample as a whole, because of the large number of low-seriousness adjudications in Mercer). Among the unadjudicated cases, those given ACDs were least serious of all, except in Manhattan.

Because of the large number of minority youths in the delinquent population, it is of interest to know whether race is a factor in the outcome of cases. Table 21 summarizes outcomes for the sample as a whole. Nonwhites (both black and Spanish-surname delinquents) were actually adjudicated less frequently than whites

---

[23] In New York, judges do not have access to a delinquent's prior record at the adjudication stage, only at the disposition stage. Thus the "proportionality" of their decisions is clearly of an accidental or "hidden hand" nature. In New Jersey, to the contrary, a juvenile's full record is available to the judge in determining the facts of a case at the adjudication stage.

Table 20 Mean Seriousness Score of Current Arrest in Vera Sample, by Outcome, by County[a]

Outcome[b]	Mercer	Westchester	Manhattan	Total Sample
Adjudicated	241.9	358.1	554.3	318.5
Not Adjudicated	227.3	230.8	410.0	336.4
Dismissed	(237.1)	(226.4)	(376.0)	(322.7)
Withdrawn	(300.0)[c]	(293.4)	(521.0)	(445.3)
ACD	(131.7)	(186.6)	(448.0)	(276.6)
Transferred	177.8[c]	246.8	361.3	275.8
Pending	391.3[c]	146.2	326.3	307.8

SOURCE: Vera Institute Violent Delinquent Study.

[a] Seven missing observations.

[b] Analysis of the variance indicates that there are significant differences in seriousness among the counties ($F = 18.01$; $df = 2$; $p < 0.001$) and among the outcomes ($F = 2.84$; $df = 4$; $p < 0.03$), but the interaction between county and outcome is not significant ($F = 0.91$; $df = 8$; $p =$ n.s.). In computing analysis of variance, the subcategories "dismissed," "withdrawn," and "ACD" were used in place of the general category "not adjudicated." In addition, the categories "transferred" and "pending" were collapsed into a single category.

[c] $N < 5$.

and dropped from court processing more frequently. Knowing that the majority of nonwhites in the sample were from Manhattan, and that the Manhattan court adjudicated delinquents at a comparatively low rate, one may suspect that the Manhattan portion of the sample masked differences in the other counties. But when each county was examined separately, the same result held true: non whites were adjudicated less frequently and dropped more frequently than whites.

There was no clear pattern of outcome with regard to the age of delinquents, suggesting that age is not a significant factor.

To test the influence of the violence and seriousness of the charge and the criminal record of the offender, as well as location and race, in a more sophisticated way, we performed a multiple regression analysis using these as the independent variables and outcome (adjudicated or not[24]) as the dependent variable. The results of the regression analysis showed race not to have a significant impact on outcome. Location, as expected, had the most

[24] The not-adjudicated category included cases that were transferred or pending as well as those that were dismissed, withdrawn, or given an ACD.

Table 21 Case Outcomes in Vera Sample, by Race[a]

Outcome	Black		Spanish Surname		White	
	N	%	N	%	N	%
Adjudicated	89	40.8	23	23.5	70	54.7
Not Adjudicated	103	47.2	57	58.2	48	37.5
Dismissed	(80)	(36.7)	(37)	(37.8)	(27)	(21.1)
Withdrawn	(16)	(7.3)	(13)	(13.3)	(6)	(4.7)
ACD	(7)	(3.2)	(7)	(7.1)	(15)	(11.7)
Transferred	13	6.0	3	3.1	7	5.5
Pending	13	6.0	15	15.3	3	2.3
Total	218	100.0	98	100.1[b]	128	100.0

SOURCE: Vera Institute Violent Delinquent Study.

NOTE: Chi square $= 39.86$; $df = 8$; $p < 0.001$. The categories "transferred" and "pending" were collapsed into a single category for computing the chi square.

[a] Sixty-six missing observations (12.9 percent).

[b] Error in percent is due to rounding.

powerful influence, followed by the violence of the offense and its seriousness. Recidivism, measured by the number of prior offenses, had a comparatively weak although still measurable impact.[25]

This statistical test reconfirms our initial observation that the degree to which petitioned delinquents are processed all the way through to adjudication depends, first and foremost, on which court they are in. The test also shows, however, that the more serious and violent cases are more likely to be carried through to adjudication in these three counties. Moreover, length of the defendant's prior record also tends to raise the probability that he or she will be adjudicated. Race, however, is not an influential factor in this regard.

In sum, the three court systems studied appear to produce proportional outcomes in delinquency cases. Although delinquents charged with violent crimes were adjudicated less frequently than those charged with nonviolent crimes, when the number and seriousness of offenses are considered (instead of the crime code classification alone), the most serious delinquents were most often

[25] Beta coefficients for these variables were as follows: location, 0.4278; violence, 0.1281; seriousness, 0.1164; number of offenses, 0.0998; and race, 0.0192. (Overall multiple $R = 0.46489$.) These results were confirmed by a discriminant function analysis.

adjudicated. Racial discrimination was not demonstrated to be a factor in court outcomes, although nonwhites' cases failed to hold up in court more often than whites' cases.

Disposition. How proportional were the courts in meting out dispositions for the 191 cases that were adjudicated? To answer this question, dispositional proportionality was measured by the degree to which the judicial system exercises relatively more control over the more serious or violent adjudicated delinquents. It should be noted that the relatively small numbers of cases receiving each disposition, particularly at the county level, lower the confidence with which these results can be generalized. Nevertheless, they are instructive.

We begin again by looking at the number of offenses. The distribution of dispositions in the most recent offense according to offense number is shown in Table 22. More of the adjudicated chronic

Table 22 Dispositions in Vera Sample, by Offense Number[a]

Disposition	One-time Offenders		Recidivists		Chronic Offenders	
	N	%	N	%	N	%
Placed	1	1.4	6	9.7	11	20.4
Probation	31	41.9	35	56.5	23	42.6
Suspended Sentence	—	—	2	3.2	11	20.4
Released	37	50.0	13	21.0	3	5.6
ACD	(32)	(43.2)	(9)	(14.5)	(3)	(5.6)
Dismissed/ Withdrawn	(5)	(6.8)	(4)	(6.5)	(—)	(—)
Paroled to Guardian	(—)	(—)	(1)	(1.6)	(1)	(1.9)
Suspended Sentence	—	—	2	3.2	11	20.4
Transferred	3	4.1	1	1.6	3	5.6
Pending	2	2.7	5	8.0	3	5.6
Total[b]	74	100.1	62	100.0	54	100.2

SOURCE: Vera Institute Violent Delinquent Study.

NOTE: Chi square = 35.55; $df = 6$; $p < 0.001$. Four categories were used in calculating chi square: "placed," "probation" (including "suspended sentence"), "released," and "transferred/pending."

[a] One missing observation.
[b] Errors in percent are due to rounding.

offenders were placed in institutions than recidivists, and more recidivists were released with no official sanction. Probation also appeared to be used in a fairly proportional manner. Considered to be a middle-level sanction, it was used most frequently with recidivists, who in our scheme are middle-level offenders. One-time offenders tended to be released when not put on probation, and chronic offenders tended to be placed or given suspended sentences when not put on probation. Official control over an adjudicated delinquent—defined as placement, probation, or a suspended sentence (which at a minimum involves threat of placement, should the delinquent commit another offense, and frequently also involves some kind of probation supervision)—increased in probability as offense number increased. Forty-three percent of adjudicated one-time offenders, 69 percent of recidivists, and 83 percent of chronics were put under some form of official control. This kind of proportionality in the overall system also prevailed in each county.[26]

With regard to dispositions for violent offenders, the overall system again proved to be proportional. Whether the measure of violence is commission of a violent offense on any occasion or only in the case at hand, or commission of two or more violent offenses, violent offenders were placed more frequently, put under some form of official control more frequently, and released less frequently than nonviolent or less violent offenders. (See Tables 4-A and 5-A, Appendix A.) Mercer and Westchester courts were both proportional along this dimension, except for the use of ACDs in half the cases of offenders charged with violent crime in Mercer, compared to only 30 percent of those charged with nonviolent offenses. The Manhattan court, however, was merely random in its treatment of violent and nonviolent delinquents. Roughly the same proportion in each group was placed or put on probation, and a slightly greater proportion of violent offenders was released. Note again, however, that the limited number of dispositions in Manhattan (thirty) restricts the reliability of this conclusion.

[26] The opposite conclusion is suggested by the Philadelphia cohort study. "The slight variation between the probabilities of a first court disposition at each offense seems to suggest that the number of previous police contacts has little to do with the type of disposition." (Wolfgang, Figlio, and Sellin, op. cit., p. 234.)

Table 23 Mean Seriousness of Current Offense in Vera Sample, by Disposition, by County[a]

Disposition[b]	Mercer	Westchester	Manhattan	Total Sample
Placed	125.8	390.5	1126.9	603.3
Probation	279.2	414.7	380.6	322.2
Suspended Sentence	213.2	29.0[c]	—	199.0
Released	208.3	261.6	316.7	231.6
ACD	(208.3)	(234.8)	(—)	(213.1)
Dismissed/ Withdrawn	(—)	(333.3)[c]	(316.7)	(322.2)
Transferred	200.0[c]	154.8	100.0[b]	153.4
Pending	251.0[c]	539.0[c]	400.0	440.7

SOURCE: Vera Institute Violent Delinquent Study.

[a] One missing observation.

[b] Analysis of variance indicates that there are significant differences in seriousness among the counties ($F = 5.14$; $df = 2$; $p < 0.01$) and among the dispositions ($F = 2.23$; $df = 6$; $p < 0.05$), but the interaction between county and disposition is not significant ($F = 2.58$; $df = 9$; $p < .01$). In computing the analysis of variance, the subcategories "ACD" and "Dismissed/Withdrawn" were used in place of the category "released."

[c] $N < 5$.

Table 23 addresses the issue of the relationship between the seriousness of the crime charged and the severity of disposition. Once again the three systems taken together seemed to perform proportionally. The higher the average seriousness of the offense, the more restrictive the disposition. Manhattan showed the greatest proportionality. Manhattan delinquents who were placed committed crimes that were on average nearly three times as serious as the crimes of delinquents who got probation and nearly four times as serious as crimes of released delinquents. (The crimes of placed Manhattan delinquents were nearly *ten* times as serious as those of placed Mercer delinquents.) The other two counties showed a different pattern, however. Placed delinquents in both Mercer and Westchester had lower mean seriousness scores than those given probation, but those given probation had higher scores than the ones who were released.[27]

[27] A similar "proportionality" was found in a 1972 study of dispositions in three jurisdictions (Denver, Colorado; Memphis-Shelby County, Tennessee; and Montgomery County, Pennsylvania) that concluded that variations in the nature and severity of dispositions were most strongly influenced by whether a formal petition

When mean seriousness scores for the total of all crimes charged to each delinquent were measured (in levels instead of by means; see Table 6-A, Appendix A), each county showed proportional court treatment with regard to dispositions. Delinquents whose combined crimes fell into higher levels of seriousness tended to receive more severe dispositions on the latest offense.

Table 24 Race and Disposition in Vera Sample[a]

	Black		Spanish Surname		White	
	N	%	N	%	N	%
Placed	8	9.1	5	21.7	5	7.1
Probation	49	55.7	9	39.1	30	42.9
Suspended Sentence	9	10.2	—	—	4	5.7
Released	16	18.2	5	21.8	27	38.6
ACD	(14)	(15.9)	(1)	(4.3)	(25)	(35.7)
Dismissed/Withdrawn	(2)	(2.3)	(4)	(17.4)	(2)	(2.9)
Transferred	—	—	1	4.3	4	5.7
Pending	6	6.8	3	13.0	—	—
Total	88	100.0	23	99.9[b]	70	100.0

SOURCE: Vera Institute Violent Delinquent Study.

NOTE: Chi square $= 16.77$; $df = 6$; $p < 0.05$. Four categories were used in calculating chi square: "placed," "probation" (including "suspended sentence"), "released," and "transferred/pending."

[a] Ten missing observations (5.2 percent).
[b] Error in percent is due to rounding.

The relationship of race to disposition proved interesting. In the overall sample (see Table 24), nonwhites were released following adjudication at about half the rate of whites (21 percent to 39 percent). In particular, nonwhites were granted ACDs at the discretion of the courts only one-third as often as whites. In Mercer County, 22 percent of adjudicated nonwhites received ACDs compared to 47 percent of whites. In Westchester County, no adjudicated nonwhites, but 22 percent of whites, received ACDs. In Manhattan, no adjudicated delinquents of any race received

had been filed or not, which in turn was most strongly related to the seriousness of the offense charged. (Lawrence E. Cohen, *Delinquency Dispositions: An Empirical Analysis of Processing Decisions in Three Juvenile Courts*, National Criminal Justice Information and Statistics Service, 1975.)

ACDs. A slightly larger proportion of nonwhites (12 percent) than whites (7 percent) were placed in institutions, and nonwhites were also given probation somewhat more frequently (52 percent of nonwhite cases) than whites (43 percent). Thus, overall, nonwhites were put under official control more frequently (72 percent of nonwhite cases) than whites (56 percent).

To test the relative strength of race and other characteristics as influences on the disposition of cases, a multiple regression analysis was once again employed. Race, number of prior offenses, and the violence and seriousness of the current charge were the independent variables. The dependent variable was disposition, simplified as the imposition of official control (placement, probation, or suspended sentences) on the one hand, or release (ACD, dismissal, or withdrawal) on the other.

The analysis revealed that the number of prior offenses had by far the strongest impact on disposition, followed by the seriousness of the current offense and race. Whether the current offense was violent or not had only a slight influence on disposition.[28] Race does appear to have some effect on disposition, although the prior record and the seriousness of the offense are more significant.

The rather strong tendency to grant ACDs to white delinquents more often than to nonwhite delinquents (Table 24) may be due to external conditions bearing on the cases instead of to racial discrimination on the part of judges. One external condition may be greater availability of social services and supports for white delinquents than for nonwhite delinquents. Judges frequently grant ACDs on the understanding that the youth in question will receive some nonjudicial assistance. If such assistance is not likely to be forthcoming, judges may prefer to issue judicial dispositions, either to help secure services or else to assure that the delinquent will remain under some form of control. Hence, to the extent that nonwhites are denied access to support services, they may be given fewer ACDs by the courts. Differential availability of services is an issue that will be addressed further in this chapter.

Older delinquents were more likely to be placed or receive sus-

[28] Beta coefficients for these variables were as follows: number of offenses, 0.40513; seriousness, 0.21317; race, 0.15590; violence, 0.12925. (Overall multiple $R = 0.44801$.)

pended sentences than younger delinquents, while younger delinquents were more likely to get ACDs.

To sum up, evidence in the Vera study suggests that dispositions are reasonably proportional, at least within the analytical framework used here. On the average, each of the courts studied tended to apply more restrictive dispositions to those delinquents who had longer offense records, who were more violent, and whose offenses had more serious consequences. A disquieting pattern of racial differences also appeared in the allocation of dispositions, but the data are not adequate to clarify the reasons for these differences.

Preadjudication Detention. Data in court files also permitted analysis of the relationship between number of offenses, violence, and seriousness, on the one hand, and the probability of detention before adjudication, on the other. Information with regard to detention for the most recent offense was available for 93.7 percent of the sample.

Delinquents in Manhattan were detained about twice as often (22 percent of all cases) as delinquents in Westchester (13 percent) and Mercer (10 percent). On the surface, this is not unreasonable, given the more serious offense histories of Manhattan delinquents. Delinquents charged with violent crimes were more likely to be detained in secure facilities (27 percent of such cases) and nonsecure facilities (11 percent) than delinquents charged with nonviolent crimes (6 percent and 2 percent of such cases, respectively). The greater the number of offenses (and violent offenses) a delinquent had committed, the more likely he or she was to be detained. Similarly, the higher the seriousness score for the offense charged or for all offenses combined, the higher the probability of detention. The older the delinquent, the greater the likelihood of detention. There appeared to be no significant racial differences in detention rates that could not be explained as well by the number of seriousness of offenses. Consequently, it appeared from the Vera data that detention decisions were proportional.[29]

[29] A recent study based on 1972 data from three jurisdictions (Denver, Colorado; Memphis-Shelby County, Tennessee; and Montgomery County, Pennsylvania)

All of this evidence taken together suggests that, by and large, a delinquents' record, the propensity to be violent, and the seriousness of the act committed have the effect one would expect in a system that is "proportionally" selective. Chronic and violent delinquents are kept in preadjudication detention more often than less serious and nonviolent delinquents. At fact-finding hearings, chronic delinquents and those whose offenses are most serious also tend to be adjudicated with greater frequency. And at the dispositional stage, the court's response tends to be harshest for the most serious delinquents. Offense number has the most powerful determining effect on disposition of the measures studied, particularly in Mercer and Westchester counties. In Manhattan, the seriousness of the offense charged (although not necessarily the "violence" of it) also shows a strong direct relationship to the severity of the disposition, a relationship that is absent in the other two counties. This overall pattern was not borne out on every measure applied, but it occurred with sufficient consistency to warrant a general conclusion that, with regard to seriousness and violence of delinquent behavior, juvenile court processing is "proportional."[30]

This study was not specifically designed to test for racial discrimination, but there were a few indications that judicial processing in some respects tends to favor white delinquents in the counties studied. Evidence was least ambiguous with regard to the granting of ACDs (adjournments in contemplation of dismissal) at the discretion of the court. Judges granted ACDs to 31 percent of all white delinquents but only 9 percent of all nonwhite delin-

---

reached a different conclusion. In each court, defendants who had a prior court referral, who were idle (not working or in school), and who came from broken homes were more likely to be detained than their counterparts who did not have these attributes. (Lawrence E. Cohen, *Pre-Adjudicatory Detention in Three Juvenile Courts—An Empirical Analysis of the Factors Related to Detention Decision Outcomes*, National Criminal Justice Information and Statistics Service, 1975.)

[30] Research on processing of delinquents in Massachusetts points to the opposite conclusion. A report by the Harvard Center for Criminal Justice shows that the kind of disposition received tends to depend on the kind of prehearing detention a child was subjected to. Prehearing detention, in turn, seemed to be more related to social class and availability of facilities than to "dangerousness" or likelihood of absconding. (Robert B. Coates, Alden D. Miller, Lloyd E. Ohlin, "Exploratory Analysis of Recidivism and Cohort Data on the Massachusetts Youth Correctional System," Center for Criminal Justice, Harvard Law School, July 1973, pp. 26–39.)

quents, combining results at both the adjudication and disposition stages. Although our data were not adequate to pinpoint the specific reason for this difference, preferential granting of ACDs may be a result of factors such as the greater availability of nonjudicial services for white delinquents instead of racial discrimination by the courts. In any event, the multiple regression analysis showed race to be an important factor (although not the most important factor) in determining disposition.

A significantly larger proportion of nonwhite delinquents (46 percent) than whites (26 percent) had their cases dismissed or withdrawn prior to adjudication. The data do not permit any conclusive judgment as to why this might have happened, although they suggest that this result is more strongly related to the disproportionate number of withdrawals and dismissals in the Manhattan court and the disproportionate number of minority delinquents there than to direct racial differences. Other explanations are sometimes offered: that police arrest nonwhite juveniles on inadequate evidence more often than they do white juveniles; that victims and witnesses more often fail to cooperate in prosecution of nonwhite delinquents than in prosecution of white delinquents; or that the courts do not regard intraracial crimes by minorities in the same way that they regard interracial crimes or crimes committed by whites against whites. In any case, proportionately more nonwhites than whites were subjected to the ordeal of court processing without a strong case being made against them.

Our evidence also showed that 11 percent of nonwhites' cases were still pending, at either the adjudication or disposition stage, seven months or more after petitions were brought, compared to only 2 percent of whites' cases. Again, it is not possible to say why this result occurred, although the disparity is influenced by the large number of nonwhite cases and small number of white cases in Manhattan, where cases generally moved more slowly through the courts. It may be that the delinquents themselves share responsibility by failing to appear at hearings or to cooperate in other ways. Perhaps, too, the fault lies in discriminatory behavior by outside agencies on which the court relies for evaluation or other services needed to expedite cases. Or, it may simply be that the wheels of justice turn more slowly for nonwhite delinquents.[31]

Finally, there is the question of efficiency. In Manhattan, the "drop-out" rate (the proportion of cases dismissed or withdrawn) was more than twice as high as in the two other counties. No obvious explanation for this emerged from the data. The correlation between the high dismissal rate and the high proportion of minority delinquents in Manhattan suggests the possibility of discrimination along some of the lines discussed above. But that explanation is not wholly satisfactory. Another partial explanation may lie in the volume and complexity of cases that come before the Manhattan court compared to the other courts. The burden of dealing with so many difficult cases, even after diversion at intake, may force the court to look for shortcuts to resolution, shortcuts that involve dismissals or withdrawals. Even if there is no stated policy in this regard, one need only spend a day observing a family court at work to realize that the long delays, adjournments, confusion, and crowded, uncomfortable facilities inevitably discourage some participants (victims, witnesses, prosecutors, and offenders alike) from staying with a case until it is concluded.

Yet another factor often cited as influencing the high drop-out rate is the relative strength of legal representation available to juveniles in New York City. Law guardians working for the Legal Aid Society in New York are aggressive, well-informed, and dedicated to securing the release of their clients. There is an unmistakable adversary orientation to their work that is not so evident in the other jurisdictions studied where law guardians, like probation staff, appear to function frequently as part of a court "team" that sees its principal mission as serving the "best interests of the child" more than securing all the child's legal rights and opportunities.

More penetrating studies than this one are required to determine the relative weight of these and other factors in the processing of delinquency cases. What has been clearly demonstrated, however,

[31] The Philadelphia cohort study showed that race was the single most important factor in determining both whether a juvenile would be sent to court by police and what disposition he would receive from the court. "[T]he weight of history and previous research on race and official response to race strongly suggest that differential disposition based on race may be the result of discrimination, prejudice, bias." (Wolfgang, Figlio, and Sellin, op. cit., pp. 221, 252, 406.)

is that Manhattan, the county that charges its juveniles most often with the most serious and violent kinds of delinquency, also has the greatest difficulty bringing these cases to a judicial conclusion. The fact that it has equal or even greater difficulty bringing less serious cases to judicial resolution should not obscure the importance of this disparity, if reduction in juvenile violence is to be an objective of public policy.

This observation returns us to the philosophical issue raised earlier in this chapter. Is a high proportion of drop-outs from the judicial system good or bad? The answer depends fundamentally on whether delinquents are guilty of the serious crimes with which they are charged, and that we cannot know. If they are, however, then there is a strong presumption that something should be done either for them or to them. When delinquents are diverted or dropped from the judicial system, the chance is nil that anything will be done to them, and minute that anything of substance will be done for them.

If they do remain within the system, the maxim that the time interval between act and consequence should be as short as possible for the greatest amount of learning to occur is almost certain to be violated. Our study showed that 15 percent of all delinquents in Manhattan had cases pending seven months or more after the petition was brought. A study in New York City by the Juvenile Justice Institute showed that of all cases before the courts between July 1, 1973 and June 30, 1974 involving eleven categories of crimes against the person, 18 percent required seven to nine months to complete, 13 percent required ten to twelve months, and 12 percent required thirteen months or more. In other words, 43 percent of the most serious cases brought to court were not resolved within seven months. Less than one-third were concluded within three months.[32]

These findings raise troubling doubts about the impact of court processing on juvenile violence in the place where it appears to be the most serious problem. But the issue must be taken one step further. In the relatively few cases that are carried through to disposition, is the final result likely to be helpful or not? A full

[32] Juvenile Justice Institute, op. cit., pp. 45–46.

discussion of this question would involve an analysis of probation services for violent delinquents, in addition to an analysis of placement options. There is room here only to summarize what a number of probation studies have shown: probation alone is largely ineffective as a sanction or as a treatment. It may be more effective with less serious delinquents if it is combined with other supportive services or if the probation officer is particularly well qualified and has sufficient time for personal contact with each probationer. But these conditions rarely exist, particularly in large metropolitan centers like New York City.[33] When probation or other intermediate sanctions fail, as they are quite likely to do with more serious delinquents, residential placement is the probable next step. This response and its impact are the issues to which we now turn.

Institutional Placement. Residential placement is generally viewed as a last resort, invoked either to provide intensive rehabilitative services to a delinquent, to protect the community from depredations, or to punish the delinquent. Judges vary, of course, in the threshold at which they react with placement. Their decisions are likely to be governed not only by their own values and those of the community, but also by the number and quality of alternative dispositions available. As a rule, however, until a juvenile shows a pattern of recidivism or engages in a particularly violent or bizarre offense, he or she will progress slowly up the dispositional ladder, from diversion to ACDs to probation to voluntary participation in social or rehabilitative services.

A substantial body of opinion supports this avoidance of more severe dispositions. The reasoning behind it is that they appear to do no good and may well do harm. The Philadelphia cohort study concluded:

Not only do a greater number of those who receive punitive treatment (institutionalization, fine or probation) continue to violate the law, but they also commit more serious crimes with greater rapidity than those who experience a less constraining contact with the judicial and correctional systems. Thus, we must conclude that the juvenile justice system, at its best, has no effect on the subsequent behavior of adoles-

[33] See pp. 115–116, supra.

cent boys and, at its worst, has a deleterious effect on future behavior.[34]

This conclusion was reinforced in two self-report studies by
Martin Gold that showed that juveniles apprehended by the police
subsequently committed more offenses than matched unappre-
hended juveniles. Doleschal, in reviewing these studies, summarizes them by saying "what legal authorities now commonly do
upon apprehending a juvenile has worse effects than not apprehending him at all—a serious indictment of current procedures."[35]

Even though traditional means of handling delinquents may do
more harm than good, there remains a need, in the view of many
authorities, for some children to be put under meaningful social
control. In Russell's words, "Many of the children . . . diverted
from the authority, control and discipline of courts and probation
are children whose principal adjustment problems represent, in
part at least, a lack of applied and internalized discipline in their
lives."[36] This observation emphasizes two factors required to deal
with serious delinquents—control coupled with effective help in
internalizing discipline. Diversion programs provide neither.
Traditional punitive responses may provide control (although they
are often faulted on that score), but evidence such as that from the
Philadelphia study and Gold's self-report studies implies that they
do little to provide internalized discipline.

In most jurisdictions, courts have access to one or more "nontraditional" programs that attempt to provide delinquents with experiences leading to the development of self-control within a less
restrictive context. (The varieties in which they come are described in Chapter 5). More often than not, they are operated by
private, voluntary agencies, although a number of public-sector
alternatives to old-fashioned incarceration are also being developed. In comparison to what has existed in the past, these
programs offer hope of more humane and perhaps even more successful treatment of delinquents. Yet they have an unfortunate

[34] Wolfgang, Figlio, and Sellin, op. cit., p. 25. This conclusion might be challenged
because the study did not control precisely for the characteristics of the offenders or
the nature of the offenses for which they were adjudicated.
[35] Doleschal, op. cit., p. 557.
[36] Russell, op. cit., p. 8.

(if understandable) record of preferring the less troubled, less violent delinquent to the one who most needs help.

The "hard-core" delinquent is usually identified late, after a fearsome record of antisocial behavior has been acquired. By that time, the delinquent is an unwanted person. The odds are high that he or she was long ago rejected by his or her family, or rejected them. They are equally high that he or she is a failure in school and a misfit in most other social settings. He or she is probably part of a small, deviant peer group that reinforces destructive behavior, but even in that group the sense of belonging and security is likely to be tenuous. Lack of social relatedness, even on that level, is probably his or her most salient characteristic.

This kind of youth is virtually certain to be rejected by any agency that has a choice. The delinquent whose alienation from society may not run so deep, but who has a serious violent crime on his or her record, is also at high risk of being refused on that basis alone. The less seriously violent youth has some chance to be admitted to a nontraditional correctional or treatment program, but must compete for limited space with many other kinds of applicants. If the delinquent should be a compulsive "runner," however, who cannot remain long within an institutional setting, an open community-based facility will be of little use, and closed facilities with good rehabilitation programs are rare indeed.

A pattern of discrimination against the most difficult delinquents by voluntary child care organizations in New York City was delineated in a 1972 report by the Committee on Mental Health Services Inside and Outside the Family Court in the City of New York. The Committee found that admission policies of voluntary agencies have been tightened so much in recent years that it has become "virtually impossible to place delinquent or seriously acting-out children with them. . . . Virtually all of the agencies will reject the child who is a fire-setter or a persistent runaway or who engages in aberrant sexual activity."[37] The Committee also found discrimination against minority children; children without "cooperative" families; children with serious emotional problems, low IQ levels, and poor reading levels; children heavily involved with drugs; and older children—in other words, the children most

[37] Committee on Mental Health Services, op. cit., pp. 54–55.

likely to become violent.[38] This conclusion was recently reconfirmed in a study by the New York State Board of Social Welfare that reported that "only 39.5 percent of the children judged as not normal and with three or more specific problems were in the preferred placement." The report noted that this finding illustrates "how hard it is to find the appropriate placement for a child who exhibits difficult behavior."[39]

The results are plain to see. In the Juvenile Justice Institute study referred to earlier, which deals with all petitions for eleven categories of violent crime brought in the year between July 1, 1973 and June 30, 1974, 197 children were reported as placed. Only 22 percent were accepted for placement in voluntary agencies, and another 2.5 percent in open facilities operated by the state. This group of forty-nine included twenty-six children charged with robbery and thirteen charged with assault. It included only eight of forty-two children (19 percent) charged with homicide, kidnapping, sex offenses, or arson. All but twelve of the remaining 148 children (all but three charged with the more serious offenses) were sent to the state's training schools.[40]

Street and Vinter, in a 1966 study of six agencies dealing with delinquents in Massachusetts, found a similar pattern in that state. In general, older delinquents with more serious offenses, disruptive family backgrounds, and lower IQ's were more likely to be placed in custodial, nontreatment institutions.[41]

It is important to note that the institutions refusing to accept the most troubled delinquents are largely supported by public funds, either direct government subsidies or tax-exempt private contributions. But the voluntary organizations are not alone in their discrimination. The Committee on Mental Health Services report also found among state and municipal psychiatric hospitals and schools for the retarded a pattern of rejecting court-referred mentally ill children considered to be management problems.[42] In Massachu-

[38] Ibid., pp. 21–32.
[39] New York State Board of Social Welfare. *Foster Care Needs and Alternatives to Placement: A Projection for 1975–1985*, November 1975, p. 23.
[40] Juvenile Justice Institute, op. cit., pp. 40–45.
[41] David Street and Robert Vinter, *Organization for Treatment* (New York: The Free Press, 1966).
[42] Ibid., pp. 67–104.

setts, one official of the Department of Youth Services reports that the only public mental health services available to delinquents are fifty beds for preadolescents.[43] In Minnesota there is only one secure mental hospital that accepts delinquents, and it is in danger of being closed.[44] Even child guidance clinics and court-related clinics have been found to screen out the most difficult cases, including older children and children who break the law.[45]

The sad fact is that most seriously disturbed delinquents who need mental health and other rehabilitation services end up in training schools, because those are the only places that *must* take such children and the only places that have some capability of preventing them from running away. In spite of much rhetoric to the contrary, treatment and rehabilitation are largely absent from the training school setting. California and Florida have experimented with several treatment approaches in their juvenile institutions. Kentucky and one or two other states are reported to be restructuring their juvenile corrections systems to facilitate short-term, intensive diagnosis and treatment. Massachusetts has done away with its traditional training schools altogether and substituted a service and rehabilitation model of corrections. But most states will retain a network of prisonlike training schools in which the most serious delinquents are mixed with many less serious offenders in an atmosphere offering little in the way of rehabilitation.[46]

The report of the Committee on Mental Health Services Inside and Outside the Family Court in the City of New York described many of the deficiencies of training schools in New York State. Despite the fact that training school placements are now reported

[43] Interview with Ed Budelmann, Assistant Commissioner of Clinical Services, July 14, 1975.

[44] Juvenile Division, Fourth Judicial District Court, Hennepin County, Minnesota, "In the Matter of the Welfare of J.E.C.: Findings and Order," February 25, 1975. In addition, compelling anecdotal evidence of the situation in Pennsylvania is given in a book by Judge Lisa Richette, *The Throwaway Children* (Philadelphia: J. B. Lippincott Co., 1969).

[45] James Teele and Sol Levine, "The Acceptance of Emotionally Disturbed Children by Psychiatric Agencies," in Stanton Wheeler, ed., *Controlling Delinquents* (New York: John Wiley & Sons, 1968).

[46] A graphic and chilling description of life inside a secure training school in Ohio is given in Clemens Bartollas, Stuart J. Miller, and Simon Dinitz, *Juvenile Victimization: The Institutional Paradox* (New York: John Wiley & Sons, 1976).

to cost an average of $23,000 per child per year in New York,[47] these institutions were characterized by the Committee as understaffed and underprogrammed. "Not one school is equipped to provide even minimal mental health treatment for the seriously disturbed children it receives. This is not because of budget cuts. No school has ever had mental health personnel able to provide more than diagnoses and staff consultation." Regarding academic, vocational, and recreational programs, the Committee concluded that job freezes and budget cuts had seriously undermined their already questionable effectiveness.[48] Discussions with child-care professionals confirm that this situation has changed little since the Committee filed its report in 1972.

Apart from failing to provide rehabilitation, the training schools in New York have also been under fire for failing to retain custody over delinquents for adequate periods of time. Severe pressures on limited space, coupled no doubt with an awareness by administrators of the limited benefit training schools have for their charges, have resulted in an implicit policy of "early release." Children who, by order of the court, could be kept in training schools for up to eighteen months are returned to the community after an average stay of only nine or ten months.[49]

The State Division for Youth (DFY) has an aftercare service with responsibility for following up released juveniles and aiding them in reintegration with the community, but the service is woefully undermanned and underfinanced. Six fully staffed and fourteen partly staffed aftercare teams are available to do the work of twenty-nine full teams. Each aftercare worker has a caseload of fifty-two or fifty-three juveniles, although DFY estimates that "sensitive" cases, including those who commit the most violent offenses, cannot be dealt with effectively in caseloads of more than

[47] According to a report published by the New York State Board of Social Welfare, the cost per child per day was $62.81 in 1974, or $22,926 per year. (New York State Board of Social Welfare, op. cit., p. 45, footnote 7.)

[48] Committee on Mental Health Services, op. cit., pp. 33–39.

[49] Nanette Dembitz, "Treatment of Dangerous Delinquents," *New York Law Journal* (February 5, 1975): 1, 7. In New Jersey, the law permits juveniles to be confined three years, until the age of 21, or the term of the adult sentence for the crime committed, whichever is shorter. The average term of confinement in a training school, however, is between ten and eighteen months.

ten. It would cost an estimated $900,000 annually to bring the aftercare program up to a minimum standard.[50]

While this description applies specifically to New York, similar problems have often been attributed to the juvenile corrections systems of other states.[51] Training schools, by default at least as much as by design, are institutions whose principal virtue is their ability to isolate criminal youth from the community in relative security.

Yet, determination of the need for secure placement is an exceedingly difficult task. When incapacitation to prevent future violence is the objective, limitations on predictive capability present serious problems. It may be easier to determine that secure custody is needed for the juvenile's own benefit, to prevent self-destructive behavior or escape from treatment, but that is still no simple matter. A straightforward punitive rationale would yield the clearest standard for determining the need for secure custody, but that is not the current orientation of the juvenile court. Even when a punitive standard is applied in practice, there is little uniformity among states or even among jurisdictions within states regarding how and to whom it is applied.

Although there is no clear standard for ordering secure custody, it is widely assumed that the number of delinquents in secure institutions is well in excess of the number who "need" to be there. The limited amount of research available on the subject tends to support that assumption.

In 1973, psychiatrists in Massachusetts court clinics examined 567 juveniles referred by the state's Department of Youth Services, all of whom would have been candidates for training schools under previously existing policy. The objective of the examination was to recommend a disposition to DYS. The clinics recommended "secure intensive care" (the most restrictive alternative available) for twenty-eight cases, or 5 percent of the sample. They recommended that 269 other delinquents, 47 percent, be placed in various kinds of less restrictive residential care away from home.[52]

[50] Figures from a memorandum by Henry Saltzman, Citizens' Committee for Children, to "Concerned Civic Leaders," April 24, 1975, pp. 4–5.
[51] See, for example, Bartollas, Miller, and Dimitz, op. cit.
[52] Russell, op. cit., pp. 21–22.

In an earlier study, 100 "assaultive" youths in closed placement were referred to the Judge Baker Clinic in Boston for evaluation regarding the "safety" of their release to the community. That study reached a somewhat different conclusion. Thirty-one of the 100 were found to require closed rehabilitative programs or placement in mental hospitals. Another twenty-one were recommended for open placement and the remainder, forty-eight, for return home with parole supervision.[53]

These two studies together imply that only 5 percent of serious delinquents (those referred by courts to the state placement agency) require closed placement, whereas about one-third of those who have assaultive histories should be in closed placement. In addition, half of the serious (but not necessarily assaultive) delinquent population and 20 percent more of the assaultive group would benefit from nonsecure (open) placement away from home.

These studies are based, of course, on the predictive approach that has been subjected to so much criticism, and must therefore be treated with caution. A follow-up study of the 100 assaultive youths by another researcher showed no difference between the subsequent assault rates of the youths recommended for closed placement and the rates of the others, controlling for time spent in confinement by those who were actually placed. No more than one-third of those judged to be in need of confinement, or 10 percent of all the assaultive youths examined, actually committed another assaultive offense.[54] Based on these results, it could be argued that only one-tenth of assaultive youths who normally would be put in closed placement actually need such confinement, although determining which delinquents fit that category is, to repeat, a difficult proposition.

Studies conducted on the Community Treatment Program in California concluded that between 50 and 75 percent of delinquents in Youth Authority institutions in that state could be released to the community with no effect on recidivism.[55] Recidivism is a broader measure of success or failure than assaultiveness, so it is reasonable

[53] Russell and Harper, op. cit.

[54] Mary Jill Robinson Harper, "Courts, Doctors and Delinquents: An Inquiry into the Uses of Psychiatry in Youth Corrections," *Smith College Studies in Social Work* 44, no. 3 (June 1974): 158–178.

[55] *Corrections Magazine* (September 1974): 50.

to assume that a somewhat larger proportion would represent no serious threat to the community if treated in open facilities.

Even with their serious limitations, these studies support the conclusion that a large proportion (between 50 and 95 percent) of delinquents placed in secure institutions under current policies do not need such restrictive confinement.

Several states have acted on this conclusion by taking steps to reduce the number of delinquents in secure custody. Massachusetts's Department of Youth Services has adopted a policy that no more than ninety-six youths should be kept in secure facilities at any one time, although in mid-1975 there were 110 delinquents in secure care: 19 percent of all delinquents receiving services from DYS, and an even smaller share of the total delinquent population in the state. Longitudinally, about 25 percent of delinquents referred to DYS end up in intensive care at one time or another.[56] Kentucky has established a new secure treatment center to handle forty "high-risk" delinquents. This figure, the number that state authorities think will require secure custody at any given time, is 6 percent of the total delinquent residential population and 0.1 percent of children brought before the courts in the state.[57]

Only the most general conclusions can be drawn from this scattered and incomplete evidence. First, the proportion of all delinquents who require placement of any kind is small, certainly less than 20 percent and perhaps less than 5 percent. Second, it appears that a significant proportion (50 percent or more) of delinquents incarcerated in closed institutions under current policies could be released without incurring further risk to the community or sacrificing any significant benefit to the offender. Third, among delinquents guilty of assaultive or violent offenses, the proportion requiring secure incarceration may be higher than the proportion of the delinquent population as a whole, but a substantial part of this group, too, does not necessarily need to be in secure institutions.

Certainly one way to reduce the need for incarceration in these

---

[56] Interview with Robert Coates, Harvard Center for Criminal Justice, July 14, 1975. See also footnote 29, this chapter.

[57] *Corrections Magazine* (March/April 1975): 27–28.

institutions would be timely intervention at one of the many earlier opportunities that are usually presented. A typical path followed by delinquents who eventually end up in secure facilities is the following. After a period of lesser delinquent activity that results in arrest, diversion, rearrest, probation, arrest again, he commits a violent act that puts him on a somewhat different track. Pending a hearing, he is held in a children's shelter or juvenile detention center where the staff's principal concern is maintaining order and minimizing assaultive behavior by detainees. He may or may not be eventually released while the case moves slowly through the court. Perhaps the judge will order mental health observation and diagnosis in a hospital during the pretrial period, but crowded facilities and disinclination to cope with troublesome cases will probably result in release after a short period of time.

Once the case is settled, and the child has been found to be a delinquent "in need of supervision, treatment or confinement," a search may be undertaken to find a community-based residential program for him. Since many programs refuse to consider applications filed simultaneously with more than one agency, the search process is usually lengthy. One rejection is likely to be followed by others. Meanwhile, the child may either remain on the street, with no attention or services, or be put back into a shelter or detention center, again without meaningful services in most cases.

Eventually it will be determined that there is no place for him except a state training school. There he will mingle with others in similarly desperate circumstances. Should the child have an episode of serious mental instability, he will probably be sent to a state hospital until he "stabilizes," at which point he will be returned quickly to the training school. He may try to run away, but if he does not, he will almost certainly be returned to the home community in a relatively short time, untreated and possibly further damaged.

Overwhelmed probation and aftercare staff will have little time to keep track of the child's activities in the community, much less to help him readjust or gain access to mental health, educational, or other kinds of services. After a time, he will be in trouble again, perhaps on a grander scale, and repeat the process until the age is reached at which the child becomes the responsibility of the adult criminal justice system.

This cycle of neglect, rejection, transfer, and failure reinforces his sense that he belongs nowhere and fans the alienation that contributes to violent behavior. The seemingly endless chain of policemen, probation officers, judges, social workers, doctors, and correction officers who pass through his life, rarely to reappear, conditions the child to expect little from relationships with adults except professional curiosity, indifference, or interference. He also learns that he can survive this process without his worst fears of annihilation being realized, which merely emboldens him. And he may well have picked up more sophisticated techniques along the way.

The process is costly to society, as well. Training school is expensive, with little return except some temporary protection, which must be weighed against the heightened anger, antisocial resolve, and criminal sophistication that may be generated. And the cost of many other ineffective public inputs along the way (court, probation, detention, and mental health services) must be counted, too.

This scenario is somewhat overdrawn, of course. Not every violent child experiences every step in the process. Certainly there are also individual delinquents who, through exceptional personal resources or exceptional good fortune, manage to find their way out of this cycle at one point or another. But the most serious indictment of all may be that deliverance from it depends on chance or sudden access to previously untapped reserves of strength instead of a rational social policy for dealing with violent juveniles.

It is my conclusion that, although police practices and court inefficiency are problems that would have to be addressed in a comprehensive overhaul of the public's response to violent delinquency, the gravest and most pressing problems arise in providing effective treatment, rehabilitation, and control for violent juveniles. The target group is a relatively small one, but it is destructive far out of proportion to its numbers. And current intervention practices seem to encourage and enhance the group's destructive potential.

Summary

In the past decade, many arrested children have been steered away from the judicial and correctional systems through diversion programs. Diversion generally favors less serious offenders. Delinquents who are not diverted but are referred for court processing "drop out" of judicial proceedings for one reason or another at rates ranging from 35 to over 80 percent, with the highest rates occurring in large cities. It appears from data in the Vera study that this drop-out process works more to the advantage of the less serious delinquent than the hard-core delinquent, as one might expect it should. As a result, at the final stage of court processing (disposition), judges must contend with a relatively serious group of delinquents, particularly in large urban centers like Manhattan.

In terms of the degree of control mandated in dispositions, the courts in the Vera study appeared to respond proportionally: the harsher and more restrictive dispositions were meted out to delinquents who had the longest records, who had committed violent crimes, and whose crimes were most serious in their consequences. Beyond this level of analysis, however, it is apparent that treatment and correctional responses for violent delinquents are often anything but proportional especially to the needs of the individual delinquent, the standard by which the juvenile justice system is supposed to operate.

Violent or seriously disturbed delinquents, the ones most in need of rehabilitative treatment as well as control, are frequently denied access to effective help. They are subjected to long delays in processing and multiple rejections by voluntary treatment programs as well as public mental health facilities. In the end, the great majority given residential placement are sent to training schools, where they may be brought under temporary control but almost certainly will receive no constructive assistance. From the point of view of public safety, the number of delinquents who require isolation in securely locked institutions is probably much smaller (perhaps by as much as 50 to 95 percent) than the number currently being placed in such settings. Many of these would be much better served by treatment in open, community-based programs.

Part of this problem stems from the scarcity of good treatment facilities for adolescents. Another part, however, can be traced to outright discrimination against this kind of delinquent on the part of voluntary and public agencies. Still another part of the problem is lack of effective control over the referral and treatment process by the public agencies that bear ultimate responsibility for dealing with violent (and other) delinquents. The result is ineffective and perhaps damaging treatment, discontinuously applied.

5 Treatment of Violent Delinquents

THE CONCEPT of treatment for criminal offenders is the contribution of the "positivist" school of criminology. Born in the late nineteenth century, positivism was a reaction to the "classical" school, which held that people become criminals through misapplication of their free will and must be controlled, humanely, through punishment and incapacitation. Positivism shifted the emphasis from failure of will to "underlying causes"—be they biological, psychological or social—and sought rehabilitation through treatment of these causes.[1]

After nearly a century of reign, the positivist philosophy of correctional treatment has begun to come under heavy attack. The argument against treatment is made on several grounds: (1) Treatment has been the excuse for interference in the private lives of offenders far in excess of what could be justified under any alternative theory, and is thus a threat to human rights. (2) When comparisons are made between "treated" and "untreated" groups of criminals, the untreated groups seem to fare at least as well as the

---

[1] For a brief summary of the development of penology theory, see Eugene Doleschal and Nora Klapmuts, "Toward a New Criminology," *Crime and Delinquency Literature* (December 1973). Also, Herbert Block and Gilbert Geis, *Man, Crime, and Society* (New York: Random House, 1962).

treated in terms of recidivism. Treatment is therefore ineffective. (3) No known treatment works because criminal behavior is not an illness or deficiency that can be "cured." It is, instead, a complex and perhaps necessary phenomenon of modern social structure.

It must be admitted that the available evidence provides impressive support, at least for the first two arguments. Numerous examples can be cited of unacceptable damage done to human rights and dignity in the name of treatment. Yet in principle this need not be so. It seems that excesses might well have been prevented had there been sufficient consciousness of the dangers and vigilance in defending individual rights. The second argument, that treatment does not work, is a more damning one, because it puts the burden of proof squarely on advocates of treatment, a burden that becomes heavier and harder to displace as time goes by.

The argument that criminal behavior is not an illness or deficiency that can be cured is one that may never be resolved, although it is certain to be debated for many years to come. It is true, however, as we saw in Chapter 3, that a theory regarding the origins of violence (to focus on this particular kind of criminal behavior) on which treatment can be based is at best weak. The most that can be said with confidence is that determinants of violence potentially include a number of factors, some inherent in the individual and others found in the surrounding environment, some congenital or developmental in origin, others more in the nature of direct stimuli. In a sense, treatment of violence has followed a path similar to the treatment of cancer. In the absence of specific knowledge about the causes of violence (or cancer), treatment (to the extent it has been attempted at all) has been pragmatic, borrowing techniques used in treating similar "disorders" and discarding those that seem to have little or no effect.

This chapter will review some of the most common treatment modalities, including what is known about their effects on violent delinquents. Treatment of psychiatric disorders has provided the basic model for a large number of intervention techniques, and it is fair to say that the treatment of violence continues to be dominated by psychiatrists. For that reason, psychiatric models are given the most attention in this review. In spite of this dominance, however, psychiatrically based treatment has not produced large-scale or dramatic successes in dealing with violence, for a number of reasons that will be discussed. Nor have the alternative models that have traditionally been employed, notably those based on social work techniques, achieved major breakthroughs. In light of this limited success, the search for new approaches and more powerful theories of treatment continues, while challenges to the legitimacy of treatment as a response to criminal behavior, violent or otherwise, keep pace.

Varieties of Treatment

Psychiatric Treatment. Psychiatric intervention is probably the first thing that comes to mind when treatment of offenders is mentioned. Psychiatry, grounded in the "medical model," has had a profound influence on both juvenile and adult corrections. Widespread disillusionment with psychiatry has set in, however. As one New York Family Court judge put it, the problem with psychiatry is that "it may have identified the right problem—these children are sick, not bad—but it isn't very good at telling us how they are sick, and it hasn't come up with any effective solutions yet."

Much of the disappointment in psychiatry can probably be traced to unrealistic expectations (and sometimes claims) of what it can accomplish. As most thoughtful practitioners will admit, psychiatry is an exceedingly complex and still evolving science, particularly when applied to adolescents. Adolescence is always a period of intense emotional turmoil, episodic regression to childhood behavior, and impulsive experimentation with new sexual and social identities; in other words, it is a period of normal insanity. Detecting signs of long-lasting, deep-rooted pathology amid the transitory chaos of adolescent development is therefore difficult. Furthermore, because identity is in flux and the capacity for introspection and self-appraisal not yet fully developed in adolescents, the foundation of psychotherapeutic treatment is often shaky. Under these circumstances, the effectiveness of psychiatry with adolescents is bound to be limited.

Disillusionment with psychiatric treatment also stems from a rather widespread misunderstanding of its techniques and purposes. To oversimplify a bit, psychiatry uses two general forms of intervention: more or less traditional medical techniques, such as drug therapy, electroshock treatment, psychosurgery, and the like, on the one hand, and psychotherapy on the other.

Traditional medical techniques are usually reserved for mentally ill psychotics with serious disturbances of thought processes, and for severely depressed patients.[2] The purpose of medical intervention is to restore a degree of stability adequate to permit the patient to function in society and to begin the process of rehabilitation. When medical techniques work, the results can be dramatic. Bizarre or self-destructive behavior may disappear, gloomy depression may lift.

As noted in Chapter 3, however, few delinquents are sufficiently disturbed to be candidates for this kind of treatment. Hospitalization of people who are not truly mentally ill is likely to produce no benefit and may well have harmful effects. At a minimum, the hospital environment, in which patients are responded to on the basis of staff perception of their needs, may encourage the development of manipulative and dependent behavior. Drugs are frequently used to manage behavior, but neither drugs, psychosurgery, nor shock treatment is widely used to "cure" violence.[3]

The second mode of psychiatric treatment, psychotherapy (with its more specialized relative, psychoanalysis), consists of one-to-one personal interaction between a trained therapist (or analyst) and a patient. It is used with people who are not seriously ill (or whose illness has been brought under some control), and who suffer from internalized, unrecognized conflicts (psychoneuroses) that cause anxiety, compulsive behavior, or other symptoms. Effective psychotherapy requires that patients have some capacity for

[2] People who require medical intervention are usually not violent, or at least no more violent than "normal" individuals. Studies have revealed that the percentage of murderers among former mental patients is lower than that among the general population in the United States. Donald T. Lunde, *Murder and Madness* (Stanford, Calif.: Stanford Alumni Association, 1975), p. 35.

[3] Kozol, Boucher, and Garofalo, op. cit., p. 388. "Dangerousness is too subtle to be materially modified or affected by specious modalities of treatment. Neuroanatomical and neurophysiological research has not progressed to the point where simple extirpation of brain centers or pharmacological intervention can be generally applied. There may be rare exceptions to the latter when epileptic-like phenomena are demonstrated in association with explosive outbursts of violence. Such exceptions, even when demonstrated, only prove the generality of our position."

reflection and self-awareness and be motivated to participate in their own treatment. Its purpose is to help the patient recognize the sources of his or her neuroses and come to grips with them, to understand his or her behavior and thereby gain control over it. Psychotherapy also plays a role in socialization, since its success depends on the development of bonds of emotion and trust between the therapist and the patient.

The limitations of psychotherapy are that it usually progresses slowly, requires some stability and willingness to cooperate on the part of the patient, and can be disrupted readily if basic needs (e.g., for physical well-being and security) are not met first. It is also expensive.

In his review of correctional treatment methods, Martinson[4] uncovered nine studies of individual psychotherapy for youth offenders. (None singled out violent delinquents, however.) Most showed no effect on recidivism rates, including the only two that dealt with females. One did suggest that if a boy was judged to be successfully treated, his recidivism improved. Another, at the Deuel School in California, divided subjects into two groups, "amenable" and "nonamenable," and subjected both to psychotherapy. "Amenable" boys did better than boys who were given no treatment, but "nonamenable" boys actually did worse than a nontreated group. On the basis of this study, Martinson concluded "that there is something to be hoped for in treating properly selected amenable subjects [with psychotherapy] and that if those subjects are *not* properly selected, one may not only wind up doing no good but may actually produce harm."[5]

These results underscore the point that some personality disorders are not effectively treated by psychiatric techniques. Such disorders, often found in violent adolescents, are not grounded in clinically detectable mental illness, nor are they regarded by the affected person as a problem, which makes them difficult to deal with in the psychotherapeutic context. What Donald Russell calls "sociosyntonic behavior," an adaptive response to a youth's environment or peers, is of this kind (see discussion under "Psychiatric

[4] Robert Martinson, "What Works?—Questions and Answers About Prison Reform," *The Public Interest* 35 (Spring 1974): 22–54.
[5] Ibid., p. 29.

Characteristics," Chapter 3). So, too, is much of the behavior labeled "sociopathic" or "psychopathic." Regardless of how destructive it is (and it can be *very* destructive), it is not often amenable to standard techniques of psychiatric intervention.

Nevertheless, psychiatrists are frequently expected to treat such cases. More than that, they are sometimes expected to produce the dramatic results found occasionally with medical techniques, but to do so in the less dramatic manner of psychotherapy—with a group of patients not suited to either mode. It is, at least at this stage in the development of psychiatry, an impossibility.

What, then, can be expected of psychiatrists and psychotherapists in the treatment of violent juvenile delinquents? They can perform three limited but vital functions. First, together with professionals from other disciplines, psychiatrists should take part in assessment and diagnosis, in order to identify the few children who are genuinely psychotic and require medical treatment, the children who have no pathology at all and should not be subjected to treatment of any kind, and the children with developmental or neurological impairments for which specific treatment has been devised. Psychiatrists who participate in diagnosis should have broad exposure to a large number of delinquent children in order to be able to understand each individual against a background of similar children instead of a background of children from entirely different social and psychological environments.[6]

Second, psychiatric hospitals should treat delinquents who are found to be mentally ill, using the best medical techniques available. As discussed in the previous chapter, there is a widespread belief within the juvenile justice system that the mental health system discriminates against children with records of serious delinquency and aggressive behavior who need hospitalization and medical treatment. To the extent that such discrimination is based on management problems, and not on a lack of appropriate treatment methodologies, it should not be tolerated.

Finally, psychotherapy should be available to violent delin-

[6] Russell and Harper (op. cit., p. 393) argue, on the basis of their study of 100 assaultive and fifty nonassaultive delinquents, that "psychiatric evaluation should be stressed not only for assaultive juveniles, but should be considered as necessary for many other delinquents as well." More of the nonassaultive category were judged to be severely disturbed than the assaultive.

quents when their antisocial impulses have been brought under control, when other basic needs have been met, and when they are ready for it. Because these conditions will not always exist, psychotherapy must be selectively used and not expected to accomplish miracles.

Group Techniques. Group techniques for correcting antisocial behavior have come into general use in recent years, for several reasons. One is the ineffectiveness of individual psychiatric and psychotherapeutic methods in treating a variety of personality disorders. The scarcity of trained professionals to conduct one-to-one therapy, and the high cost of such treatment, are also important factors. An additional consideration in the use of group techniques for adolescent delinquents has been the observation that their peer relationships may have a more significant impact on their behavior than their relationships with adult and authority figures.[7] It was seen in Chapter 3, for example, that delinquents committing violent acts were more likely to do so in the company of others than alone.

The objective of group techniques, like that of individual psychotherapy, may be to produce insight or understanding of the causes of delinquent behavior as a step toward change. Or group techniques may be used to alter behavior patterns directly, circumventing (at least in the short run) reliance on insight.

A wide variety of group techniques have been developed in recent years, but most share many common features. Only a few methods typically applied to delinquents will be described here.

Group therapy is an umbrella concept that generally refers to periodic meetings of a fixed group of peers, nearly always "guided" by a professional or trained paraprofessional, in which the emotional and behavioral problems of the members are discussed. The goal may be to help group members come to grips with their internal conflicts, vent their emotions in a controlled way, understand how their behavior affects others and interferes with the development of close personal attachments, or learn to control

---

[7] Recent studies by Hirschi (cited in Glaser, op. cit., p. 54) concluded that delinquents' attachments to peers, while not as strong as the peer attachments of nondelinquents, were nonetheless stronger than their attachments to any other group.

their impulses. There is usually a mix of these objectives, although some group approaches concentrate more on development of self-awareness and internal controls, while others are more concerned with straightforward training to improve behavior.

An example of the former is transactional analysis. TA, as it is called, is a structured method for analyzing interpersonal relationships in a group setting in order to reveal dysfunctional behavior patterns. It assumes that "motivation for change lies within the person, not without, and that the individual is free to change if he becomes aware of alternatives to problematic roles he usually adopts."[8] It was tested in a California research project in which 15- to 17-year-old delinquents were randomly assigned to TA or to another treatment mode (behavior modification, described below). The results indicated lower parole violation rates for TA participants in comparison with youths receiving no treatment, but no better or worse than rates of those in the behavior modification group. Interestingly, when results were analyzed by personality type, TA was found to be more effective with "aggressive, acting-out, manipulative" boys than with "low-maturity, passive" boys.[9]

Another form of group counseling, guided group interaction (GGI), places somewhat more emphasis on external incentives to behavioral change. In addition to using the group as a device for analyzing members' behavioral problems and exploring solutions, GGI often gives the group considerable responsibility for making decisions regarding individual progress and for managing rewards for improvement. Originally developed at the Highfields program for delinquent youth in New Jersey, GGI has become one of the most commonly used treatment methodologies in institutions for delinquents around the country.

Practitioners of GGI report enthusiastically on its success, especially as an institutional control device. But there is little reliable evidence of its long-term impact on delinquent behavior. A study of the Silverlake Experiment in Los Angeles in the mid-1960s showed that the effects of that program (which used GGI) were

[8] Stevens H. Clarke, "Juvenile Offender Programs and Delinquency Prevention," *Crime and Delinquency Literature* 6, no. 3 (September 1974): 381.
[9] Ibid., pp. 380–383.

not significantly better, in terms of twelve-month recidivism rates, than those of a highly regimented residential environment.[10] A long-term follow-up study of the original Highfields program showed that treated boys had lower recidivism rates at twelve and thirty-six months than a control group from a regular reformatory, but *not* at twenty-four and sixty months.[11] On the other hand, a third study showed that GGI used with juvenile gang members in a community setting did "somewhat reduce the percentage that were to be found in custody six years later."[12]

No evaluations of GGI focusing specifically on its effects with violent delinquents have been found. Overall, however, group counseling techniques for incarcerated offenders, while popular, have not convincingly demonstrated a significant effect on subsequent rates of recidivism.[13]

Behavior modification is a more rigorously structured method of inducing behavioral change in a group setting. Both positive and negative reinforcements may be employed to train participants to replace "bad habits" with good. Positive reinforcements are often provided through "token economies," in which privileges, increased autonomy, or graduated authority over other group members can be earned in exchange for approved behavior. Negative reinforcements include verbal "haircuts," denial of privileges or prolonged detention.

Aspects of behavior modification can be found in nearly all correctional programs, but in formal behavior modification programs the techniques are refined and packaged into an elaborate system. Contracts may be written detailing exactly what behavior is desired and how it will be rewarded. Group roles may be highly stratified and regimented to permit visible movement up (or down) the ladder of responsibility and authority, as progress dictates. The basic point is to make all expectations and all consequences as explicit as possible. In putting the emphasis on

---

[10] Clarke, op. cit., pp. 379–380.

[11] Martinson, *op. cit.*, p. 34.

[12] Ibid., p. 40.

[13] See Robison and Smith, op. cit., pp. 72–76. Also Nora Klapmuts, "Community Alternatives to Prison," *Crime and Delinquency Literature* 5, no. 2 (June 1973): 325–328.

behavior as opposed to insight, behaviorism "assumes people will feel better if they first act better."[14]

As mentioned, an experiment in California found a behavior modification program for 15- to 17-year-old delinquents to be as effective, overall, in reducing parole violations as transactional analysis. Behavior modification, however, was more successful with "passive" and "cultural conformist" types than with "aggressive, acting-out" youths.[15] One of the most famous behavior modification programs is located at Achievement Place, a group residential program for court-referred youths in Lawrence, Kansas. Research on this experiment, which has been challenged as being methodologically weak, shows considerable improvement in recidivism rates of participants compared with training school residents and delinquents on probation.[16]

In the view of one child psychoanalyst who has observed a behavior modification program over a period of time but practices an entirely different kind of treatment himself, the technique appears at this point (with acknowledged inadequate observation) to be an effective device for controlling a child's aggressive antisocial impulses. It only takes a child up to a point, however, leaving him or her essentially dependent on a supportive environment to sustain changed conduct. To prepare the child for eventual autonomy in a not-so-supportive society at large, additional individualized treatment in the form of psychotherapy may be required.[17]

Milieu therapy may be the ultimate in group techniques. Milieu therapy is a catchall category for a wide range of treatment approaches that share two common features: twenty-four-hour residential care and reliance on intensive peer pressure as the key therapeutic tool. In essence, milieu therapy seeks to convert every aspect of the child's environment into a reinforcement of treatment. It is undertaken in an institutional setting, usually isolated from the surrounding community. Because of their self-contained nature, milieu therapy programs are often called "therapeutic communities." Drug rehabilitation programs like Synanon and Daytop

---

[14] Richard R. Parlour, M.D., "Behavioral Techniques for Sociopathic Clients," *Federal Probation* (March 1975): 3–11.

[15] Clarke, op. cit., pp. 380–383.

[16] Ibid.

[17] Interview with Robert Evans, M.D., June 13, 1975.

Village pioneered the therapeutic community (TC) model and continue to typify it today.

Within a given "community," a variety of treatment methodologies may be used, from individual psychotherapy to many forms of group treatment (sensitivity groups, attack therapy, primal scream therapy, TA, GGI, etc.). Behavior modification techniques, including a highly stratified organizational structure through which residents progress and a system of enforced rewards and punishments, are almost universally employed.

The community is designed to provide both control and support. Organizational divisions between staff and clients are blurred. Both are expected to interact in the same manner with all other members of the community. Although staff members have final authority and decision-making responsibility, they are as vulnerable to criticism and challenge as residents, and the entire group takes some role in decisions regarding the progress of individuals and their eventual "graduation" from the program. Everyone thus becomes an agent in the rehabilitation of all residents. Moreover, every group meeting, every encounter between individual members, every activity from community maintenance functions to individual educational efforts is treated as an opportunity for analyzing and correcting behavior. In short, milieu therapy is designed as a total attack on antisocial and self-destructive behavior patterns. (One example of a milieu therapy program open to violent delinquents, Elan in Maine, is described in Appendix D.)

Milieu therapy has had its longest and most extensive test in the drug treatment field, where results have not been strongly encouraging. Therapeutic communities have been criticized for excessive dropout and recidivism (return to drug use) rates, which are reported to run as high as 70 percent and sometimes higher. This criticism is, of course, less valid for compulsory treatment in secure institutions than it is for the largely voluntary drug treatment programs. Not many compulsory programs exist, however. Milieu therapy has also been challenged, like the behavior modification techniques on which it is partially based, for the harshness of its peer pressure methods and for leaving participants dependent on the "community" for support in order to continue functioning successfully. One reviewer of drug treatment programs noted the possibility that an addict "may be replacing his addiction to heroin with an 'addiction' to being an ex-addict and to the encounter therapy. The philosophy of the TC becomes a religion for the addict. It is something to believe in and a message to spread to his fellow addicts in the world."[18]

Conclusions based on experience with milieu therapy in treatment of drug addiction may not be wholly fair, however. As the same reviewer observed:

> In the long run, it may turn out that the TC is much more interesting outside the drug context than within it. By setting itself the task of rehabilitating drug addicts—a notoriously hard group to rehabilitate —the TC movement may have destined itself to look bad. The real contributions that such methods might make to improvements in the condition and functioning of more tractable populations are easily lost sight of by appraisers who are concerned with the drug problem.[19]

The basis for such optimism is that some problems or personality types may respond better to milieu therapy than others. In fact, some reports have observed that "the TC works best for the sociopath who is tough enough to take the encounters but not for those with less serious psychological problems or those who are the least alienated."[20] Along this line, there is a widely shared opinion among people working with hard-core violent delinquents that milieu therapy has the best chance of all methodologies for treating this group effectively. This view was typified in a comment by Judge Nanette Dembitz of the New York City Family Court.

> Judging from court records and from the opinions of psychiatrists both in and out of court, only a minority of persistent and violence-prone delinquents can be treated by present one-to-one psychiatric techniques with sufficient success to stop their criminality. For the majority of these dangerous youths, "Milieu therapy"—meaning a caring, constructive environment—is the best possibility.[21]

Available research on milieu therapy in correctional institutions yields a mixed picture. The studies reviewed by Martinson (none

[18] James V. DeLong, "Treatment and Rehabilitation," in Patricia M. Wald et al., *Dealing with Drug Abuse* (New York: Praeger, 1972), pp. 192–193.
[19] Ibid., p. 196.
[20] Ibid.
[21] Dembitz, op. cit.

of which, apparently, focused specifically on violent delinquents, for these programs also include many drug addicts and nonviolent youths) suggested that the technique tends to work better with juveniles and older youths than with adult inmates in correctional institutions, and better with males than with females. Among nine studies on young males, two showed clearly positive effects, one showed a statistically unreliable negative effect, four showed no effect either way, and two reached mixed conclusions. (Two of the four studies that showed no long-lasting improvement in young male experimentals' recidivism rates compared to controls, nevertheless did indicate that new offenses by experimentals were less serious than those of controls.) Martinson concluded that "youth in these milieu therapy programs at least do no worse than their counterparts in regular institutions and the special programs cost less."[22]

The cost argument is an important one. Training schools in New York State are said to cost approximately $23,000 per child per year. Psychiatric hospitals are in the same range or higher.[23] By placing heavy reliance on paraprofessional staff and heavy responsibility on the peer group for management of the community as well as surveillance of residents, therapeutic communities can often provide full-time residential treatment at a third to a half of this cost, with results that appear to be at least as effective as those of the other institutions.

Milieu therapy is interesting as a focal point for additional research and experimentation for yet another reason. Something of a "grab-bag" approach, it has been used both compulsorily and voluntarily; it encompasses a variety of therapeutic inputs within a generally similar philosophical framework and physical setting; and it has shown a somewhat greater willingness to deal with hardcore social deviates than have other approaches. Because of these attributes, milieu therapy offers an opportunity to examine some complex and important treatment issues, including the following.

[22] Martinson, op. cit., p. 35.
[23] In New York City, the cost per child of care in the Department of Mental Health's children's psychiatric hospital was $78 per day in 1974, or $28,470 per year. Training school cost $62.81 per child per day, or $22,926 per year. (New York Board of Social Welfare, op. cit., p. 45, footnote 7.)

- Can violent antisocial behavior patterns be changed permanently at a relatively late developmental stage (adolescence or later) by changing the environment surrounding a person?
- Are only a few individuals amenable to change, or are many? And what distinguishes those who are from those who are not?
- If change is possible, must participation be voluntary, or will it also work in a compulsory setting?
- To what degree are specific therapeutic methods the key to change, as distinct from general environmental influences or interpersonal relationships?

The answers to questions like these remain largely unknown. Before a systematic effort could be made to address them through further experimentation with milieu therapy, it would be necessary to create some order out of the vast diversity of programs that now come under that rubric. Milieu therapy programs differ from each other along the following dimensions, among others: the nature and variety of therapy techniques used; the amount of authority accorded to the peer group; the nature of rewards and punishments used in the behavior modification aspect of the program; the formality and rigidity of the organization structure; the level of involvement by psychiatric and social work professionals; the degree to which autonomous functioning outside the group, as contrasted with adjustment to the group itself, is a goal; the amount of contact permitted with society outside the program; and the nature and extent of supportive inputs like education and vocational training. Variations along each of these dimensions, and others, would have to be controlled, in the research sense, if answers to basic questions are to be forthcoming.

In general, group therapy techniques like those just described share a common philosophical reference point with individual psychiatric and psychotherapeutic techniques: both locate the basic source of antisocial, self-destructive behavior inside the individual and seek to bring about changes in the individual. Group techniques differ among themselves in the emphasis they place on insight and understanding as the medium of change, as contrasted with structured "training" in new behavior patterns.

Therapy-centered strategies regard their major task as helping delinquents to develop the capacity to relate to other human beings with trust, respect, and concern. To accomplish this, they seek to help participants develop (or, more accurately, redevelop) an awareness of their own feelings and a capacity to verbalize them, gain a core of self-respect, and learn to control their impulses. The fact that these are tasks all people confront on the way to maturity suggests that violent behavior is viewed in psychiatrically oriented treatment as the result of a short circuit in the developmental process. The short circuit may occur because of an adolescent crisis, or at an earlier stage because of the failure of "upbringing," or perhaps because of some trauma resulting in neurological damage. In any case, these therapies attempt to provide the setting and ingredients necessary to permit the growth process to begin again.

Some success with violent delinquents has been claimed by each method, probably with justification. On the other hand, no methodology has yet been demonstrated to be broadly effective in treating this particular group. There is evidence that fitting the type of treatment to the characteristics and needs of the individual is beneficial. In the general opinion of experts dealing with delinquents, and in the scant and not always reliable research available, group techniques (and particularly milieu therapy) appear to have an edge over individual psychotherapy in dealing with violent youths, at least in producing short-run behavioral changes. The advantage may stem from the greater ability of the group to control the individual, the somewhat greater willingness of such programs to take in hardcore delinquents, and the lower cost of treatment in the group setting. It may also have to do with a special capacity of those who themselves require help to clarify destructive patterns and induce a desire to change in others.

Social Services. Unlike individual and group therapy, the provision of social services is an approach to treatment that emphasizes deficiencies in the external social environment. Implicitly or explicitly, the theory that environmental deficiencies are responsible for delinquent behavior underlies a large number of programs designed to improve the social conditions of delinquent youth. Most of these programs have been aimed at three areas of need: shelter or substitute family care, income, and education. This section will briefly review what is known about the effects of programs in these areas.

Shelter or substitute family care is one of the first needs to be considered when children get into trouble. It is provided in public facilities, private voluntary agencies, group homes, or foster families; it can be temporary during an emergency or extend over an entire childhood. As far as we were able to determine, no empirically based research has been done on the effects of shelter care per se on delinquency, no doubt because serious theoretical and methodological problems are involved in separating the effects of the structure from the effects of program content, which is usually the focus of research. It is generally believed, however, that the quality of care goes up as the size of the unit goes down and as the permanence or at least the continuity of care is assured. On both of these counts, private agencies, and particularly group homes and foster homes, tend to be superior to public agencies. Yet it is widely conceded that the more violent and dangerous a youth appears to be, the less likely he is to be admitted to a private shelter-care program.

The growth of public-sector group homes for delinquents outlined in Chapter 4 may mean that more desirable kinds of care will become increasingly available to violent youths, although it can safely be predicted that new openings will be allotted first to the less serious cases. Individual foster homes are even rarer for violent delinquents, and openings for this group will probably not expand in the future without a major stimulus from the public sector. One authority questions whether foster homes are the most appropriate option for adolescents in any case.

> Few foster placements seem to have worked well for older juveniles, and it would be expected that an adolescent from a damaging home experience could not thrive or develop simply being placed in a "good" home. For most adolescents, group placements are necessary.[24]

Others doubt that foster care is much superior to institutional care if it is not established in such a way as to promote permanent

[24] Russell, op. cit., p. 25.

bonds between foster parent and foster child.[25] One foster care program that seems to meet these objectives and is available to some violent delinquents is the Downeyside program in Massachusetts. It is described in Appendix D.

Income is seen as a second critical need, particularly of older children, and adolescent employment programs have long been promoted as a means of preventing delinquency. The assumption is that delinquency is at least partially motivated by economic concerns and can be alleviated by increasing economic opportunity. Empirical support for this approach may be found in the fact that property crimes are by far the most frequent form of delinquent activity. Moreover, statistics indicate that delinquents who pass the age at which leaving school is permitted, and thus become eligible to get jobs, show a significant decline in property offenses.[26]

The most comprehensive youth employment effort ever undertaken was the Neighborhood Youth Corps (NYC) program begun by the Federal Office of Economic Opportunity in the 1960s. NYC was aimed at thousands of impoverished ghetto adolescents who were given summer and, to a lesser degree, year-round jobs in community service projects. Studies of this program failed to show any long-term effect on participants' criminal behavior, however. An evaluation of the Cincinnati NYC program revealed that there was little difference between controls and experimentals in terms of the percentage charged with serious crimes over the fourteen months after the experimentals were enrolled, and no difference between the two groups after the program ended. Interestingly, experimentals with no prior police record were charged with serious offenses more frequently (12 percent) than controls with no prior record (10 percent).[27]

The Court Employment Project in New York City, which intercedes on behalf of young (but not juvenile) offenders at the presen-

---

[25] Joseph Goldstein, Alfred Solnit, and Anna Freud, *Beyond the Best Interests of the Child* (New Haven: Free Press, 1973), pp. 25–26.

[26] Glaser, op. cit., p. 46. Elliott and Voss, although confirming that delinquency declines following dropout, found the employment-delinquency relationship to be a complex one, with postschool marriage a more significant deterrent to delinquency than postschool employment. (Elliott and Voss, op. cit.)

[27] Clarke, op. cit., pp. 390–392.

tencing stage to attempt to arrange employment and counseling as an alternative to conviction, once claimed, on the basis of a matched control research project, that the program resulted in reduced recidivism for participants. A subsequent analysis of that research by Franklin Zimring showed, however, that the positive effects could be explained by inadequacies in the research design. Zimring called for research based on a random-assignment design, which has only recently begun.[28]

No carefully controlled employment experiment aimed especially at violent delinquents has been reported in the literature, as far as we were able to determine. A juvenile "supported work" project providing work experience in a structured, supportive setting is underway at the Henry Street Settlement House in New York City. It enrolls court-referred children, including some with records of violent behavior. The results of the project, once reported, may be instructive. In the meantime, youth employment projects should be regarded as a possible, although not yet proven, treatment approach, if for no other reason than the logic behind them and the broad support they receive from professionals working in the field.

Nearly every delinquency prevention or treatment program has some kind of educational component. Given the high reported incidence of serious reading problems and the low level of skill development among delinquents, and given the necessity of basic educational and vocational ability in modern society, this is eminently sensible. Yet education programs, standing alone, are another in the long list of ideas whose effectiveness is yet to be proven. In reviewing a large number of studies of both basic and vocational education programs aimed at reducing recidivism among young incarcerated male offenders, Martinson came to a familiar conclusion: "One can be reasonably sure that, so far, educational and vocational programs have not worked."[29]

But he also put his finger on a probable cause of failure. "The difficulty," he wrote, "may be that they lack applicability to the

---

[28] Franklin E. Zimring, "Measuring the Impact of Pretrial Diversion from the Criminal Justice System," *University of Chicago Law Review* 41 (1974): 224–241.
[29] Martinson, op. cit., p. 28.

world the inmate will face outside prison."[30] The point is not that educational programs are not needed, but that they must be closely related to the environment the delinquent normally lives in. For the hard-core delinquent, it is a world lacking the usual incentives for learning: a college opportunity, the promise of a better-paying job, intellectual stimulation. Consequently, educational planning for this group is a challenging assignment. Run-of-the-mill approaches will not work. One suspects, too, that even highly innovative approaches will not be of much benefit if they are expected to carry the full weight of rehabilitation by themselves, because educational deficiencies are not usually perceived by delinquents as the heart of their problems. (Whether that perception is accurate or not—it probably is in most cases—it must be given weight in designing programs for this group.) Education can help delinquents develop self-esteem and an increased sense of control over their environments, and for those reasons should probably never be absent from rehabilitation programs. Genuine rehabilitation, however, must include a fuller program of personal and social development attuned to the environmental realities of the delinquent's world.

The education programs reviewed by Martinson all took place within or in conjunction with correctional institutions. Thus, their target was the individual whose social maladjustment had progressed far enough to land him or her in reform school or prison. But educational innovation has also been tried with a different group, predelinquents or "preserious" delinquents. "Preventive" special education programs for chronic truants and children with behavioral problems have been developed in many cities. Few have been studied with regard to their effect on subsequent delinquent behavior. But an early one that was (a program in Quincy, Illinois, studied by researchers from the University of Chicago) showed a sharp decline in police contacts among youths enrolled in experimental classes for slow learners compared to a control group enrolled in regular classes. The delinquency rate of the control group tripled during the ages of 16 to 18 relative to the rate in prior years, whereas the delinquency rate of the experimentals de-

[30] Ibid.

clined by more than one-third. Moreover, the experimental group had fewer serious violent offenses than the control group. Interestingly, these results occurred in spite of the fact that there was no significant difference between the two groups in learning.[31]

Many special education programs are viewed by their staffs as having an impact on the delinquent behavior of enrolled students. Although no reliable data are available from these programs to support this perception, the suggestion that special education programs can prevent delinquent (and perhaps violent) behavior among children with learning and behavior problems appears to be sufficiently strong to warrant serious study.

Education and most other social services are probably necessary but insufficient inputs, particularly when the target is the hardcore, violent delinquent. By the time a child's life situation has deteriorated to the point where he or she resorts to violent antisocial behavior, it is reasonable to assume that the task of rehabilitation involves more than replacing missing material necessities. Perhaps the most convincing evidence of this comes from the self-report studies discussed in Chapters 2 and 3, which point out the limited correlation between delinquency and social class. If children with an adequate level of material comfort can be as frequently and as seriously delinquent as deprived children, it seems unlikely that removing material deprivation alone will result in decreased delinquency. At the same time, concentration on psychological, moral, or spiritual reconstruction is likely to be wasted effort if nothing is done to improve the basic resources available to a child (and his or her family) for surviving and advancing in the real world. Those basic resources must include, at a minimum, a secure and comfortable place to live, a means of earning money, and an education.

Treatment approaches that emphasize changes in the environment of the delinquent might be viewed in terms of the "stress" model outlined at the conclusion of Chapter 3. Reading programs, job training, diet therapy, foster care—each in its own way is an

---

[31] Paul H. Bowman, "Effects of a Revised School Program on Potential Delinquents," *Annals of the American Academy of Political and Social Sciences* 322 (1959): 53–61. The article notes that these results are preliminary and refer to an experimental population of insufficient size to yield statistically reliable conclusions.

effort to reduce the stress that bears on a delinquent and is presumed to account for his or her behavior. The fact that delinquent behavior is frequently preceded by multiple kinds of stress may partially explain why some degree of success is achieved by so many different forms of intervention. It may also explain why success is so often temporary; even when specific stresses that initiate or exacerbate violent behavior can be identified and eliminated in the treatment setting, unless the child's defense or coping mechanisms (whether biological, psychological, or social) can be adequately strengthened, temporary gains registered in treatment programs may be (and all too often are) lost when the child returns to the high-stress environment from which he or she came.

Other Intervention Approaches. If the generally poor track record of treatment programs aimed at changing either the personal makeup of the offender or his or her environment is not yet sufficient reason to give up on treatment, it should at least be a stimulus to try other ways of approaching the problem. Some interesting possibilities merit brief discussion here. They involve unorthodox methods that have treatment overtones but are fundamentally concerned with prevention of or response to crime.

One approach centers on community conflict resolution. Given the relatively high rate of assaults by juveniles and older youths (see Table 4 in Chapter 2), many of which arise out of conflict with friends, neighbors, and family, the need for new means of resolving conflict seems evident.

Several models have been tried. One is the Forum of the Neighborhood Youth Diversion Program located in the Bronx, New York. The Forum consists of a small group of people from the community who meet periodically with parents and children in conflict with each other and attempt to find nonjudicial solutions to the problem. Forum panel members are chosen for their community roots and for their wisdom and experience, but not necessarily for any special background or training. Much emphasis is placed on getting parents and children to verbalize feelings and needs, for which practical answers are then sought. The children who participate in NYDP programs, including the Forum, do so as part of a family court diversion program, and thus are under threat of return to court. In practice, however, the threat is a weak one, and participation has a quality of voluntarism.[32]

A similar idea has been implemented in East Palo Alto, California, where a court diversion project called the Community Youth Responsibility Program has instituted community panel hearings, in which delinquent youths are brought before a group of community residents to have their cases explained and dispositions determined. Unlike the NYDP Forum, which is limited to obtaining consensual acceptance of solutions to conflicts, the East Palo Alto Panel can impose community service tasks on delinquents as a form of punishment, although capacity to enforce compliance is also somewhat limited. What both programs have in common is that the community itself takes responsibility for intervening in the problems of its youth and for devising and helping to implement solutions to those problems.

Conflict resolution models for adults are more common than those for juveniles. In New York City, the Institute for Mediation and Conflict Resolution has developed a Dispute Center to which police bring both complainants and defendants in lieu of formal booking for selected offenses ranging from harassment to assault. Trained community mediators on the Center's staff try to resolve the dispute that led to the arrest by obtaining the consent of both parties to a negotiated settlement. The conditions of the agreement can be put into a formal contract, enforceable in civil court if need be. Police and city officials were sufficiently pleased with a pilot in Harlem that they have recently expanded the model to other parts of Manhattan. Similar projects in Boston and in Columbus, Ohio, handle cases that are referred by the courts or by prosecutors.

The concept of third-party involvement in the resolution of problems that lead to delinquent behavior has been institutionalized in Scottish juvenile law. Informal hearings by children's panels, composed of three lay citizens, are responsible for disposition of most cases in which a child is found (or pleads) guilty. The Scottish panels have been criticized for being dominated by

---

[32] For a fuller description of the Forum, see William P. Statsky, "Community Courts: Decentralizing Juvenile Jurisprudence," *Capital University Law Review* 3, no. 1 (1974): 1–51.

middle-class members, but the principle of community responsibility remains nevertheless.[33]

At present, neither the American nor the Scottish models are likely to deal with children whose behavior has become repeatedly violent. But both must encounter some children in the early stages of their delinquent careers who are at risk of developing violent behavior patterns, and no evaluations of their effectiveness in preventing this development have been done (although such studies would be useful). Certainly, no *prima facie* case can be made for why this procedure could not be applied to more violent youth in an experimental form. In fact, logic would support such an effort because interpersonal conflict is, if anything, more likely to result in violence than in property crime. Reducing conflict could thus be expected to have a corresponding impact on violence.

Another unorthodox approach involves restitution by the offender for the crime he or she has committed. The restitution approach attempts to provide offenders an opportunity to do something constructive to compensate victims or society in general for their crimes instead of simply "doing time." Its advocates view it as more appropriate, less costly, and less damaging than incarceration and rehabilitation aimed at changing the character of offenders. However, some authorities and observers feel that restitution, in the form of either direct compensation to a victim or service to the community at large, may also have a therapeutic effect on the offender. That effect may stem from reduction in guilt and increase in self-esteem once a debt has been paid, or it may come from an increased sense of social belonging derived from participation in community service.[34]

Restitution experiments in England and Scandinavia have been based on the community service approach. The English model, begun on a trial basis in 1973, offers offenders the option of 40 to 240 hours of community work as a noncustodial sentencing alternative. It is used with offenders on whom other methods of treat-

[33] For a description of the Scottish system, see Sanford Fox, "Juvenile Justice Reform: Innovations in Scotland," *American Criminal Law Review* 12, no. 61 (1974).

[34] The Task Force on Crime of the Violence Commission observed, for example, that psychiatrists think social activism can work to restore an individual's self-esteem. See Mulvihill, Tumin, and Curtis, op. cit., p. 463.

ment have been tried unsuccessfully, and who otherwise would be faced with a prison term. It is generally regarded as inappropriate for persons who do not have ties to a particular community. Community service assignments are sought that fit the offender's skills, capacities, and interests. During the first eighteen months of the experiment, in which approximately 1,200 offenders were given community service sentences, the program worked reasonably well: best for those with shorter criminal records and those who had not previously served time in prison, least satisfactorily for their opposites. The kind of offense committed appears so far to have little bearing on successful completion of community service. As a result of the experiment, England has decided to institute community service throughout the country.

Community service as a dispositional alternative for juvenile offenders has been tried, as noted, in the East Palo Alto Community Youth Responsibility Program, although the sanctions available to assure completion of service assignments have few teeth. Community service for juveniles is also a central feature of the program of the Centro de Orientacion y Servicios in Ponce, Puerto Rico, which attempts to steer delinquents and potential delinquents away from crime by involving them in projects alongside adults and "role-model" advisors.

A restitution model based on direct compensation of the victim by the offender can also involve elements of conflict resolution by bringing the offender and the offended together to work out a reasonable solution. One such program at the Minnesota Restitution Center permits men and women incarcerated for nonviolent property offenses to obtain work-release assignments in order to earn money for compensating their victims. Face-to-face negotiations and contracts between victims and offenders were initially an important feature of the program, although their use has declined recently.[35]

Restitution is another idea that is likely to be tried first and most frequently with the least serious offenders. But, like community conflict resolution, it may be both desirable and possible to experi-

[35] "The Minnesota Restitution Center," *Corrections Magazine* (January/February 1975): 13–20.

ment with restitution for violent offenders, particularly those guilty of robbery.

These two approaches, community conflict resolution and restitution, are based on assumptions about criminal behavior that are different in an important way from the assumptions that underlie treatment programs. They are not rooted in a belief that the essential cause of antisocial behavior is some deficiency in the offender or some missing social or economic resource. Instead, conflict resolution attempts simply to create an atmosphere that produces alternatives to violent behavior as a solution to problems, while restitution aims to develop a more relevant, equitable, and efficient response to crime. Yet both approaches do have treatment overtones, in that they offer opportunities for behavioral change. Consequently, they lie in a middle area of the spectrum of intervention modes that ranges from treatment at one end to prevention or deterrence at the other.

Selecting a Treatment Mode

The fundamental goal of all treatment programs for offenders is to bring about a cessation or at least a decrease in antisocial behavior. How people come to change their behavior is still not well understood, however. Some delinquents seem to "grow out" of destructive behavior on their own, perhaps because as they mature they gain more control over their impulses or their environment, or both. Others seem to "burn out," showing little or no change in motivation, self-image, or self-control, but simply exhausting themselves, often through the effects of drugs, alcohol, or other forms of self-destruction. Still others, a minority, just seem to get worse. The last two groups (and from a social cost point of view, especially the third) are the ones on which intervention strategies should focus; however, for many reasons, including the difficulty of predicting which delinquents will eventually fit into which category, intervention is probably practiced on a good many of those who would grow out of the antisocial phase on their own.

In assigning individuals to treatment, certain basic distinctions are necessary in order to focus first on the most basic and urgent problems, to avoid wasting time and resources on inappropriate interventions, and to avoid inflicting additional damage. For example, a malnourished child or one who requires major medical or dental treatment is unlikely to be as amenable to psychiatric intervention as a healthy child. Similarly, a child with no functioning family and no adequate substitute may feel too threatened to respond to an education program.[36] Mentally retarded youths and those with organic brain damage who will be unable to respond to many kinds of treatment should be placed in programs addressing their special needs. Psychotic youths should be treated in psychiatric hospitals, a setting that offers nothing to nonpsychotics and may, in fact, do them harm. Children with severe sociopathic tendencies can be highly destructive in programs designed for less disturbed children and should be placed in environments permitting a higher degree of control.

Beyond such basic distinctions, a number of attempts have been made to identify characteristics of personality or psychological makeup that correlate with success in various modes of treatment. The most extensively used and most famous of such classification schemes is the "I-level" system, first developed in California's Community Treatment Program (CTP) for juvenile offenders, which classifies individuals according to seven levels of "interpersonal maturity." Opinions regarding the success of this particular effort vary. Some studies showed, for example, that youths classified on this scale as "neurotics" did better in community treatment than in institutions, while those classified as "power oriented" responded in the opposite manner,[37] or that transactional analysis was more effective with "aggressive, acting-out, manipulative" boys than with "low-maturity, passive" boys, while the reverse was true for behavior modification.[38] On the other hand, a major evaluation of the CTP by Paul Lerman in 1975 concluded that the I-level

---

[36] The concept of a hierarchy of needs, both biological and psychological, has been explored by Dr. Abraham Maslow. See, for example, *The Farther Reaches of Human Nature* (New York: The Viking Press, 1971), Appendix D: "Criteria for Judging Needs to be Instinctoid."

[37] "The Community Treatment Project," *Corrections Magazine* (September 1974): 52.

[38] Clarke, op. cit., p. 381.

system was flawed and failed to produce significant differences in treatment outcome. Lerman maintained that the system as applied in CTP was an inappropriate measure of personality for black youths and may also be invalid for middle-class whites. On the whole, he found no significant differences between the parole success of those sent to institutions and those treated by CTP in the community that could not be explained by the differential behavior of the adult parole agents.[39]

Glaser has proposed a less complex distinction among offender types, based on whether they are "conflicted" about their delinquencies or are committed to "careers" in criminality. He cites research showing that behavior modification is most appropriate for the "career" types, while "flexible and rapport-oriented" treatment is best for the "conflicted" youth.[40] Many studies reviewed by Martinson and others have also demonstrated better results with youth for whom the applied treatment was judged in advance to be appropriate.

While these results should not be taken lightly, it would be a mistake, given the present state of knowledge about human behavior, to place a great deal of faith in fine diagnostic distinctions. Much of the research demonstrating differential reaction to treatment according to offender types has been subject to methodological criticism, in particular for showing signs of a "labeling effect" in which the way a subject is initially identified affects the subsequent treatment he or she gets and hence the outcome. Moreover, given the difficulty of identifying subtle personality traits in the turmoil of adolescence, accurate diagnosis is problematic at best. This is not to say that no effort should be made to fit an individual to an appropriate treatment method. But it warns against following an initial diagnosis to the point that flexibility in treatment becomes impossible.

An approach that may be useful in resolving the conflict between the need for individualized treatment and the simultaneous need to avoid rigid diagnostic labeling is one being tried as part of Massachusetts's intensive care program for serious delinquents. In-

[39] Paul Lerman, *Community Treatment and Social Control* (Chicago: University of Chicago Press, 1975). It should be noted that CTP excluded all youths convicted of murder, armed robbery, rape, or other violent crimes.
[40] Glaser, op. cit., p. 120.

tensive care is provided in a half dozen separate facilities, some of which are public institutions and some private. The common characteristics of all these facilities are that they are secure, in the sense that it is difficult for residents to leave without permission (although not all are locked); they are small, housing between twelve and twenty-five youths each; and they generally include both sexes. All intensive care facilities have a rehabilitation orientation, but their approaches to rehabilitation vary considerably. One uses milieu therapy. Another emphasizes physical challenge on the Outward Bound model. Others stress individual and family therapy. In this way, the intensive care network seeks to provide treatment tailored to the needs of each juvenile. Transfers among these facilities or from intensive care into community-based programs are permitted, so that when one method fails, or when the needs of the youths change, another more promising option can be made available. In this way, a "best guess" about treatment needs is possible without being sanctified as a definitive diagnosis or resulting in immutable placement decisions. In such a system, however, the importance of the initial diagnosis should never be underplayed, because frequent shifting of children from one setting to another may do as much psychic damage as the use of inappropriate intervention techniques.

Treatment in the Punishment Context

As noted at the beginning of this chapter, the role of treatment as a response to criminal behavior is one of the most controversial issues in modern penology. One of the landmark studies of treatment for juveniles offenders, Paul Lerman's analysis of California's Community Treatment Program, produced some revealing data concerning the interaction of treatment and punishment. CTP, devised as an alternative to incarcerating juvenile offenders, provided intensive treatment in a variety of community-based facilities whose programs were "matched" to the personality types and needs of the youths. CTP's managers and social workers were given considerable discretion regarding the assignment of youths to programs and the content of the treatment applied.

Extensive research was done on the results, using a comparison group of youths who were incarcerated and subsequently released on parole. In the course of CTP's development over the years, its staff adopted a policy permitting periodic detention of participants when agents felt it would have some therapeutic value. Although detention was thought to be used sparingly, Lerman discovered that in a sixteen-month period CTP participants were subjected to an average of fifty-six days of detention each, compared to thirty-five days for the control group of parolees. Moreover, CTP youths were subjected to detention for more arbitrary and noncriminal reasons than the parolees. Even more shocking, Lerman found that the fifty-six days of detention contrasted with only 9.8 days of "direct treatment services" to CTP participants over the same period.[41]

Detention in CTP is an example of punishment introduced into (and eventually dominating) a treatment-oriented program in the community. In prisons, the reverse situation applies: treatment is introduced into an environment heavily conditioned by punishment motives. The question posed is whether, in this context, treatment can be effective. Critics argue that it is doomed to fail, and they cite volumes of research like that already described to support their argument. Some go further than this, however, noting that treatment inside prisons runs the grave risk of becoming the handmaiden of punishment, permitting the use of measures that would be intolerable in a free society without the presumption that they are intended for the ultimate benefit of the prisoner.

One of the key issues in this controversy is the indeterminate sentence, defined broadly by Marvin Frankel as "any prison sentence for which the precise term of confinement is not known on the day of judgment but will be subject within a substantial range to the later decision of a parole board or some comparable agency under whatever name."[42]

Indeterminancy in one degree or another is the rule in sentencing for serious offenses in virtually all states and in the federal system. In its most common form, it involves a maximum upper

41 Lerman, op. cit.
42 Marvin Frankel, *Criminal Sentences: Law Without Order* (New York: Hill and Wang, 1972), p. 86.

limit (and perhaps a minimum) coupled with a parole board's discretion to release within some specified time interval before the maximum is reached (e.g., when one-third to two-thirds of the sentence has been served). At the extreme, indeterminate sentences can be completely open-ended, as with Maryland's "defective delinquent" statute, which permits those to whom judges apply this label to be incarcerated at the Patuxent Institute until staff psychiatrists declare them to be cured—a practice that has occasionally resulted in many years of imprisonment for individuals originally charged with minor offenses.[43]

The justification for indeterminate sentencing is that it permits a flexible response based not only on the nature of the offense committed but also on the rehabilitative potential and progress of the individual, thus increasing the likelihood that one of the purposes of imprisonment (rehabilitation) will be accomplished and providing greater safety to the public. The problem with this rationale, as its critics have pointed out, is that no rehabilitative techniques have been found that are broadly effective with prisoners, nor are there sufficiently reliable techniques for predicting the likelihood of success in individual cases.

In the absence of such tools, parole boards or other bodies empowered to make release decisions are reduced to making guesses (educated sometimes, to be sure, but guesses nonetheless) regarding the degree of rehabilitation that has been accomplished and the relative safety of returning individuals to the community. At its worst, this situation breeds despair or indifference among decision makers and leads to arbitrary and capricious choices. Short of that, it forces authorities to search for whatever subtle, elusive evidence they can find on which to base their decisions.

In the comparatively sterile prison environment, treatment programs are among the few areas in which a prisoner can demonstrate "progress" and earn early release. Thus in the shadow of indeterminate sentencing, treatment takes on a compulsory aspect, whether it is truly mandatory or not. Coupled with the intrusiveness of many treatment modalities, this compulsory aspect renders prison treatment distasteful to many. It may also be one of

[43] See Phil Stanford, "A Model Clockwork Orange Prison," *New York Times Magazine* (September 17, 1972): 9ff.

the causes of its ineffectiveness. Prisoners are fully aware of the importance attached by parole boards to their performance in treatment programs and often react by tailoring their behavior accordingly, a kind of "countermanipulation" that undermines genuine rehabilitation.

As an alternative to the rehabilitation model and the ethical and practical problems it has raised, imprisonment based on what is sometimes called the "justice model" has gained a large following in recent years. Broadly, the justice model seeks to minimize the exercise of discretionary authority over the lives of prisoners by formalizing and safeguarding their civil rights while in prison, by assuring due process and adequate grievance procedures when rights are abridged, and by narrowing the scope of indeterminacy and discretion in the sentencing structure. Movement toward the implementation of these principles has been urged by a number of experts, study groups, and commissions, including the National Advisory Commission on Criminal Justice Standards and Goals of the Federal Law Enforcement Assistance Administration. It has also been spurred on by a burgeoning case law that has substantially extended the civil rights of prisoners in this decade.

In the field of juvenile corrections, impetus has recently been given to the justice model by the Juvenile Justice Standards Project, a four-year study sponsored jointly by the American Bar Association and the Institute of Judicial Administration of New York University Law School. The Project's final report declared that "the rehabilitative ideal has proved a failure" and called for a national sentencing policy for juveniles based primarily on the seriousness of the offense committed, in place of the current standard based on the needs and the best interests of the juvenile. (The Project's guidelines would also permit consideration of the child's prior record, age, and degree of guilt.) To curtail indeterminacy, the Project proposed that sentences, once imposed, not be reduced except by special petition to the court, although a 5 percent reduction could be granted for "good behavior."[44]

Among the diverse critics who find themselves grouped under the banner of the justice model, there seems, therefore, to be broad

[44] *New York Times,* November 20, 1975, pp. 1 and 58.

agreement on two points: that indeterminate sentences should be abolished, and that participation in treatment should not be compulsory or coerced.

The issue is thorny, however, and even on these two points agreement is not universal and positions are not rigid. Even an outspoken opponent of indeterminate sentencing such as Marvin Frankel, for example, does not argue, in his words, "that an indeterminate sentence could never be wise and fair"—only that the presumption should be strongly against the practice. He believes that:

> there is probably a suitable ground for indeterminate sentencing in the service of incapacitating dangerous people . . . upon detailed showings in specific cases involving (1) demonstrated needs for rehabilitation and incapacitation and (2) rationally organized means for serving those needs.[45]

"To be slightly more concrete," he adds, "there are specific kinds of defendants for whom we have plausible, if by no means certain, hopes of rehabilitation. It appears, for example, that there are some meaningful hypotheses about 'treatment' for some drug users, some sex offenders, and, most hopefully, some of our numerous young offenders." Even with regard to these groups, Frankel warns, "the hopes must be modest, scaled to the meagerness of our knowledge and our niggardliness in allocating resources to such concerns."[46]

On the issue of compulsory treatment, the Commission on Standards and Goals states flatly that "no offender should be required or coerced to participate in programs of rehabilitation or treatment nor should the failure or refusal to participate be used to penalize an inmate in any way in the institution."[47] On the other hand, the Commission concludes its commentary on this point with a hedge. "This principle, *as it applies to juveniles*, must be qualified under the parens patriae concept, but nonetheless it would also appear to have considerable validity here also."[48] Norval Morris, in his de-

[45] Frankel, op. cit., p. 101.
[46] Ibid., p. 98.
[47] National Advisory Commission on Criminal Justice Standards and Goals, *Report on Corrections* (Washington, D.C.: U.S. Government Printing Office), 1973, p. 44.
[48] Ibid., p. 45 (emphasis added).

scription of a model prison for repetitively violent criminals, would make initial exposure to treatment compulsory, over a four- to six-week period, but would then give the offender free choice as to whether to continue in treatment or not.[49]

The question of how to relate treatment to punishment is plainly far from simple. Few critics of current practice who are not extremists maintain that there is no place whatever for treatment in a correctional program. (In fact, courts have shown increasing willingness to uphold a right to treatment in prison, and the Standards and Goals Commission has formulated a standard that would make that right explicit.) The difficulty comes in finding its proper role and in defining the limits of our expectations for it.

I have little to add to the voluminous discussion of these issues that has been carried on by experts for years, although I favor the position that stresses voluntarism after sufficient exposure to make the decision a knowledgeable one. It is worth reemphasizing, however, that disagreement between "treaters" and "antitreaters" tends to diminish as the age of the offender in question decreases and the violence (or "dangerousness") of his offenses increases. There is both greater hope for successful treatment of younger offenders and greater demand for treatment of those who are violent. Consequently, it seems to me imperative to continue the search for treatment approaches that work and for the environmental conditions that facilitate their success, at least with regard to violent juveniles.

Summary

The evidence mustered in the debate over the effectiveness of correctional treatment of violent offenders, by both the partisans and the opponents of treatment, is flawed. In the first place, there is little of it on either side because, as we saw in the previous chapter, delinquents with violent histories or other characteristics that may be interpreted as indicators of potential violence are routinely denied access to the treatment-oriented programs that provide the basis of our knowledge regarding the success or failure of

---

[49] Morris, op. cit., pp. 10–19, 100–107.

treatment. Data are thus scarce with regard to demonstrably violent individuals, except perhaps sex offenders, for whom special facilities are sometimes available. Moreover, much of the evidence that is said to prove the failure of treatment comes from programs that involve adult offenders. By and large, the results of programs for juvenile offenders tend to be more ambiguous.

Research on treatment of violence is flawed in other ways as well. Experiments with treatment have usually relied on that rather broad and slippery outcome measure, recidivism, and thus gloss over subtle but important changes that may occur in offender behavior. As a result, we know little about the effects of various kinds of treatment on subsequent violent behavior, apart from other kinds of criminal activity. To make matters worse, most of the studies that have been done have employed inadequate research methods. Few have been designed and executed with sufficient rigor to make their conclusions reliable and generalizable.

In spite of the scantiness and unreliability of the data on treatment, several broad and tentative conclusions can be formulated.

1. There is not yet a specific treatment for violence. Instead, there are interventions aimed at reducing antisocial behavior generally, of which violence is only one form. There is some evidence that some forms of treatment are more effective than others with certain personality types frequently associated with violent behavior, but this evidence remains highly tentative.

2. Rarely (if ever) will a single method of treatment succeed in changing the violent behavior of a delinquent. Effective treatment usually involves several kinds of interventions and supports, which should not be surprising in view of the multiple problems that characterize most violent offenders. Consequently, a range of treatment options, together with good diagnostic, planning, and management capabilities, is necessary for success in any significant degree.

3. Among the forms of treatment usually applied to delinquents, group techniques appear to hold more promise than individual treatment methods on the basis of both cost and effectiveness in reaching large numbers. Milieu therapy is an especially

interesting approach for delinquents with histories of serious, repetitive violence or self-destructive behavior. Each treatment method, however, may benefit some delinquents at various stages of their rehabilitation, which again points to the need for a thorough and continuous assessment of each individual.

4. Treatment cannot be expected to bring about complete "cures" within a short period. Incremental progress toward constructive reintegration into society is a more reasonable goal, and one that may require social and therapeutic supports long after the delinquent's legal debt to society has been repaid.

Perhaps the most important reason not to abandon treatment is that, particularly with regard to violent juveniles, it is unacceptable public policy to do nothing. Release to the community with no treatment or control may invite further violence and certainly invites a backlash of public opinion. Simply locking violent delinquents in prisons, on the other hand, contradicts what we know about the destructive effects of that approach and offends our hopes that they can change. What kind of treatment to offer, how much to insist that participation in treatment be voluntary, how to integrate rehabilitative objectives with punishment objectives: these are exceedingly difficult questions. But they should be confronted directly through carefully controlled research and experimentation that pay scrupulous attention to human rights. They are too important to ignore just because they are difficult.

6

Some Thoughts on Strategies for Preventing Juvenile Violence

THE READER was warned at the outset that this study would be concentrated on known juvenile offenders, delinquents caught by the police and charged with violent (and other) crimes. The discussion so far has dealt with their characteristics, their processing in the juvenile courts, and the measures taken to sanction their behavior and prevent its recurrence. In the final chapter, the one that follows this, some recommendations for improving our understanding and handling of juvenile violence will be offered, and once again they will focus mainly on apprehended delinquents.

This choice of focus was dictated largely by expediency: more is known about arrested delinquents than about those who get away, and they are, of course, much easier to reach with treatment, services, or sanctions. Furthermore, an empirical excursion into the dark continent of unreported or unsolved juvenile violence would have required time and money that were beyond the means of this limited effort. There is, however, a wholly reasonable opinion, widespread in professional circles and in the public, that dealing with arrested delinquents merely scratches the surface of the problem. The opinion is supported by data discussed in Chapter 2—the rather low reporting and clearance rates for offenses, and the self-report studies indicating high levels of undetected delinquency.

It is important to enter a qualification with regard to more serious and violent offenses. We know that clearance rates for crimes of interpersonal violence (which often involve defendants and victims known to each other[1]) are generally somewhat higher than clearance rates for property offenses. We have also learned from self-report studies that the more frequently a juvenile commits offenses and the more serious those offenses are, the higher the probability that he or she will be caught. Nevertheless, the conclusion that we must look beyond our court and penal systems for the solution to the problem of violence is, for the most part, an accurate one.

The National Advisory Commission on Criminal Justice Standards and Goals declared in 1973 that "the greatest potential for reducing the incidence of crime in America lies in activities directed at preventing the occurrence of crime."[2] Although the commission may well be right, the "potential" in crime prevention is extraordinarily difficult to realize. Public expectations for crime prevention run far ahead of current reality, in which effective prevention strategies are inhibited by technological limitations, inhospitable social conditions, and constitutional standards that cannot be compromised. As one of the authorities cited by the Commission observed, "The field of prevention is by far the least developed area of criminology: current popular views are naive, vague, most erroneous, and for the most part devoid of any awareness of research findings."[3] The Commission's own recommendations were based largely on what it called "programs and activities directed toward removing the desire or need for an individual to commit crime," herculean tasks such as improving the delivery of public services, increasing educational and employment opportunities for disadvantaged and minority youths, shoring up the integrity of politicians and government officials, and reducing corruption and organized crime.

---

[1] See, for example, *Felony Arrests: Their Prosecution and Disposition in New York City's Courts* (New York: Vera Institute of Justice, 1977).

[2] National Advisory Commission on Criminal Justice Standards and Goals, *Report on Community Crime Prevention* (Washington, D.C.: U.S. Government Printing Office, 1973), p. 1.

[3] Peter Lejins, cited in National Advisory Commission, *Community Crime Prevention,* p. 1.

There can be no question that a democratic society must advance on all these fronts if it hopes to maintain respect for law and order among its citizens. Although crime is certainly rooted to some extent in the sheer perversity of human nature, more of its roots lie in the fertile soil of poverty and inequality. Long-run permanent reductions in the rate of crime and violence will depend to a great degree on how we deal with these problems.

It is not the purpose of this study, however, to dwell on such generalities, undeniably important as they are. We are concerned instead with the search for measures to prevent juvenile violence in the short to middle run that can be undertaken within an experimental framework. And here the going gets tough; the catalog of programs that have been tried is thin, the list of successes shorter still, and reasonable ideas for future experimentation scarce.

To impose some order on the analysis that follows, it will help to group preventive approaches in four general categories.

- Preventive "treatment" to lower the potential delinquent's propensity to offend.
- "Incapacitation" or "removal" to isolate the potential offender from potential victims.
- "Deterrence," which increases the incentive not to offend.
- "Target hardening" to reduce the opportunity to commit crimes.

Others may prefer different classification schemes or object that practical programs are not so neatly distinguished as this division suggests, which is certainly true. Nevertheless, this scheme seems to me to serve the purpose of isolating the main functions of crime prevention programs.

Preventive Treatment

Preventive treatment, as the term is used here, is in substance virtually identical to rehabilitative treatment. It encompasses interventions or supportive measures designed to reduce an individual's propensity to commit crimes. With regard to violence, these measures include all of those discussed in Chapter 5 as approaches to rehabilitation.

What makes the concept of preventive treatment different from that of rehabilitative treatment is its object: it is not necessarily aimed at high-risk delinquents deemed to need "rehabilitation" in order to turn them away from further offending. Instead, preventive treatment would be directed toward all those for whom the intervention is considered to be appropriate and potentially helpful, regardless of their prior criminal records. For example, a reading program for dyslexic delinquents in a training school would be considered rehabilitative treatment; however, the same program for school dropouts in the community might be considered a preventive measure.

Hence the critical distinction between preventive and rehabilitative treatment programs concerns the size and nature of the target group. In general, preventive programs would involve larger numbers of juveniles at somewhat lower average risk of committing violent acts than would a rehabilitative program.

These differences in scale and in the nature of participants raise several problematic issues. The first is that the wider net cast by preventive programs presumably entails larger costs at the same time that it lowers the potential average payoff, because the average risk to society posed by participants is lower. Together, these two factors may weaken the justification for such programs in terms of their impact on crime reduction. They cost more and may have smaller payoff. A decision about the desirability of extending a program to a lower-risk individual would have to be made in each case by balancing the marginal cost of doing so against the potential benefit from reducing his or her delinquency potential—always easier said than done. Some preventive programs might pass this test, but most probably would not. This is not to argue that preventive programs failing the test should never be undertaken, however. It argues only that they would have to be oriented toward (and justified in terms of) a larger set of social objectives to offset the difference between their cost and their more limited return in reduced delinquency.

One kind of program that might meet this test with delinquency prevention as the sole or major objective is alternative schooling for children with learning and behavior problems. The marginal cost of these programs, particularly if they operate within or in close relationship to, the regular school system, may be relatively small. Preliminary research shows, on the other hand, that making the school experience less painful and frustrating, even if not more directly productive, may reduce delinquent behavior considerably.[4] Certainly more research and experimentation in this area are called for.

Another field that merits further scrutiny in this context is family assistance. The importance of the family in stimulating or inhibiting the development of delinquent tendencies has been confirmed by psychiatric theory and observation, by a vast number of correlational studies, and by the testimony of offenders themselves, to mention some of the more significant sources.[5] Although the evidence regarding violence is less definitive than the evidence regarding delinquency generally, it seems scarcely questionable that defective family relationships are one of the principal factors that influence violent behavior. Given the relatively large amount of public assistance that already goes to provide social services for troubled families, it is probable that some service programs could be restructured, at acceptably low marginal cost, to permit evaluation of their worth in reducing violence. Testable hypotheses regarding the influence of family structure and interaction on subsequent violent behavior of children certainly exist. The greatest need (and one of the most difficult to meet) is for long-term research funding to permit observation from the subjects' infancy (since there is wide agreement that the earlier an intervention takes place, the greater the likelihood of its success) through their late adolescence, which is the period of highest risk of violent behavior.

Feasible preventive treatment programs will in all likelihood be limited to those that are viewed by the recipients as an unqualified "good." Treatment interventions perceived as "bad," coercive, or restrictive face an objection that is probably fatal. As noted in

---

[4] See discussion under "Social Services" in Chapter 5.
[5] See discussion under "Family Structure" in Chapter 3.

Chapter 2, no available technique for predicting future violence has proven accurate even half the time. The safest prediction, statistically, is that no one will be violent in the future. Moreover, the further one moves away from the group with known histories of violent behavior, the weaker the power of all predictive techniques, whether based on clinical or statistical evidence. Even if coercive treatment programs could be justified in cost-benefit terms, therefore, subjecting individuals to them not on the basis of some offense already committed but on the basis of a highly speculative prediction of their future dangerousness raises virtually insurmountable moral and legal questions.

Incapacitation

Incapacitation involves a straightforward preventive technique: incarceration of potential offenders in secure facilities. (It may also involve capital punishment, but that and forms of incapacitation long since abandoned, such as dismemberment, hardly seem worth discussing, certainly not in the context of delinquency prevention.) Incarceration makes it impossible for the offender to prey on noncriminal society, although he or she may well continue to prey on fellow inmates.[6] Renewed interest in the benefits afforded society by incapacitating offenders has been generated by several studies that claim to show that policies producing higher rates of incapacitation following conviction would yield a substantial reduction in the number of offenses.[7]

In analyzing this issue with regard to juveniles instead of adults, however, Stevens Clarke reached the opposite conclusion. Using arrest and incarceration data from the Philadelphia cohort study, he found that a policy that produced a doubling in the number of juvenile offenders incarcerated would result in a reduction in crimes of injury, theft, damage to property, and sexual assault of 1

---

[6] See Bartollas, Miller, and Dimitz, op. cit.

[7] One of the more recent of these studies, by Shlomo and Ruel Shinnar, indicates that "the rate of serious crime would be only one-third of what it is today if every person convicted of a serious offense were imprisoned for three years." Cited in James Q. Wilson, *Thinking About Crime* (New York: Basic Books, 1975), p. 201.

to 4 percent. Given the cost of implementing such a policy, he concluded that it would not be justified.[8]

The figures on which his conclusions were based are now quite dated, of course. Additional studies using such estimating techniques and based on new data would update and possibly add to our knowledge on this point. Experimentation is probably not a feasible approach, however, given constraints imposed by the equal protection clause of the Constitution.

Deterrence

Deterrence might be said to take place when an individual chooses not to commit a crime that otherwise would have been committed because he or she judges the risk of punishment to be too great and the probable cost of that punishment to outweigh the potential gain from the crime. Increased deterrence has traditionally been thought of in terms of raising the probability of detection and apprehension through improved police practices; raising the probability of conviction once apprehended, by making criminal and juvenile court prosecutions more efficient; and raising the probability of punishment once convicted, perhaps through limiting court discretion or increasing the number and variety of punishment opportunities (such as jail cells) available to the court. Deterrence is also frequently discussed in terms of raising the severity of the punishment for certain crimes.

Given what has been learned about rates at which delinquents are arrested, about the efficiency of court processing (particularly in large urban centers like Manhattan), and about the frequency with which efficacious punishments are applied, there would appear to be plenty of room for improvement on all these fronts. A popular explanation offered for the rise of juvenile violence is that delinquents realize that the system—from arrest at the outset to punishment at the end—offers little real threat to them. Since the risk is low, the crime rate is high.

---

[8] Stevens H. Clarke, "Getting 'em Out of Circulation: Does Incarceration of Juvenile Offenders Reduce Crime?" *Journal of Criminal Law and Criminology* 65, no. 4 (1974): 528–535.

There are many reasons to try to improve the performance of the juvenile justice system in each of these respects. The most basic is that if society has decided to deal with crime in this particular way, it ought to do it as well and as efficiently as possible. Modest hope for success has also been found in some experiments, including increasing the number of police officers in subways during high-risk nighttime hours and using special police decoy teams, which have lowered offense rates or raised arrest rates.

But it is far from clear that improving arrest rates, conviction rates, and punishment rates will actually deter delinquency. Robert Martinson says that we know "almost nothing" about the deterrent effect of punishment on criminal behavior, and has called for a "family" of studies on this matter.[9] In James Q. Wilson's view, most of the studies that have been done suggest that the certainty of punishment does indeed have a deterrent effect on crime, but that the length (or severity) of sentences has rapidly diminishing returns, if any.[10] Others, like Norval Morris, say that while "we have some knowledge of the deterrent effects of certain punishments . . . such slight evidence as there is indicates that we tend to exaggerate their efficacy."[11] With regard to the effect of punishment on future criminal behavior of delinquents who are caught, evidence from the Philadelphia cohort study and Martin Gold's self-report studies suggest that increased severity of punishment actually increases the risk of future criminality.[12] This finding says nothing, of course, about the deterrent effect of stiffer punishments on delinquents who are not caught.

More research on this issue will almost certainly be forthcoming. Whether it will be able to surmount the theoretical and practical problems that have confronted past studies (e.g., the difficulty of measuring how real changes in the risk of punishment are communicated to and evaluated by potential criminals, and the difficulty of controlling the many factors exogenous to the formal policies of the criminal justice system that impinge on risk) remains to be seen.

[9] Martinson, op. cit., p. 50.

[10] Wilson, *Thinking About Crime*, pp. 174–179.

[11] Norval Morris, "Punishment and Rehabilitation." National Council on Crime and Delinquency, 1965, p. 24. (Mimeo.)

[12] See discussion under "Self-Report Surveys" in Chapter 2.

One aspect of the deterrence issue tends to be overlooked or treated as an afterthought. As Wilson has pointed out, the deterrence equation has two sides to it: the risk and cost of punishment relative to the benefit to be gained from success in the crime. He says, for example, "What the government can do is to change the risks of robbery and the rewards of alternative sources of income for those who, at the margin, are neither hopelessly addicted to thievery nor morally vaccinated against it," and adds that "simultaneously decreasing teenage unemployment and increasing the risks of youthful crime may be the most rational response society can make to property crime."[13] Most of the interest in deterrence has centered on raising the risks; little of it (at least little that is more than just rhetoric) has been concerned with increasing the benefit to be derived from not engaging in crime.

Thinking about the other side of the deterrence equation suggests an interesting but sensitive and difficult line of exploration. Young minority males living in inner-city ghettos, the group with the highest risk of committing violent crimes, are often said to have little "stake" in staying on the good side of the law. Job and income prospects are poor. School is more a trial than a pleasure. Family life is stressful and frequently as harmful as it is helpful. Under these circumstances, even if the delinquent is caught, convicted, and incarcerated, his or her perceived "loss" of benefits is much smaller than it would be for others for whom freedom brings many benefits denied to this group. Why not experiment with raising the "stake"?

A number of programs that purport to have this goal have been tried. But their goals are rarely limited to crime prevention, and the rules and regulations relating to participation in them muddy the issue. For example, youth employment programs are frequently offered as a solution to delinquency, but participation in them (and therefore access to the reward—income) generally depends on overall good behavior (measured by attendance, punctuality, etc.) instead of avoidance of crime. An experiment might be designed that offers a "stake" with only one string attached: do not commit a crime. The stake could be almost anything that is truly

[13] Wilson, *Thinking About Crime*, pp. 177–178.

valued by the participant—a cash grant, clothes, meal tickets, a car, access to recreation and entertainment opportunities. The important point is that it be something of sufficient value to offset the temptation to commit crimes. Such a program would not be "treatment," because it would not aim to change anything within the offender. It would accept the offender as he or she is and merely try to change one of the many influences that bear on the decision to commit a crime or not. Among the many problems with a scheme of this kind, two need to be confronted directly. One is that material or social incentives may be effective only where material or social gain is one of the objectives of the criminal behavior. This might exclude most categories of violent crime. Robbery would be an exception, however, and since robbery is the most frequent single violent offense committed by juveniles, it might be worth limiting the program to potential robbers. The "stake" could be withdrawn only if robbery is committed, irrespective of what other violence is committed.

The other problem involves detecting violations of the no-robbery rule when there is no arrest. Clearance rates are, as we noted, relatively low for this crime. Thus, unless the risk of apprehension could be raised simultaneously, the message of the program might be translated from "do not rob" to "do not get caught robbing." Even that, however, might have a payoff in terms of less frequent offending or fewer offenses of a high-risk nature that would justify the program's cost.

Obviously there is something morally disturbing about bribing juveniles not to commit crime. Nevertheless, a simple experiment of this kind might provide valuable information about the motivation that underlies a crime like robbery and contribute significantly to the eventual design (and evaluation) of more complicated programs that are less offensive to the public's sense of propriety.

Target Hardening

Although different in important ways from the rehabilitative interventions described earlier, the preventive strategies discussed in this chapter up to now share an important attribute with rehabilitation: preventive treatment, incapacitation, and deterrence are still, for the most part, offender-centered. Target hardening is an approach that attempts to prevent crime with complete disregard for who the potential offender is, what the motivation might be, how rational the offender is, what the offender's capabilities are. It seeks to make it physically impossible, or more difficult, to carry out a crime.

Target hardening has had its most notable successes in the prevention of property crimes, through the development of devices such as locks for automobile steering columns, improved burglar alarms, electronic sensors to identify shop-lifted items, and the like. Some innovations have also had an impact on violent street crime, however. Improved street lighting is an example.[14] Improved building design allowing surveillance of public areas is another.[15] Homicide, assault, and rape seem to be particularly difficult crimes to prevent through target hardening strategies, because of the complex and unpredictable forces that lead to these kinds of violence. Conflict resolution services to deal with family and neighborhood quarrels seem more promising than target hardening as a means of reducing homicide and assault. A campaign to disseminate public information on techniques for preventing rape attacks, like that recently sponsored by women's movement organizations, may have a positive impact on the incidence of this crime as well.

Robbery, because of the less complicated motives behind it and the greater ease in identifying potential targets, is probably the violent crime most amenable to this particular preventive strategy. Development of target hardening approaches to robbery would begin with an analysis of the victims. Who gets robbed by juveniles? Although data in the Vera study offer no statistical verifica-

---

[14] National Advisory Commission, *Community Crime Prevention,* pp. 198–199.

[15] In 1972, architect Oscar Newman, in a book called *Defensible Space* (Macmillan and Co.), awakened public interest in this form of crime prevention. He provided a detailed analysis of the relationship between architectural design and crime rates and offered a number of recommendations for improving the deterrence impact of building design. These included readily visible public areas, open spaces that encourage a sense of "territoriality" in residents, and electronic monitoring devices in elevators.

tion, it is commonly and probably justifiably assumed that most victims of juvenile robbers are either other juveniles or elderly people—two relatively vulnerable groups.

Hardening the elderly target might be done in a number of ways. Providing escort services to groups of elderly people during shopping trips and other excursions from the relative safety of their apartments; installing better entryway protection, door locks, intercom, and alarm systems, or hiring elevator operators in buildings with large elderly populations; mailing social security and welfare checks directly to bank accounts—these are all devices that might prove effective against robbery of the elderly. Many of these ideas have already been tried, although as far as I am aware, not in a systematic, experimental way and not with reduction of juvenile offenses as an explicit goal.

Target hardening with regard to juvenile victims seems more problematic. Unlike the elderly, juveniles generally do not have set routines that can be anticipated and controlled. In addition, they tend to seek out the company of other juveniles, or at least not to avoid it so assiduously, and thus expose themselves, one might say deliberately, to higher risk. Even so, it might be possible to interpose protective measures in situations where numbers of juvenile victims are likely to be exposed to juvenile victimizers; schools are one good example. The growing demand for more school guards may mean that this is one preventive idea whose time has come. But there is some reason to doubt that preventive steps in the school setting will actually deter many of the most serious violent crimes. Although a large number (perhaps even a majority) of petty robberies and assaults do occur in schoolyards, armed robbery, rape, and aggravated assault seem more likely to occur in alleys, abandoned buildings, and other less well-traveled or more anonymous areas. This is merely an impression, however, not an assertion that I can support with data. It should be examined more carefully, and if it turns out that areas where juveniles congregate in large numbers (like schools) are indeed the setting for a substantial amount of the most serious violence, target hardening measures in such places would be a desirable initiative.

Arson is another crime considered by many to be violent. In New York City, it is said that a majority of arson offenses are committed by males between the ages of 13 and 16.[16] Arson may have a variety of motives, ranging from pyromania to economic gain, but it is also possible to design preventive measures, such as sealing abandoned buildings and apartments, which could reduce the incidence of arson and thereby cut down on another juvenile offense with violent overtones.

Successful target hardening strategies would, of course, deter potential offenders other than juveniles. In weighing the value of particular proposals, therefore, consideration would have to be given to their overall impact on crime. Yet properly designed studies could also provide useful information regarding their specific impact on juvenile delinquency. In such studies, the "displacement" effect, whereby a gain in reduced robberies against juveniles or the elderly may be partially (or wholly) offset by increases in other crimes and other victims, would have to be taken into account.

I fear that these thoughts do not reach very far beyond the "naive" and "vague" level deplored by the Standards and Goals Commission. Certainly they do not match the public's aspirations for better means of preventing juvenile crime, which have been boosted by the apparent success of some simple, concrete, and yet elegant projects. Most of these, however, have addressed the problem of property crime—auto theft, shoplifting, burglary. Simple, successful programs aimed at preventing violence are much more difficult to identify. One important reason is our ignorance of the specific factors that nurture violent inclinations and trigger violent episodes and our ignorance of the factors that determine who the target of violence will be.

Although the gap between the number of violent crimes and the number of arrests is wide, one has to wonder how much further it can be closed in the near future without resorting to a "fortress" mentality or to measures of surveillance that are unsuited to a free society. On the other hand, the road toward crime prevention by way of greater social equality and economic opportunity, one that

[16] "The City of New York: 1976 Comprehensive Crime Control Plan," Criminal Justice Coordinating Council, 1976, pp. 1–18. (Mimeo.)

must be traveled regardless of its measurable return in reduced crime and violence, is long and uncertain. Unfortunately, no easy solutions to the problem of violence will be found in crime prevention any more than they are to be found in punishment and treatment of arrested offenders.

7 Concluding Reflections and Recommendations

THE TRAIL has sometimes been obscured by inadequate or contradictory data, but on the whole the evidence gathered in the course of this study supports a conclusion that juvenile violence is a serious and growing problem. The juvenile arrest rate for violent crimes has increased much faster than the adult rate, particularly for robbery and aggravated assault. By 1975, the arrest rate of 15–17-year-olds for violent crimes had surpassed the rate for people 18 or older. Data in the Vera survey suggest, however, that most robberies and assaults by juveniles are of a less serious nature (i.e., they involve neither weapons nor serious injuries to the victim).

Apart from its growth, juvenile violence deserves special attention for another reason. The Philadelphia cohort study showed that arrests for violent crimes increase as juveniles get older, whereas arrests for property and other index offenses either decrease or are unaffected by age. In commenting on a follow-up study of a subsample in the Philadelphia cohort, Marvin E. Wolfgang noted that the best predictor of adult violence is juvenile violence. Thus violence, compared to other kinds of juvenile crime, seems less likely to be a problem that will solve itself as juveniles "age out."

In spite of the large, rather steady increase in arrests for violent crimes, it is important to recognize that violence still represents only a small part of the illegal activities of the young. Approximately 10 percent of juvenile arrests for serious offenses in 1975 (less than 4 percent of all juvenile arrests) involved charges of robbery, aggravated assault, rape, or homicide. Only 0.7 percent of juvenile arrests that year were for the crimes of rape and homicide, offenses that generate the most publicity about a "wave" of juvenile violence. Most juvenile crime, serious or otherwise, consists of offenses against property. Status offenses are the second most prominent category.

Deciding which delinquents (as distinct from crimes) can legitimately be labeled "violent" was one of the more vexing issues confronted in this study. As a minimum standard, we considered violent only those delinquents charged at least once with murder, rape, robbery, or assault. By that standard, approximately 44 percent of delinquents brought before courts in three New York metropolitan area counties in 1974 could be regarded as violent. Projecting that figure to all juveniles arrested that year, 25 to 30 percent had been charged at least once in their careers to that point with a violent offense. A rough, although not perfect, comparison can be made with the Philadelphia cohort study, which showed that 31 percent of delinquents (or 11 percent of all male juveniles) were arrested at least once for a crime resulting in injury to the victim. That figure excludes an unknown number of boys arrested for robbery, which we have considered a violent offense.

When minor offenses labeled as violent (those not involving weapons or serious injury) are screened out of the violent subgroup in the Vera sample, however, 29 percent remained who had been charged at least once with a *serious* violent crime. Projected to all juveniles arrested in the target area that year, this figure suggests that between 15 and 20 percent had at least one serious violent offense on their records—still a rather high figure. The single offense standard is less than satisfactory, however. We know that many juveniles who engage in violent acts are not arrested for them. Furthermore, we know from the Philadelphia study and other sources that a large proportion of delinquents caught once in a violent crime never repeat, although they may go on to commit other kinds of offenses. Consequently, to identify delinquents whose behavior is measurably and significantly more violent than that of the majority, an observed pattern of violence (at least two detected offenses) is a preferable standard. In Vera's cross-sectional sample, only 14 percent of delinquents brought to court had been charged twice or more often with violence, and only 6 percent had been charged twice or more often with serious violence. Again projecting from the sample, roughly 3 to 5 percent of arrested juveniles, or about 0.06 percent of the total juvenile population, had shown the beginning of a pattern of serious violence. In the Philadelphia cohort, 7 percent of all male delinquents (2.5 percent of the cohort) were charged twice or more before their eighteenth birthdays with committing injury offenses. (Again, this figure excludes boys who committed robberies but did not commit offenses that necessarily involve injury.)

From this pool come the children whose social and moral development may be so stunted that violence is an acceptable, even "normal" means of problem resolution or self-expression. Through their violence, these children will inflict a degree of damage on society far out of proportion to their relatively small numbers unless somehow stopped. Consequently, they deserve high priority in public policy toward delinquency.

Data in the Vera study and from numerous other sources provide a description of some common characteristics of violent delinquents. They are most likely to be minority-group males living in lower-class or slum neighborhoods of large urban centers. Like most delinquents, they tend to come from broken homes and have poor relationships with parents. Most likely they are school failures, and they may well have learning disabilities. Few of them are psychotics, but many have psychological disturbances.

Elements of this general profile are useful in addressing another important question. What is the likelihood that juvenile violence will continue to increase in years to come? To an important degree, the answer depends on what happens to the growth of the juvenile population in the future. Birthrates have dropped significantly in recent years and show every indication of remaining at low levels in the future. Does that not mean that a corresponding reduction in juvenile violence can be expected?

Not necessarily. Although the total number of juveniles will indeed decline from the present high level, the group at highest risk of committing violent crimes (urban minority males) will probably increase in number. In a recent analysis of youth crime for the Office of Juvenile Justice and Delinquency Prevention of LEAA, Franklin Zimring projected future population levels for young males. The number of all males aged 15 through 20 years will be down about 17 percent in 1990 from a peak in 1975, but urban nonwhite males in the same age range will increase in number by about 3 percent.[1] Zimring acknowledged a wide margin of error in these calculations, but they bear the clear implication that faith in demographic changes as a cure for juvenile violence may be misplaced.

The fact that the group at highest risk may increase in size does not prove that violent delinquency will get worse, of course. A change in one or more of the forces that stimulate violence in this segment of the population could offset an increase in the number of potential actors to produce a leveling off or even a decrease in the number of acts. But in the absence of significant changes in family structure, economic opportunity, social mobility, or other broad influences on delinquency, it is reasonable to expect an increase, or at least no decrease, in juvenile violence where it is already at its worst—in the cities.

Yet we cannot rely on changes in the social or political fabric of the nation to solve this problem either. Although it is fair to say that social and political forces have always had more influence on the pattern of crime and delinquency than specific responses of the criminal or juvenile justice systems, and presumably will continue to do so, improvements in social mobility and economic opportunity never come easily. Moreover, when they do occur, their effects on criminal behavior may be weak, even perverse, in the short run. The decade of the 1960s was simultaneously the period of the most rapid social and economic progress for minorities and the period of the most dramatic increase in reported crime in recent American history. Social and economic progress should, of course, be pursued for the sake of a long-run reduction in social

[1] Franklin Zimring, "Dealing with Youth Crime: National Needs and Federal Priorities." September 1975, pp. 33–41. (Mimeo.)

tension, but not in expectation of immediate reduction in juvenile (or adult) criminal violence.

Meanwhile, the juvenile justice system must respond to violence as best it can. And the record of the recent past suggests that there is room for much improvement. Data in the Vera study indicate that the proportion of delinquency cases adjudicated (resulting in a "guilty" finding) varies significantly according to the size of the jurisdiction and the structure of the court system. Mercer County, with the smallest population, the least violence, and only one presiding juvenile court judge, adjudicates 64 percent of juveniles charged with delinquency. Manhattan, at the other extreme, with the largest population, the most violence, and eleven judges, adjudicates only 14 percent. By themselves, high or low adjudication rates are hard to evaluate, but a disparity of this magnitude eludes a satisfactory rationale. At the minimum, it points to an enormous expenditure of time and resources and a high degree of potentially damaging exposure to the judicial process that occurs without a corresponding return in the form of court-mandated services and control in the jurisdiction with the most severe problem of delinquent violence. The fact that this inefficiency is slightly less characteristic of cases involving serious or violent delinquents than nonviolent cases is of limited comfort.

An equally troubling conclusion of this inquiry concerns the failure of the juvenile justice system to intervene effectively, once a juvenile has been adjudicated of a violent crime, to bring an end to his or her violence. The correctional responses most frequently applied to violent delinquents, probation or training school, appear to have little or no constructive impact on subsequent criminal behavior. At the same time, treatment-oriented programs have, for the most part, been closed to juveniles with violent offenses in their records.

In spite of all the evidence of shortcomings in the juvenile justice system, no obvious solutions to these problems have appeared. The leap of faith required to conclude that juvenile violence is likely to get worse in the absence of special intervention is only a hop when compared to the leap required to say what form intervention should take. Improving police efficiency in making arrests has long been urged for all crimes and age groups, with little measurable effect on overall crime rates. Court processing certainly needs to be made more efficient, but there is no evidence that doing so would have a major impact on juvenile violence; in fact, there is considerable opinion that processing more children through to probation or corrections might only do more harm. With regard to treatment, no methodology yet devised has convincingly proven its power to stop or even reduce criminal behavior in adults or juveniles. On the other hand, few have been given a sufficient (or sufficiently researched) effort, particularly with violent juveniles, to say for certain that they do not work for this group. Against such a background, almost any set of recommendations (whether to do something or do nothing) could probably be justified.

In my view, the arguments for further experimentation outweigh arguments for doing nothing, and I will outline briefly the directions in which I think this experimentation should proceed. Because this analysis has focused on a description of delinquents who get caught and subsequently processed through the juvenile justice system, my recommendations are heavily weighted toward ways of improving the system's handling of that group. In other words, they are largely offender-centered recommendations.

I recognize the limitations of this emphasis. Delinquents who are arrested and processed through the system may or may not be representative of all delinquents. Without a doubt, the offenses for which they are brought to court represent a small minority of offenses committed by delinquents. When one considers that only about one-third of crimes against the person are reported to the police,[2] that only about one-fourth of reported violent crimes are cleared with an arrest,[3] and that about one-half of the children arrested in New York City for such crimes are brought to court, it is apparent that the courts probably deal with less than 5 percent of the crimes against the person committed by juveniles. Martin Gold's self-report studies showed that a delinquent's chances of

---

[2] U.S. Department of Justice, National Criminal Justice Information and Statistics Service. *Criminal Victimization Surveys in 13 American Cities* (Washington, D.C.: U.S. Government Printing Office, June 1975).

[3] Based on New York City police figures in 1971, as reported in Vera Institute of Justice, *Felony Arrests,* p. 5.

being arrested increase with the frequency and seriousness of his offenses. Even so, only a relatively small proportion (about one-third) of even the most delinquent juveniles are ever arrested.[4]

Consequently, an offender-centered strategy that worked perfectly could still prevent only a small share of crimes against the person by juveniles, and it would affect no more than about one-third of those committing such offenses. A logical conclusion, therefore, is that other kinds of intervention strategies at least deserve serious consideration. Some ideas along those lines were outlined in Chapter 6 and will not be repeated here.

Data Collection and Basic Research

Anyone seeking to understand the problem of juvenile violence is struck immediately by the lack of adequate information at all levels. Despite the abundance of research on delinquency, data on the incidence of violence among the delinquent population and on the characteristics of violent delinquents must be put together from a variety of sources. Numerous case histories of violent individuals exist, but they usually have a narrow disciplinary focus (e.g., psychiatry) and frequently deal only with the more bizarre cases (murderers, a small and atypical group, are a favorite). Their generalizability and practical impact are thus limited. Follow-up studies of treated delinquents almost always lump violent offenders (to the small extent they are admitted to treatment in the first place) with nonviolent offenders and then ignore differences in the nature of subsequent offenses committed. As a result, we know little about the impact of treatment on violent behavior. Least of all do we have adequate information on the causes of violence. Remedying these deficiencies must be an objective of a long-run strategy for dealing with juvenile violence. A few specific suggestions for new or expanded research follow.

Cohort Studies. The most meaningful and widely cited source of data on delinquency is the Philadelphia cohort study by Marvin

[4] See Martin Gold, "Undetected Delinquent Behavior," *Journal of Research in Crime and Delinquency* 3, no. 1 (1966): 27–46.

E. Wolfgang and his colleagues. The cohort format makes possible an understanding of the pattern of criminal behavior over an individual's entire "career." When done on the scale of the Philadelphia study, it also permits analysis of the relationship of delinquent behavior, and changes in delinquent behavior, to many other factors.

An optimum research strategy would call for more such cohort studies. The value of information obtained would be enhanced if several studies were carried out simultaneously in jurisdictions of varying size and social character, having significant variations in juvenile laws as well as court and correctional procedures. One of the locations studied should be Philadelphia, in order to provide a comparison with the earlier Wolfgang study, which could yield useful information about changes in delinquent behavior over time.

As with other kinds of research, more emphasis should be placed on analysis of violence in future cohort studies.

Delinquent Careers.   Short of full-blown cohort studies, there is a need for more research on changes in individual criminal behavior over time. Such research should examine the "normal" path of delinquent behavior and the factors associated with an increase or decrease in individual offense rates. It should also attempt to determine what distinguishes those who cross over the line between violent and nonviolent behavior from those who do not, and whether there are distinct types of violent delinquents in terms of both offense patterns and personal characteristics.

An indispensible tool for this kind of research is an offender-based data bank that would include information not only on arrest charges throughout an individual's career, but also on dispositions, changes in charges between arrest and disposition, salient facts about the offense other than charge category, correctional and treatment methodologies applied following each conviction, and the time spent in various stages of the process. Creation of such a data bank would pose some risk to the privacy and civil rights of individuals whose criminal careers were recorded, which cannot be ignored. A data bank of this kind should therefore be developed only if methods can be devised to code identities and control access to the file in such a way that that risk is reduced to an acceptable level.

Court and Correctional Processing. Several studies, including the Philadelphia cohort study and some of Gold's self-report research, have shown that the deeper a delinquent moves into the court or correctional processes, the more delinquent his or her subsequent behavior is likely to be. The Philadelphia study was unable to say whether this is because the courts accurately select the "harder core" for more serious treatment or because more serious treatment creates a harder core. Gold's research, using matched pairs of self-confessed delinquents who received different treatment, suggested that offender characteristics were less important than the effects of processing. Both studies, however, support a conclusion, in the words of one, that "the judicial process and the correctional system do not seem to function effectively to restrain, discourage, or cure delinquency."[5]

We need to understand both sides of this issue better: does court and correctional processing make serious offenders out of nonserious offenders or merely respond to preexisting characteristics, and why is it that, in either case, the system fails to reduce subsequent delinquent behavior? In addition, more attention must be paid to the matter of racial differences in outcome and disposition of juvenile cases. Is discrimination a factor in the harsher treatment received by minority youths, or does this treatment appropriately reflect greater harm done to society by minority youths? An offender-based data bank of the kind described above would contribute much of the data necessary for this kind of research.

Self-Report Studies. The only longitudinal comparison of self-reported information on delinquent behavior (Gold and Reimer) sharply contradicted police arrest data regarding changes in delinquent activity. The reasons for the discrepancy in the two data sources have not been adequately explained. Moreover, self-report studies have not yet clarified our understanding of changes in rates of commission of the most violent kinds of delinquent acts. Addi-

[5] Wolfgang, Figlio, and Sellin, op. cit., p. 243.

tional studies of this kind aimed at these issues should be encouraged.

The Causes of Violence and Delinquency. An issue that has barely been touched in this study, but that is obviously crucial to the development of preventive and rehabilitative strategies, is the cause of violent and delinquent behavior. Cohort studies and other kinds of research have generated a large volume of information comparing delinquents and nondelinquents on broad social measures. For example, it is by now well established that lower-class and minority youths are more prone to arrest and more frequently charged with violent crimes than middle- or upper-class youths. Much less is known, however, about the specific influences that keep a youth from becoming (or being labeled) delinquent (e.g., whether personal qualities, family behavior and resources, social values or the responses of official agencies play key roles, and if so, how).

There is a great need for theories of causality with more explanatory and predictive power, theories capable of bridging the gaps that now exist between biological, psychological, and sociological explanations. One potentially fruitful avenue of exploration involves anthropological methods of observation focusing on social mores and values regarding violence, their transmission through family and institutional influences, and the circumstances that govern individual receptivity. Studies of this kind might lead to sounder and more comprehensive theories, which in turn could provide the basis for more efficient experimentation.

Experimental Intervention Programs

Although more information about the scope and nature of juvenile violence, its causes, and the effects of current judicial and correctional practices is vital, information alone will not solve the problem. Experimental intervention must also be encouraged.

Innovations in corrections and treatment programs are becoming commonplace. The literature is bulging with descriptions of new community-based and institutional treatment programs for offenders. Yet we still know surprisingly little about their effects on violent behavior, for all the reasons that have been mentioned throughout this study. There is some anecdotal evidence of success in the few treatment programs willing to take violent delinquents, but hard evidence of long-term success is scarce. Even so, there is still reason to hope. Stevens Clarke reviewed eight studies of treatment programs for delinquents and found that the only three that showed a significant effect in reducing subsequent delinquent behavior (all three, unfortunately, having methodological deficiencies) were the ones that served the most serious kinds of delinquents. This result, in Clarke's words, "suggests the tentative conclusion that it may be easier to achieve a reduction in delinquent behavior with serious juvenile offenders than with nonserious juvenile offenders."[6] Thus more experimentation with treatment for the serious delinquent seems warranted.

A prime candidate for further evaluation is milieu therapy. In view of widespread disillusionment with treatment based on the medical or psychiatric model and many studies that lend support to that disillusionment, this may seem to be a rather misguided recommendation. Research on milieu therapy has, however, produced more ambiguous (or less discouraging) conclusions than research on other treatment modalities. Furthermore, while psychiatrists and other mental health professionals are admitting in increasing numbers the ineffectiveness of many of their techniques in reaching severely delinquent children, many still feel that milieu therapy offers promise, particularly for young people with histories of serious antisocial behavior. Their optimism is shared by a number of judges, probation officers, and corrections officers. Unlike some forms of psychiatric intervention, milieu therapy can also be provided to relatively large numbers of delinquents in relatively secure settings at relatively low cost. Thus it may be a practical alternative to incarceration—if it works.

Part of the reason we still do not know for certain that milieu therapy works is that the term covers such a variety of programs, in terms of therapeutic content, that precisely what has been studied so far is not clear. One need in future experimentation,

---

[6] Clarke, "Juvenile Offender Programs," p. 392.

therefore, is for some degree of uniformity, or at least order, among the programs studied so that results can be compared among experiments and with control groups. Some of the characteristics on which milieu therapy programs often differ, and on which variation would have to be controlled, were described in Chapter 5.

Another idea of some promise is embodied in the Downey Side program in Massachusetts (see Appendix D). Downey Side arranges "permanent" group foster care for wards of the state with no functioning families. Placements are permanent in the sense that the family, the youth, and the state agree to a placement period of at least three years, usually until the youth reaches 18. Most children placed in the program have delinquent records, including some with histories of violence. No recidivism data are available, but staff estimates that 121 out of 175 placed children have formed permanent relationships with their foster families, an indication of general success with a difficult group. The keys to success are the quality of the foster parents and the permanence of the commitment to each youth. Downey Side's setting is nonurban, but its director feels it could also work in an urban environment with violent youths who can be managed within the community.

Outward Bound, a program of high-stress physical challenge in a wilderness setting designed to produce self-awareness and strengthen interpersonal relations, has been found successful in reducing the frequency of delinquent behavior in the short-to-medium run and the seriousness (but not frequency) of delinquent acts over the long run (see Appendix D). Adaptations of the Outward Bound model developed for inner-city delinquent youth show encouraging results. The model is probably most appropriate for youths who are in (or soon to be released to) community treatment programs. Its most significant drawback is its short duration. Experimentation with the model should stress extending or renewing exposure over a longer period of time and integrating the wilderness or equivalent stress experience with the environment in which the participant will spend most of his or her life. One possible modification might be to substitute a demanding work challenge for the challenge of wilderness survival. A pilot project with these features applying the Outward Bound method to a group of New York City's most serious delinquents has just recently been initiated under the sponsorship of the Fund for the City of New York. It deserves to be watched closely.

Because of the high correlation between school failure and delinquency, education has always been a tantalizing realm in which to seek causal explanations and devise preventive or corrective programs. The movement to develop alternative classroom settings for students with learning or behavior problems has produced a number of experiments that have among their goals, explicitly or implicitly, the prevention of delinquency, including violence. A few, like the Quincy, Illinois, program of the 1950s,[7] have been evaluated in terms of their effect on delinquency—in that particular case with strongly positive results. Most, however, have not. Several programs that were observed in the course of this study, notably those at the Argus Community in the Bronx and the Henry Street Settlement House in Manhattan's Lower East Side, left a strong impression that they are having a preventive impact. But that impression is yet to be validated by research.

Such programs usually contain a mixture of children, not all of whom have committed or will commit delinquent acts. Yet by focusing on inner-city youths who have a demonstrated pattern of truancy or maladjustment in the classroom, they enroll a high-risk group. Carefully designed studies of the preprogram, in-program, and postprogram delinquency records of a sufficiently large group of students receiving special educational assistance of this kind—and a control group could provide valuable data about their effect on delinquency.

The association between school failure and delinquency, the decline in delinquent behavior that follows dropping out of school,[8] and the high proportion of property crimes in juvenile offenses all suggest the desirability of experimenting with models that replace traditional classroom schooling with opportunities to develop skills while earning income. The range of possible program models is large, running from adding income-producing work components to vocational education programs, to substituting apprenticeships in skilled crafts for schooling, all the way to a national youth service corps for unemployed school dropouts.

[7] Bowman, op. cit.
[8] Elliot and Voss, op. cit.

For the violent delinquent, supported work (jobs that rehabilitate) is an idea that needs further study. Features of the supported work concept appear to be relevant to problems commonly associated with juvenile violence. First, of course, it provides income. (Half of all juvenile arrests for serious violent crimes are for robbery, an economically motivated crime.) It also provides a controlled environment for peer interaction in which cooperation, discipline, and conflict resolution techniques can be taught. Moreover, supported employment can help to enhance self-esteem through community service and through promotions for work well done. It could also offer an outlet for youthful energy (hard physical labor might be preferable for aggressive delinquents).

So far, supported work has been applied principally to adult former drug addicts, offenders, and chronic welfare dependents. The results of the longest standing supported work project, Wildcat in New York, remain inconclusive with regard to its impact on criminal behavior, although the impact appears to be greatest in the first year after enrollment.[9] Supported work programs for juvenile delinquents in New York and Massachusetts are too new to evaluate.

Finally, notice should be taken of some specific physical problems that have been linked in a preliminary way to the presence of violence or other delinquent behavior. One of these is learning disability, a term used to describe specific perceptual problems that inhibit children from reading and writing in the normal way.[10] The causal relationship between learning disability and delinquent behavior has not been established, but an association between these two problems has been observed in a number of studies and by many teachers and experts. Research is currently underway to understand this relationship better and may eventually lead to hypotheses that can be tested in experimental programs.

Health problems, including especially neurological disorders, have also been associated with delinquency and violence in a number of studies. More recently, attention has been focused on

[9] "Third Annual Research Report on Supported Employment," Vera Institute of Justice, December 1975. (Mimeo.)
[10] See discussion under "Education and Learning" in Chapter 3.

the relationship of nutritional deficiencies and violent behavior. Laboratory and clinical research projects have demonstrated a correlation between specific nutritional stresses (vitamin deficiency, hypoglycemia, food allergies, etc.) and hyperactive or aggressive behavior. For example, the Full Circle Residential Research and Treatment Center, a program in California, studied seven delinquents referred from juvenile halls, selected on the basis of evidence of learning disabilities and behavior problems that precluded their placement in any other therapeutic program. In six of the seven, severe behavioral responses resulting from food allergies were discovered, and all seven showed evidence of hypoglycemia. Six of the children improved markedly in behavior as a result of diet therapy.

Interventions aimed at concrete problems such as learning disability or health and nutritional deficiencies have an especially seductive appeal. They are the kind of problems that, in many cases, we can do something about. Compared to factors such as poverty, cultural influences, family background, and IQ, which are extraordinarily difficult if not impossible to change, neurological and nutritional problems seem relatively straightforward. Because of the power of this attraction, however, we must be on guard against rushing to embrace overly simplistic models. In the first place, health and nutritional damage may not be fully reversible, and even if the immediate damage can be repaired, it is far from certain that other biological and psychological side effects can be eliminated. More important, the likelihood of a simple causal relationship between an organic problem and a behavioral one like violence is, in the opinion of most experts, remote. It is entirely possible that organically based disorders can play a significant role in the development of aberrant behavior, but it is premature, to say the least, to conclude that simply by attacking such disorders we can "cure" the problem of violence.

This argument, of course, applies to all other forms of intervention as well. All too often, rehabilitation is viewed as an attack on one specific problem manifested by a delinquent. The single-solution approach flies in the face of overwhelming evidence that violence is an outgrowth of multiple deficiencies and pressures bearing on the individual. If no single cause has been isolated, why should a single solution be adequate?

Intervention strategies that make use of a combination of inputs based on identified needs of the individual and reasonable hypotheses about causes of his or her behavior must be encouraged. To a degree, of course, this happens already. Corrections programs, after all, usually provide a variety of services for participants, including special education, counseling, and perhaps vocational training. But this approach should be refined and extended much further. For example, take the case of a youth whose persistently violent behavior leads to the conclusion that milieu therapy is required in order to provide an environment that offers both control and therapeutic support. At the same time, a complete medical diagnosis may reveal food allergies that could be a contributing factor, and an educational evaluation may uncover specific learning disabilities. Instead of dealing with only one of these problems, the optimal approach might be to initiate nutritional therapy, behavioral therapy, and special education all at once. Even if, say, the food allergy were clearly responsible initially for both the behavioral problem and the learning disability, the probability that years of behavioral adaptation and learning deprivation could be reversed simply by eliminating the original activating condition seems small. Clearing away that cause would be a necessary but insufficient step. Specific remedial attention to the secondary problems would almost certainly be required, too.

In some cases, sequential instead of simultaneous use of techniques may be appropriate. Consider a violent boy from a disorganized, destructive family who has been forced to rely on his own aggressive instincts and capacities to survive in the streets. He may first need a jolting experience that enables him to adopt a new perspective on his life, followed by a period of supportive care and attention to build a new self-confidence, and finally an opportunity to develop skills that will enable him to earn a respectable, adequate living on his own. For him, a sequence that includes an Outward Bound-like experience, followed by long-term foster care and possibly supportive group therapy, and eventually vocational training, might be optimal. Each of these by itself might have little long-term impact but, when combined, the cumulative impact might be substantial.

The point is simply that the more intervention programs are designed to take account of the diversity and complexity of individual histories and needs, the more likely they are to succeed. This is not a recommendation for a shotgun approach that tries everything in the hope that something will work, which would be no better than the single shot expected to hit many targets at once. Instead, what is urged are programs capable of putting together combinations of inputs based on the best available diagnosis of individual problems and needs. A detailed model of such a program will be drawn in the following section.

At the risk of laboring the obvious, I would like to end this discussion of experimentation with two general points that seem critical to me. First, it is imperative to stop wasting scarce resources on research that is doomed from the outset (by virtue of its inadequate, nonexperimental design) to produce no reliable information about the impact of the interventions studied. Funding agencies should make the existence of a scientifically respectable experimental research design a minimum, unwaivable requirement for obtaining research support. Second, research designs that apply to projects aimed at reducing delinquency (and especially violence) should be required to include meaningful outcome measures. One of the common faults in evaluations of treatment programs is that the outcome measure used is simply recidivism, often including minor infractions or unspecified violations of probation conditions. Such a measure tells us little about the real impact of treatment programs in terms of social benefit. For, as Marvin E. Wolfgang and his colleagues concluded on the basis of data in the Philadelphia cohort study, "a major thrust of social action programs might be toward a change in the character rather than in the absolute reduction of delinquent behavior."[11] Follow-up research must therefore include measures of the nature and seriousness of crimes committed after treatment in comparison to those committed before treatment.

[11] Wolfgang, Figlio, and Sellin, op. cit., p. 111.

Continuous Case Management

Perhaps the most important requirement of all for effective re-habilitation of violent delinquents is continuity. I have discussed how violent delinquents may be shunted from detention to diagnostic centers, to the streets, to training schools, and back to the streets again, with little purpose except to comply with administrative exigencies and the preferences of the agencies involved. Often there is no one person or group of persons managing the process, which further increases the risk that decisions will bear scant relation to the needs of the child. A policeman turns a child over to a court intake worker who may refer the child to a detention center. A social worker may be assigned to see that the child gets a pre-hearing diagnostic evaluation, do a background investigation, and seek placement openings. Meanwhile, the child is also assigned a law guardian. Eventually he or she will be sent away to the custody of a training school and on release, months later, will become the responsibility of an aftercare worker. At each juncture, the juvenile's eligibility for the service or program in question must be determined, and funding must be negotiated or arranged. Rejection is possible, often likely. Important information may be lost. Even more damaging, relationships are broken and responsibility diluted.

What is needed to end this highly destructive process is a single locus of accountability on whom both society and the child can rely to help develop an appropriate response to the child as an individual; to maintain continuity among the numerous stages of the judicial, placement, and aftercare processes; to expedite those processes; and to see that the child does not lose sight of his or her responsibility and personal goals or lose touch with the positive elements in his or her environment. Many delinquents never get sufficiently entangled in the judicial and correctional web to require this kind of help. Others are lucky enough to have family or supportive adults able and willing to serve this function on their behalf. But the odds are against juveniles who commit serious violent acts, and particularly those with histories of repeated delinquency and assaultive behavior; they are more likely to find themselves deeply enmeshed in the system, later if not sooner, and much less likely to have environmental supports on which they can rely to soften and make more constructive its impact.

The call for a procedure that would assure rational planning and continuity among the various branches of the juvenile justice system that deal with violent delinquents has the ring of a high-minded ideal beyond implementation in the real world. Paradoxically, it also sounds simplistic. I do not believe that either assumption is warranted, however. I will begin my defense of this recommendation by outlining a general model of a continuous case management program for repetitively violent delinquents. Variations in state laws, existing institutional structures, and other critical factors would shape the design and mandate of such a program in each state or locality. Because I know the New York City system best, the model presented reflects in particular my understanding of current realities and needs there.

A diagram of the functions and flow of clients through a Continuous Case Management Program (CCMP) is given in Figure 2. Only those delinquents whose criminal histories and social backgrounds indicate a need for special intervention would be eligible for referral to the CCMP. Its principal functions would be: (1) assessment; (2) development of a treatment or correctional plan and recommendations to the court in that regard; (3) postdispositional referral to treatment; (4) contact with the delinquent and monitoring of treatment during the placement period; (5) postplacement follow-up; and (6) referral to (or provision of) supplementary services. As the delinquent moves through each of these steps, the CCMP would maintain contact with the agencies and individuals involved in the process—the court, legal aid, the family, the school, the correctional and treatment systems and the service agencies. The overall aim of the CCMP's involvement would be to integrate and expedite each step in the process in order to avoid delays, contradictory decisions, and damaging discontinuities.

I will elaborate briefly on these functions. Once a juvenile has been assigned to the program (which could occur as early in the process as during arrest proceedings or detention, but more likely would take place after adjudication but before disposition), its first

Figure 2 Client Movement Through a Juvenile Court, a Continuous
Case Management Program, and Other Agencies

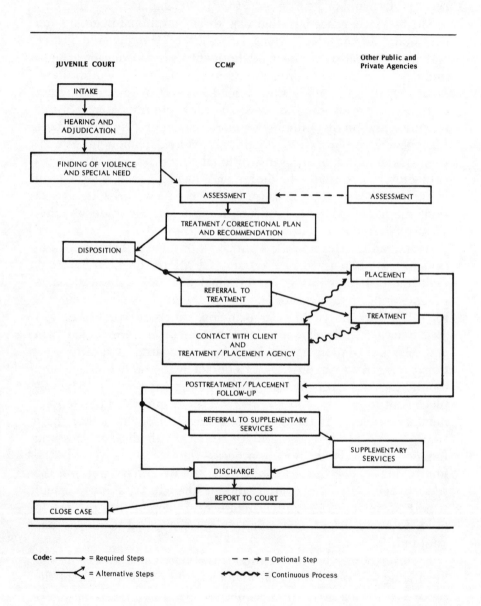

task would be to undertake a thorough assessment of the child's needs, the sources of his or her problems, and his or her potential. Part of this function (e.g., psychiatric or educational testing) might be contracted out to professional consultants, but a major share would be done in-house by a staff member, preferably someone familiar with the juvenile's community. This staff member would learn about the client's life history, the environmental influences and pressures that bear on the client, his or her interpersonal relationships, strengths, weaknesses, goals, accomplishments, failures—in short, everything of relevance to a treatment decision.[12] He or she would then be responsible for integrating this information with that provided by professional evaluators and for formulating a treatment recommendation to be presented to the judge.

The program's next responsibility would be to secure an opening for the client in an appropriate treatment program. Access to treatment is, of course, the most critical element of the entire plan. Without it, the evaluative, planning, and coordinating roles are meaningless. To obtain access to treatment on behalf of its clients, the CCMP would require a purchase-of-service budget, authority to compel acceptance of referrals (perhaps by being given a decision-making role in budget or licensing procedures), or at least a close working relationship with agencies having budgetary and licensing authority. A combination of the first two powers would be ideal, but any of the three might suffice. For juveniles for whom punishment (i.e., incarceration) seems inescapable or even advisable, the CCMP would identify the correctional environment with the most appropriate treatment possibilities, and then formulate a voluntary treatment plan for the postincarceration period.

[12] For a sense of the complexity of the assessment task, see New York State Board of Social Welfare, op. cit., Appendix C: "Summary of Criteria for Placement and Alternatives to Foster Care," pp. 101–111. It describes more than 100 criteria to be considered in weighing two dozen service or placement options. In New York City, as in many other places, the responsibility for assessment of children about to be placed by the court currently falls on the shoulders of probation staff who are frequently overworked and undertrained. The quality of background investigations varies from reporter to reporter and case to case. They are often limited to a psychiatric or psychological diagnosis, a brief rundown of the child's court record (which may be incomplete because New York City has no centralized city-wide record system), a cursory description of family structure and home life (often based on hearsay), and occasionally an educational evaluation. Together with the availability of placement openings, this information is the basis on which the court usually determines which disposition the child will receive.

Throughout the treatment process, the CCMP would maintain close contact with the client to assure that his or her needs were being met, arrange for additional or alternative services if necessary, supervise his or her return to the community during home leave, help keep him or her in touch with relatives and friends, and in general assume some of the roles that would normally be taken by a supportive family. Relations with treatment programs would have to be managed delicately to avoid counterproductive interference, but if properly handled, the monitoring role should benefit both the client and the treatment program.

It might be possible for the CCMP to develop a treatment component alongside its other functions, although some considerations would warn against that approach. In the first place, since a single treatment approach would be unlikely to meet all needs of all clients, the program would either have to develop a multiplicity of treatments or emphasize in-house treatment for some clients but not for others. In either case, the intensity and heavy demands created by a treatment component could begin to dominate, to the detriment of other aspects of the program. Furthermore, in order to serve its clients well, the program must retain flexibility and objectivity, qualities that might be jeopardized if one or more treatment methodologies were incorporated and emphasized. On the other hand, it might be entirely appropriate for the CCMP to initiate other kinds of inputs for its clients that cannot be found elsewhere.

Once a client leaves a residential treatment program, whether he or she has completed the full term under official control (including parole or probation) or not, the CCMP would continue to bear responsibility for reintegration into the community. It would arrange health care, schooling, vocational training, a job, or perhaps a supported work opportunity. It might provide a place to stay, in a group home or foster care. It would assist the client in developing constructive relationships with his or her family. It might arrange for counseling or enroll the client in special programs like Outward Bound to help further growth and development. Whatever access and resources a client required and could not be expected to provide alone would be made available by the CCMP, until he or she reached, say, 18 years of age, and perhaps even longer. The one function the program should not perform, however, is that of a parole officer or policeman whose mission is to reinstate punishment as the response to failure. When that reaction is necessary, it should be the responsibility of other official agents.

To the extent possible, the CCMP should be based in the community from which its clients come, or at least have a strong community outreach capability. The key staff members, the case managers, should be people with strong roots in the community. Young college graduates or paraprofessionals would be appropriate for these positions, but the demands of client assessment, resource management, family and client counseling, vocational and educational planning, and all the other functions of the case manager would necessitate a well-conceived and continuously implemented in-service training program. In addition, the case managers should be backed up by a core of professional administrators and perhaps clinicians, and should have access to consultants for special diagnostic treatment or crisis intervention. To the extent the CCMP undertakes its own treatment or supplementary service programs, professional and paraprofessional staff would also have to be hired to carry out those functions.

This brief sketch calls to mind elements of many other kinds of programs and may make the CCMP concept appear to be old wine in a new bottle. On the surface, it resembles the youth services bureaus that became popular in the late 1960s and early 1970s, although it would work with a more "selective" population, over a longer period of time with each individual, and provide more referral and monitoring services in addition to direct services than many of the YSBs. It would also perform some of the functions of a diversion program, but within the context of the judicial and corrections systems instead of as an alternative to them. The CCMP idea reflects aspects of intensive probation programs, but it would not rely on just one adult or one kind of service input to change the behavior of its delinquent clients. Furthermore, it would divorce the policeman's role from the advocate's role, a conflict inherent in most probation programs, and would continue functioning as a service-provider even after the termination of court-mandated control. The program also has some resemblance to a parole aftercare service, except that its involvement would begin before instead of after correctional intervention.

The most distinctive feature of the CCMP, apart from the comprehensive nature of its assignment, and probably the most controversial, is that it would deliberately reverse the existing pattern of discrimination against violent delinquents in the provision of treatment and other services. It would have its own substantial budget and direct access to other services; it would hire high-quality, well-trained staff; it would help to secure a comprehensive range of the best available social and remedial services; and all this would be for the "worst" delinquents.

This reversal can be justified because these are children who have been victims as well as victimizers; because they will exact the greatest cost from society if something constructive is not done to and for them; and because the concept makes room for measured, appropriate punishment for their crimes, including possibly incarceration, but seeks to put an end to the far more lasting and destructive punishments of neglect, delay, isolation, untreated psychological damage, and foreclosure of opportunity. It can also be justified because, as Norval Morris said in describing a special prison for violent offenders, "if some measure of success can be achieved by reforms applied to the toughest group . . . their feasibility should be established as to the entire . . . system."[13]

Why not make this service available to all children who need it, not just violent delinquents? The unfortunate reality is that there are not enough good staff, diagnostic services, treatment resources, community programs, and money for all the children who need them. A program of such scope would also require a massive, top-to-bottom restructuring of the social service establishment which, although perhaps desirable, is not realistic in most places at the present time. Meanwhile, it seems desirable to begin applying the limited resources that do exist to the children who need them most and who will be the greatest burden if they are not helped.

To avoid the predictive trap, eligibility for this program should be determined by two criteria. The first is the delinquent's record.

[13] Morris, *Future of Imprisonment,* p. 86.

Only juveniles with a clear pattern of assaultive antisocial behavior suggesting a high risk of continued violence should be considered. Wolfgang has suggested that the optimum time for intervention might be after a youth has committed three offenses, at which point the probability that he or she will desist on his or her own does not decrease.[14] That seems to be a reasonable first approximation, although to be certain of addressing a small target population that includes the most critical cases, the three offenses in question should probably all be serious and include at least one violent offense.

The second criterion should be a determination that no conventional approach is likely to succeed. Possibly the most practical way to apply this criterion would be to limit referral to the CCNP to youths likely to be sent to a training school, with the understanding that an alternate disposition would be allowed if the program could arrange one satisfactory to the court. In this way, diversion, probation, and voluntary placement would continue to follow their customary paths.

An estimate of the maximum enrollment in a New York City CCMP can be drawn from figures in the Juvenile Justice Institute study cited earlier. In 1973–74, the study reported, 136 children out of a total of 197 placed following adjudication on violent charges were sent to the State's training schools because no other program was deemed appropriate or would take them.[15] These 136 children might be good candidates for this kind of program. Another clue to the minimum size of a program at the state level was given by Governor Carey's staff following the announcement of his intention to recommend legislation providing stiffer penalties for the state's most serious juvenile offenders—14- and 15-year-olds found guilty of "major violent crime and found dangerous to society." His staff estimated that there would be approximately 150 such youth throughout the state.[16] A reasonable estimate, therefore, is that each state might have 50–200 repetitively violent youths each year who would be the target of this kind of program.

Where to lodge a continuous case management program in the

14 Wolfgang, Figlio, and Sellin, op. cit., p. 253.
15 Juvenile Justice Institute, op. cit., pp. 40–45.
16 *New York Times,* December 10, 1975, pp. 1, 29.

bureaucratic structure is a complex matter. A number of arguments can be advanced in support of putting it into a governmental agency—possibly at the state level—as contrasted to a private or semiautonomous agency. A state-level agency would have stature on a par with the judicial and corrections systems. If given authority to exercise budgetary or licensing control over treatment programs, a state agency could also enforce dispositional decisions that the court alone may not be able to enforce. If the agency were part of the state corrections system, it would have (or be able to develop) its own treatment and correctional resources, thereby avoiding the need to negotiate slots on behalf of each client enrolled. In any case, a state-level agency probably stands a better chance of securing the funding required to operate a CCMP successfully.

But there are also arguments in favor of a more locally centered program, possibly even a private program. One is the need for strong ties to the community from which violent delinquents come. A remote state agency may find it difficult to establish a credible presence in the community or to maintain the proper balance between the administrative needs of a governmental bureaucracy and the need for flexibility in dealing with complex and sensitive human problems. Another argument concerns the need to attract dedicated, community-oriented staff as case managers, and to ensure that they neither "burn out" (as staff of delinquency treatment programs so often do) nor become stale and rigid in their dealings with youths. A state agency operating under civil service regulations would not have the same freedom as a private agency to hire whom it chooses, to establish policies for rotating assignments and refreshing staff in other ways, or to terminate employees who no longer work well with clients.

On balance, the arguments for locating the CCMP in a state agency may be stronger. Authority and adequate resources are crucial if the objectives of securing access to treatment and reducing delays and confusion are to be realized. It is conceivable, moreover, that a state-level agency can so structure itself as to reduce the distance between the program and the community. It could, for example, open regional CCMP offices in major urban and metropolitan areas and provide them with enough autonomy to permit close interaction not only with the community, but also with other state, local, and private agencies operating with the same population.

In New York, several state agencies might make an appropriate home for the continuous case management program (e.g., the Departments of Probation, Mental Hygiene, or Social Services, or the Division for Youth). Among these alternatives, the Division for Youth may be the most suitable. It already has responsibility for both corrections and aftercare of delinquents, including operation of the state's training schools and other residential treatment programs. Furthermore, it has a budget for support of local programs and purchase of treatment services. Adding a CCMP component would require that DFY take over some of the functions of Probation, Mental Hygiene, and possibly Social Services with regard to the small group of delinquents eligible for the program, but the stretching of administrative lines would be much more extensive if one of the other agencies were to take over the program.

The CCMP might acquire an increment of political viability and funding appeal if it were part of an agency responsible not only for "bad" children but for "good" children as well. In New York State, however, there is no likely candidate with those credentials. Connecticut, in contrast, has a newly restructured Department of Children and Youth Services that appears to be an ideal host for a program of this kind. As of January 1, 1976, DCYS acquired responsibility for all children in need of state assistance (delinquent, dependent, neglected, uncared-for, mentally ill, and emotionally disturbed), thus uniting the political interests of both "good" and "bad" children and perhaps enhancing funding prospects for all. Moreover, DCYS has a mandate to provide all necessary services (from detention to mental health to education and vocational training) for all children in need and will be structured, if plans materialize, so as to provide the continuous case management advocated here for all of its clients. Consequently, in principle at least, violent delinquents need not be singled out for special attention in order to get the kind of attention they require.

In states that do not have a single overall agency like Connecticut's DCYS, funds for care of delinquents come from diverse sources and move in a pattern analogous to a series of parallel channels instead of tributaries feeding into a common stream. Each need is addressed by a different funding agency, so that a child requiring more than one kind of service must, in effect, obtain separate permission to enter each appropriate channel. A list of some of the funding sources in New York State for the kinds of services clients of a CCMP would require is given in Table 25. Depending on the categories of eligibility he or she falls into (AFDC dependent, Medicaid recipient, etc.), his or her needs, and even where he or she lives, a delinquent may have access to one or more of these sources.

Table 25 Some Funding Sources for Delinquent Services and Programs (New York State)

Service/ Program Category	Funding Sources	Special Eligibility Criteria
Assessment	State Department of Mental Hygiene: —State mental hospitals —Community mental health services (50% share with county governments)	
	City government: —Municipal hospitals —Diagnostic centers (50% share with State Bureau of Child Welfare)	Court order generally required
	Family Court: —Court mental health clinics (in some localities only)	
Corrections	State Division for Youth (50% share with county governments): —Training schools —Open facilities (camps, etc.)	Court order
Residential treatment	State Division for Youth: —Urban group homes —Youth development centers	Court order, voluntary admissions
	State Department of Social Services (50% share with county governments): —Public and voluntary group home and foster care	Court order, voluntary placements

Table 25 Some Funding Sources for Delinquent Services and Programs (New York State) (cont'd)

Service/ Program Category	Funding Sources	Special Eligibility Criteria
	Federal government:	
	—AFDC (50%; 25% state and county) for foster care	AFDC eligible, court placed
	—Title XX (85–90% of costs) for foster care	Funds limited, eligibility determined by state
	—Juvenile Justice and Delinquency Prevention Act of 1974 (through State DCJS)	
Other treatment	Federal government:	
	—Medicaid (50%; 25% state and county) for medical and psychiatric care	Medicaid eligibility
	State Department of Mental Hygiene: —State mental hospitals —Community mental health services (50% share with county governments)	
Supplementary services	Federal government:	
	—Title I funds for education in training schools	Placed in training school
	—Comprehensive Training and Employment Act for vocational training	
	—Juvenile Justice and Delinquency Prevention Act of 1974 (through DCJS) for a variety of supplementary programs	
	State Department of Education:	
	—Special education funds for learning-disabled delinquents	Mental, physical, or emotional handicap

This system introduces two major difficulties. One is fragmentation (and accompanying delays) in planning and meeting the needs of a child. The second is unbalanced availability of essential services created by the divergent and frequently inflexible policies of various funding agencies. For example, a considerable amount of money is spent on detention and incarceration of delinquents in New York State (nearly $8 million in 1974 on maintenance costs for New York City's single secure detention center,[17] and approximately $23,000 per child per year in the state's training schools). Yet incarcerated (and especially violent) delinquents often are not provided other services that may be more appropriate for them, either because no money for such services is available or because, where money is available, programs exclude them.

To work effectively, a CCMP would have to solve both of these problems: it would have to develop more flexible use of available funds and obtain more access for its clients to treatment and service programs.

Ideally, flexible funding would come from a pooling of the resources now being spent under the auspices of different agencies. A CCMP would have automatic access to the pool for whatever services were required whenever the need arose. In reality, however, it is unlikely that funding sources would readily relinquish the control they now have over screening and enrollment of service recipients. Another way to achieve greater flexibility would be to reassign authority (and funds) for purchasing various kinds of services for the small number of individuals who meet a CCMP's criteria from the agencies that now have it to the CCMP or its parent agency. For example, authorization to spend special education funds on behalf of the delinquents enrolled in the CCMP in New York State might be shifted from the Department of Education to the Division for Youth (perhaps with a ceiling on total annual expenditures authorized). Of course, a move of this kind would probably encounter stiff political resistance.

Instead of acquiring flexibility in these ways, it may be more realistic for a CCMP to attempt to tap existing funding sources more intensively. An obvious, although piecemeal, way of doing that would involve ascertaining each client's eligibility under all potential categories of support and taking the necessary steps on his or her behalf to secure funding from all appropriate sources. In the absence of the kinds of umbrella funding arrangements dis-

17 New York State Board of Social Welfare, op. cit., p. 47.

cussed above, this would have to be one of the principal functions of a CCMP.

Greater control of funding or increased use of available funds can be expected to produce some additional access to treatment and service programs, on the principle that who pays the piper calls the tune. But more efficient use of existing resources will probably not solve all such problems. For one thing, forcing a delinquent into a program that neither wants the child nor is structured to deal with his or her problems may do more harm than good, both to the child and to the program. For another, many treatment programs that would be appropriate for violent delinquents would have no difficulty in filling their slots without reliance on funding from a CCMP. Instead of extending the available services of the existing child care network to include larger numbers of violent delinquents, therefore, new treatment programs designed specifically for this kind of child will probably have to be developed. A CCMP might sponsor the creation of new programs with resources from existing but unused budgets. To cite some examples, a residential treatment center for highly disturbed youths might be established as an intermediate care facility with 100 percent Medicaid financing under Title XIX of the Social Security Act. Or alternative day treatment programs might be created with 90 percent federal funding under Title II of the Juvenile Justice and Delinquency Prevention Act of 1974. Of course, new programs might also require funds not presently available in any budget. And in an era of fiscal restraint, acquiring additional money is likely to be at least as difficult as redirecting the flow of current allocations.

The Continuous Case Management Program has been presented here as a new kind of intervention in its own right. This is one way to view it, especially in light of the failure of previous "case management" programs like youth services bureaus to reach out to more difficult violent youth, and the failure of other more specific intervention programs to deal with a wide range of needs over a long period of time. But the CCMP might also be considered simply a new context within which intervention strategies for violent delinquents can be studied. The CCMP context would make available for study a pool of high-risk delinquents who share many common characteristics and for whom the common objective of intervention is specific—a reduction in their future violence. It would permit (even require) experimentation with a variety of treatment approaches but in a somewhat controlled framework. And its continuous nature would facilitate follow-up research over an extensive period. Finally, if implemented in several jurisdictions at once, it could be expected to yield useful comparative information about the broader environmental conditions that enhance or impede the work of specific interventions of the kinds recommended above.

Testing the CCMP concept in more than one site is recommended for several reasons. One is the political vulnerability of such a program. A change of administration or an unfortunate incident resulting in bad publicity could threaten a project's life before its impact can be adequately measured. The risk of losing research benefits in such a case would be reduced by having several related projects under way at once. Whether political climates change or not, effectiveness is also bound to be influenced by social climate. Locating projects in several areas would permit analysis of the effect of varying social environments on outcomes. Finally, since a single model could not be expected to work perfectly under all conditions, controlled variations on a basic model in a number of settings could increase our understanding of what is essential and what is not in this concept.

Should this concept strike a responsive chord in more than one jurisdiction, it would be highly desirable—I am tempted to say essential—to knit the various pilot projects together into a common research effort by developing a standard research format to apply to all. I do not think it is an exaggeration to say that the increment to our understanding of the effects of treatment on violence that would come from a comparative research approach of this kind would be worth many times the administrative cost of organizing and implementing a common research plan. Funding for pilot projects should be available for a period of four or five years at a minimum. It will take time to build up the service capacity required for successful operation of CCMPs and to move individual delinquents through rehabilitation programs. Several years of follow-up are also required in order to be reasonably certain of the impact of programs on recidivism by participants.

The political reality is, however, that few states or localities will undertake such a major restructuring of priorities, particularly on behalf of this population, without some extra incentives initially and some reasonable assurance of success. Certainly it is unlikely that a group of localities or states could pull themselves together into a common cooperative research endeavor without outside help. Encouragement in the form of supplemental financial assistance for pilot projects (whether through federal programs, foundations, or other sources) is no doubt required; although public concern about violent delinquency is at a peak, public concern is not easily translated into public dollars. As James Q. Wilson has observed, "That we do not devote . . . additional resources in a country obsessed with the crime problem is one of the more interesting illustrations of the maxim familiar to all political scientists, that one cannot predict public policy simply from knowing public attitudes."[18]

Conclusion

Juvenile violence is as confounding as it is disturbing. In spite of years of effort to find solutions to the problem, it appears to be getting no better, and possibly it is getting worse. The more we learn, the more complex we realize the problem to be, and the line that divides the violent juvenile from the nonviolent one remains obscure.

> Adolescents everywhere, from every walk of life, are often dangerous to themselves and to others. It may be a short step from distrusting authority to taking the law into one's own hands, from self-absorption to contempt for the rights of others, from group loyalty to gang warfare, from getting "kicks" to rampaging through the streets, from coveting material goods to stealing them, from feelings of rebellion to acts of destruction. Every suburban parent knows of parties that have turned into near riots. . . . Every insurance company executive

[18] Wilson, "Lock 'em Up," p. 47.

knows how dangerously adolescent boys drive. . . . Every newspaper reader knows how often bands of young people of all kinds commit destructive and dangerous acts.[19]

If we can be sure of anything, it is that juvenile violence will continue at some level in our society in spite of our best efforts to prevent it. That does not mean, however, that we should abandon the attempt to limit it or deal more effectively with it—only that we must be realistic in our expectations of what can be accomplished. No response will be effective with all violent delinquents, but we must continue the search for treatments that will work with some.

It is also certain that we cannot continue to turn our backs on those juveniles who present the highest risk of violence and still expect to make any real progress. The risk is only compounded when they are excluded from programs that might make some difference. Even if we have not succeeded in making model citizens out of most violent offenders in the past, that is no reason to reject approaches that might at least make them less destructive offenders in the future. Even small gains would be well worth the effort.

[19] President's Commission on Law Enforcement and the Administration of Justice, op. cit., p. 41.

Appendixes

Appendix A Summary of Data Collection in the Vera Institute Study

The Sample

The sample was drawn from delinquency petitions filed in 1974 in each of the three jurisdictions studied: Mercer County, New Jersey; Westchester County, New York; and New York County (Manhattan), New York. A 10 percent random sample was sought in each jurisdiction, although time and other factors caused the actual number to vary from that target. In Mercer County, 200 petitions were included in the sample, 8.4 percent of all petitions. In Westchester, 110 petitions were sampled, 17.3 percent of all petitions. And in Manhattan, 222 petitions were sampled, 10.5 percent of all petitions filed.

The period covered by the sample was calendar year 1974 in Westchester and Manhattan, but "court year" in Mercer County—September 1, 1973 through August 31, 1974.

Petitions in each county are assigned consecutive numbers by court clerks, in the order they are filed. A table of random numbers could therefore be used to identify petitions to be included in the sample. In a few cases, this procedure resulted in sampling two petitions for the same individual. When that occurred, the most recent petition was kept in the sample and a new case was included by taking the next number in the random numbers table.

Status Offenses in Mercer County

Prior to March 1974 delinquents and status offenders were charged under the same kind of petition in New Jersey. From March on, a new law required that they be separated. Consequently, delinquency petitions in Mercer for half of court-year 1974 (September through February) included individuals charged with status offenses. Some of these status offenders appeared in the Vera sample.

For the analysis in this report, however, all cases in which the most recent charge was a status offense (twenty-two cases out of two hundred) were dropped from the sample. The resulting sample of 178 petitions was about 8.6 percent of all *delinquency* petitions filed in court-year 1974 in Mercer County.

Comparison of the Sample to the Universe

Data on the characteristics of all children against whom petitions were filed in the sample year were not available in Manhattan or in Westchester County. Consequently, we can only assume that our samples were representative of the universe in those two counties. Since the sample was random and exceeded 10 percent in each case (10.4 percent in Manhattan, 17.3 percent in Westchester), the assumption seems reasonable.

In Mercer County, where the sample amounted to only 8.4 percent of petitions, information on the universe was available. Characteristics of the universe and the sample, in terms of sex, age, nature of offense charged, and disposition, are shown in Table 1-A. The comparison suggests that the sample was reasonably representative of the universe.

Racial Data

Court and probation records in Mercer and Westchester counties contained relatively complete information on the race of delinquents petitioned. In Manhattan, however, racial data were not available on seventy-two youths—roughly 32 percent of the sample.

To obtain more complete information on race in the Manhattan group, an estimation procedure was used in cases for which that information was missing. The youths' addresses were checked against

Table 1-A Comparison of the Vera Sample and All Petitions Filed in Mercer County, Court Year 1974 (figures in percent)

	Sampled Petitions	All Petitions
Sex	($N = 200$)	($N = 2363$)
Male	81.0	80.2
Female	19.0	19.8
Age	($N = 197$)	($N = 2363$)
Less than 100	0.5	1.5
10–11	5.6	3.1
12–13	12.2	12.1
14–15	33.0	32.4
16 and over	48.7	50.8
Offense Charged	($N = 220$)	($N = 3601$)
Murder	—	[a]
Robbery[b]	1.8	2.4
Assault[b]	10.5	8.8
Larceny	15.0	10.1
Burglary	13.2	12.6
Possess Stolen Property	6.4	4.4
Weapons Charges	2.3	2.3
Drugs	11.8	11.9
Morals	4.5	6.5
Status Offenses	13.6	14.5
Traffic/Vehicular	3.2	6.9
Other Crimes Against Persons	0.9	0.2
Other Property Crimes	6.8	6.1
Other Victimless Crimes	0.5	6.6
Attempts	3.6	1.4
Miscellaneous	5.9	5.2
Disposition	($N = 200$)	($N = 2731$)
Probation	33.0	30.5
Probation Continued	3.5	6.2
Charge Dismissed	29.0	26.9
Sentence Suspended	6.0	3.4
Placement	2.5	2.9
Other	26.0[c]	29.8

SOURCE: Mercer County Office of Probation and data from the Vera Violent Delinquent Study.

[a] N = 1, negligible percentage.

[b] Assault counted as the most serious offense in the Vera sample when both robbery and assault were charged. This may account for some of the small difference between the sample and the universe.

[c] 19.0 percent were adjourned in contemplation of dismissal.

census tract information. If the youth lived in a tract in which 95 percent or more of the population was black, the youth was assumed to be black. If he or she lived in a tract in which 90 percent or more of the population was white, we assumed the youth was white. If the census tract in which the youth lived was more racially mixed than 95 percent black or 90 percent white, his or her race was coded unknown.

This procedure was not applied to Spanish-surnamed youths. If race was not explicitly indicated in the file, youths with Spanish surnames were coded as such.

This estimation procedure yielded racial data on an additional twenty-seven cases, providing racial data for a total of 79.7 percent of the Manhattan sample.

Socioeconomic Status

Information on socioeconomic status (SES) was not readily discernible from court and probation files. To obtain it, census tract data were used again. The median income of the census tract in which the youth lived was taken as representative of his or her family income. Income was then converted into an SES level by the following formulas based on information from the U.S. Department of Labor regarding income for families of four persons:

Westchester and Mercer counties:
  Lower SES = less than $9,198
  Middle SES = $9,198–$20,776
  Upper SES = $20,777 or greater
Manhattan:
  Lower SES = less than $9,852
  Middle SES = $9,852–$25,469
  Upper SES = $25,470 or greater

Additional Data

Additional data regarding court outcomes and dispositions, not presented in the text, are given in Tables 2-A through 6-A.

Table 2-A Outcome of Most Recent Petition by the Nature of the Charge (Violent or Non-Violent) (figures in percent)

Outcome	Westchester[a] (N = 109)		Mercer[b] (N = 178)		Manhattan[c] (N = 219)		Total[d] (N = 507)	
	Violent Charge	Nonviolent Charge	Violent Charge	Nonviolent Charge	Violent Charge	Nonviolent Charge	Violent Charge	Nonviolent Charge
Adjudicated	36.7	45.6	40.0	68.2	16.5	11.2	25.5	42.3
Dismissed	20.0	10.1	56.7	23.0	45.9	50.7	42.8	30.4
Withdrawn	16.7	10.1	3.3	–	16.5	10.4	13.8	6.1
ACD	3.3	20.3	–	4.1	7.1	6.7	4.8	8.6
Transferred	20.0	8.9	–	2.7	4.8	3.6	6.9	4.5
To Another Petition	(20.0)	(8.9)	(–)	(–)	(2.4)	(2.2)	(5.5)	(2.8)
To Another Jurisdiction	(–)	(–)	(–)	(2.7)	(2.4)	(0.7)	(1.4)	(1.4)
PINS Petition Substituted	(–)	(–)	(–)	(–)	(–)	(0.7)	(–)	(0.3)
Pending	3.3	5.1	(–)	2.0	9.4	17.2	6.2	8.3
Total	100.0	100.1	100.0	100.0	100.2	99.8	100.0	100.2

SOURCE: Vera Institute Violent Delinquent Study.

[a] Chi square = 9.22; df = 5; p < 0.1004.
[b] Chi square = 20.59; df = 5; p < 0.0010.
[c] Chi square = 6.66; df = 7; p < 0.4656.
[d] Chi square = 24.98; df = 7; p < 0.0008.

Table 3-A Outcome of Most Recent Petition by Number of Times Ever Arrested for a Violent Offense
(figure in percent)

Outcome	Westchester[a]			Mercer[b]			Manhattan[c]			Total[d]		
	0 (N=68)	1 (N=33)	2+ (N=18)	0 (N=118)	1 (N=44)	2+ (N=16)	0 (N=100)	1 (N=74)	2+ (N=46)	0 (N=287)	1 (N=151)	2+ (N=70)
Adjudicated	42.6	42.4	50.0	69.5	52.3	50.0	11.0	14.9	17.4	42.9	31.8	28.6
Dismissed	10.3	21.2	—	19.5	45.5	50.0	51.0	47.3	45.7	28.2	41.1	41.4
Withdrawn	10.3	18.2	—	—	2.3	—	10.0	14.9	15.2	5.9	11.9	10.0
ACD	22.1	6.1	—	5.1	—	—	7.0	8.1	4.3	9.8	5.3	2.9
Transferred	10.3	9.1	37.5	3.4	—	—	3.0	5.4	4.3	4.8	4.6	7.1
To Another Petition	(10.3)	(9.1)	(37.5)	(—)	(—)	(—)	(1.0)	(2.7)	(4.3)	(2.8)	(3.3)	(7.1)
To Another Jurisdiction	(—)	(—)	(—)	(3.4)	(—)	(—)	(1.0)	(2.7)	(—)	(1.7)	(1.3)	(—)
PINS Petition Substituted	(—)	(—)	(—)	(—)	(—)	(—)	(1.0)	(—)	(—)	(0.3)	(—)	(—)
Pending	4.4	3.0	12.5	2.5	—	—	18.0	9.5	13.0	8.4	5.3	10.0
Total	100.0	100.0	100.0	100.0	100.1	100.0	100.0	100.1	99.9	100.0	100.0	100.0

SOURCE: Vera Institute Violent Delinquent Study.

NOTE: Significance calculated on the basis of 0-5 violent offenses, instead of collapsed categories in this table.

[a] Chi square = 17.74; df = 15; p < 0.2767.
[b] Chi square = 23.37; df = 20; p < 0.2708.
[c] Chi square = 31.63; df = 35; p < 0.6314.
[d] Chi square = 40.87; df = 35; p < 0.02284.

Table 4-A Disposition of Most Recent Petition by Character of Charge (Violent or Non-Violent) (figures in percent)

Disposition	Westchester[a]		Mercer[b]		Manhattan[c]		Total	
	Violent (N = 11)	Nonviolent (N = 36)	Violent (N = 12)	Nonviolent (N = 101)	Violent (N = 14)	Nonviolent (N = 15)	Violent (N = 37)	Nonviolent (N = 152)
Placed	27.3	8.3	8.3	4.0	28.6	20.0	21.6	6.6
Probation	27.3	7.2	25.0	54.5	28.6	40.0	27.0	51.3
Probation	(18.2)	(36.1)	(15.7)	(44.6)	(28.6)	(40.0)	(21.6)	(42.1)
Continue Probation	(–)	(2.8)	(–)	(6.9)	(–)	(–)	(–)	(5.2)
Probation with Conditions	(9.1)	(8.3)	(3.3)	(3.0)	(–)	(–)	(5.4)	(3.9)
Released	9.1	27.8	50.0	29.7	35.7	20.0	32.4	28.3
ACD	(9.1)	(19.4)	(50.0)	(29.7)	(–)	(–)	(18.9)	(24.3)
Dismissed	(–)	(2.8)	(–)	(–)	(28.6)	(13.3)	(10.8)	(1.9)
Dismissed with Conditions	(–)	(2.8)	(–)	(–)	(–)	(–)	(–)	(0.7)
Withdrawn	(–)	(2.8)	(–)	(–)	(–)	(–)	(–)	(0.7)
Paroled to Guardian	(–)	(–)	(–)	(–)	(7.1)	(6.7)	(2.7)	(0.7)
Suspended Sentence	9.1	–	15.7	9.9	–	–	8.1	6.6
Transferred	9.1	11.2	–	1.0	–	6.7	2.7	4.0
New Petition	(9.1)	(5.6)	(–)	(1.0)	(–)	(–)	(2.7)	(2.0)
New Jurisdiction	(–)	(5.6)	(–)	(–)	(7.1)	(6.7)	(–)	(2.0)
Pending	18.2	5.6	–	1.0	7.1	13.3	8.1	3.3
Total	100.1	100.1	100.0	100.1	100.0	100.0	99.9	100.1

SOURCE: Vera Institute Violent Delinquent Study.

[a] Chi square = 10.60; $df = 11$; $p < 0.4772$.

[b] Chi square = 6.26; $df = 7$; $p < 0.5098$.

[c] Chi square = 2.51; $df = 5$; $p < 0.7748$.

Table 5-A Disposition of Most Recent Petition by Number of Arrests for Violent Offenses (figures in percent)

Disposition	Westchester[a]			Mercer[b]			Manhattan[c]			Total		
	0 (N=29)	1 (N=14)	2+ (N=4)	0 (N=82)	1 (N=23)	2+ (N=8)	0 (N=11)	1 (N=11)	2+ (N=8)	0 (N=122)	1 (N=48)	2+ (N=20)
Placed	10.3	7.1	50.0	1.2	13.0	12.5	18.2	9.1	50.0	4.9	10.4	35.0
Probation	37.8	57.1	25.0	56.1	43.5	25.0	45.5	27.3	37.5	50.8	43.8	30.0
Continue Probation	(24.1)	(50.0)	(25.0)	(50.0)	(17.4)	(25.0)	(45.5)	(27.3)	(37.5)	(43.4)	(29.2)	(30.0)
Probation with Conditions	(3.4)	(–)	(–)	(3.7)	(17.4)	(–)	(–)	(–)	(–)	(3.3)	(8.3)	(–)
Probation	(10.3)	(7.1)	(–)	(2.4)	(8.7)	(–)	(–)	(–)	(–)	(4.1)	(6.3)	(0.0)
Released	30.9	14.3	–	34.1	30.4	12.5	27.3	36.4	12.5	32.8	27.1	10.0
ACD	(20.7)	(14.3)	(–)	(34.1)	(30.4)	(12.5)	(–)	(–)	(–)	(27.9)	(18.8)	(5.0)
Dismissed	(3.4)	(–)	(–)	(–)	(–)	(–)	(18.2)	(36.4)	(–)	(2.5)	(8.3)	(–)
Dismissed with Conditions	(3.4)	(–)	(–)	(–)	(–)	(–)	(–)	(–)	(–)	(0.8)	(–)	(–)
Withdrawn	(3.4)	(–)	(–)	(–)	(–)	(–)	(–)	(–)	(–)	(0.8)	(–)	(–)
Paroled to Guardian	(–)	(–)	(–)	(–)	(–)	(–)	(9.1)	(–)	(12.5)	(0.8)	(–)	(5.0)

SOURCE: Vera Institute Violent Delinquent Study.

NOTE: Significance calculated on basis of 0-5 arrests for violent crimes instead of clustered figures in tables.

[a] Chi square = 22.02; df = 33; p < 0.9271.
[b] Chi square = 58.95; df = 28; p < 0.0006.
[c] Chi square = 24.01; df = 20; p < 0.2421.

(continued on next page)

Table 5-A Disposition of Most Recent Petition by Number of Arrests for Violent Offenses (figures in percent) (cont'd)

Disposition	Westchester [a]			Mercer [b]			Manhattan [c]			Total		
	0 (N=29)	1 (N=14)	2+ (N=4)	0 (N=82)	1 (N=23)	2+ (N=8)	0 (N=11)	1 (N=11)	2+ (N=8)	0 (N=122)	1 (N=48)	2+ (N=20)
Suspended Sentence	–	7.1	–	6.1	13.0	50.0	–	–	–	4.1	8.3	20.0
Transferred	13.8	7.1	–	1.2	–	–	9.1	–	–	5.0	2.1	–
To New Petition	(6.9)	(7.1)	(–)	(1.2)	(–)	(–)	(–)	(–)	(–)	(2.5)	(2.1)	(–)
To New Jurisdiction	(6.9)	(–)	(–)	(–)	(–)	(–)	(9.1)	(–)	(–)	(2.5)	(–)	(–)
Pending	6.9	7.1	25.0	1.2	–	–	–	27.3	–	2.5	8.3	5.0
Total	99.7	99.8	100.0	99.9	99.9	100.0	100.1	100.1	100.0	100.1	100.0	100.0

Table 6-A Proportion of Sample Receiving Each Disposition, by Level of Total Seriousness of Up to Six Offenses[a] (figures in percent)

Disposition	Westchester County[b]					Mercer County[c]				
	I (N=4)	II (N=7)	III (N=12)	IV (N=12)	V (N=11)	I (N=24)	II (N=31)	III (N=19)	IV (N=15)	V (N=24)
Placed	—	—	8.3	33.3	9.1	—	—	—	13.3	12.5
Probation	25.0	14.3	41.7	41.7	63.7	20.8	70.9	68.4	60.0	37.6
Probation	(—)	(14.3)	(25.0)	(41.7)	(45.5)	(20.8)	(64.5)	(47.4)	(40.0)	(29.2)
Continue Probation	(—)	(—)	(—)	(—)	(9.1)	(—)	(3.2)	(10.5)	(20.0)	(4.2)
Probation with Conditions	(25.0)	(—)	(16.7)	(—)	(9.1)	(—)	(3.2)	(10.5)	(—)	(4.2)
Released	25.0	57.2	33.3	8.3	9.1	79.2	29.0	21.1	13.3	8.3
ACD	(25.0)	(28.6)	(25.0)	(8.3)	(9.1)	(79.2)	(29.0)	(21.1)	(13.3)	(8.3)
Dismissed	(—)	(14.3)	(—)	(—)	(—)	(—)	(—)	(—)	(—)	(—)
Dismissed with Conditions	(—)	(14.3)	(—)	(—)	(—)	(—)	(—)	(—)	(—)	(—)
Withdrawn	(—)	(—)	(8.3)	(—)	(—)	(—)	(—)	(—)	(—)	(—)
Paroled to Guardian	(—)	(—)	(—)	(—)	(—)	(—)	(—)	(—)	(—)	(—)
Suspended Sentence	25.0	—	—	—	—	—	—	5.3	13.3	37.5
Transferred	25.0	28.6	8.3	8.3	—	—	—	—	—	4.2
To New Petition	(25.0)	(—)	(8.3)	(8.3)	(—)	(—)	(—)	(—)	(—)	(4.2)
To New Jurisdiction	(—)	(28.6)	(—)	(—)	(—)	(—)	(—)	(—)	(—)	(—)
Pending	—	—	8.3	8.3	18.2	—	—	5.3	—	—
Total	100.0	100.1	99.9	99.9	100.1	100.0	99.9	100.1	99.9	100.1

SOURCE: Vera Institute Violent Delinquent Study.

[a] Seriousness levels: I = 1-199; II = 200-399; III = 400-699; IV = 700-999; V = 1000+.

[b] Chi square = 58.88; df = 44; $p < 0.0661$.

[c] Chi square = 83.13; df = 28; $p < 0.0000$.

[d] Chi square = 26.90; df = 20; $p < 0.1381$.

(continued on next page)

Table 6-A Proportion of Sample Receiving Each Disposition, by Level of Total Seriousness of Up to Six Offenses[a] (figures in percent) (cont'd)

Disposition	Manhattan[d]					Total				
	I (N=4)	II (N=3)	III (N=9)	IV (N=1)	V (N=13)	I (N=32)	II (N=41)	III (N=40)	IV (N=28)	V (N=48)
Placed	–	–	11.1	–	46.2	–	–	5.0	21.4	20.8
Probation	50.0	66.7	22.2	100.0	30.8	25.0	60.8	50.0	53.6	41.7
Probation	(50.0)	(66.7)	(22.2)	(100.0)	(30.8)	(21.9)	(56.1)	(35.0)	(42.9)	(33.3)
Continue Probation	(–)	(–)	(–)	(–)	(–)	(–)	(2.4)	(5.0)	(10.7)	(4.2)
Probation with Conditions	(–)	(–)	(–)	(–)	(–)	(3.1)	(2.4)	(10.0)	(–)	(4.2)
Released	50.0	–	55.5	–	7.7	68.8	31.6	32.5	10.7	8.4
ACD	(–)	(–)	(–)	–	(–)	(62.5)	(26.8)	(17.5)	(10.7)	(6.3)
Dismissed	(50.0)	(–)	(44.4)	–	(–)	(6.3)	(–)	(10.0)	(–)	(–)
Dismissed with Conditions	(–)	(–)	(–)	–	(–)	(–)	(2.4)	(2.5)	(–)	(–)
Withdrawn	(–)	(–)	(–)	–	(–)	(–)	(2.4)	(2.5)	(–)	(–)
Paroled to Guardian	(–)	(–)	(11.1)	–	(7.7)	(–)	(–)	(–)	(–)	(2.1)
Suspended Sentence	–	–	–	–	–	3.1	–	2.5	7.1	18.8
Transferred	–	33.3	–	–	–	3.1	7.3	2.5	3.6	2.1
To New Petition	(–)	(–)	(–)	–	(–)	(3.1)	(–)	(2.5)	(3.6)	(2.1)
To New Jurisdiction	(–)	(33.3)	(–)	(–)	(–)	(–)	(7.3)	(–)	(–)	(–)
Pending	–	–	11.1	–	15.4	–	–	7.5	3.6	8.3
Total	100.0	100.0	99.9	100.0	100.1	100.0	99.8	100.0	100.0	100.1

Appendix B Vera Institute Study Research Instrument

A. *Identification*   Card ☐1 1
    1. Case ID: ☐ ☐ ☐ 2–4
    2. Location: ☐ 5
       1. Westchester
       2. Mercer
       3. New York
    3. Docket or charge #: ☐ ☐ ☐ ☐ ☐ 6–10
    4. Central file #: _____
    5. Current charge: _____
B. *Demographic Information*
    1. Sex: ☐ 11
       1. male
       2. female
    2. Race: ☐ 12
       1. black
       2. white
       3. Spanish surname
       4. other
       X. unknown

3. Religion: ☐ 13
    1. Catholic
    2. Protestant
    3. Jewish   5. none
    4. other   X. unknown

4. Date of birth: ☐ ☐ ☐ ☐ ☐ ☐ 14–19
               mo.   day   yr.

5. Place of birth: ☐ 20
    1. same as current residence
    2. same state, different town
    3. Southern state
    4. other (non-Southern) state
    5. foreign country
    6. Puerto Rico
    7. unknown

6. Current address: _____
                        block   street

                      _____
                       city or town   state

7. Socioeconomic level: ☐ 21
    1. lower
    2. middle
    3. upper
    X. unknown

8. ☐ 22
    1. urban
    2. suburban
    3. rural

C. *Family Situation*
    1. Parents living: Mother ☐ Father ☐
                             23   24

        1. alive
        2. deceased
        X. unknown

    2. Mother's age at subject's birth: ☐ ☐ 25–26
                                     yrs.

    3. Current marital status of parents: ☐ 27
        1. married   4. divorced
        2. common law   5. widowed
        3. separated   X. unknown

4. If separated, divorced or widowed,
   give subject's age at time of event: ☐ ☐ 28–29
   (blank if not applicable; X if   yrs.
   unknown)
5. Number of natural siblings: ☐ 30
   (10 or more code 0; blank
   if none)

                                    31   32
6. Parents' occupations: Mother ☐   Father ☐
      1. professional or managerial
      2. manufacturing or construction
      3. civil service
      4. domestic service, cleaning, other unskilled
      5. clerical
      6. self-employed
      7. unemployed
      8. retired
      9. other (specify) _____
      X. unknown
7. Child *currently* lives with: ☐ ☐ 33–34
      1. mother and father   9. father & relative
      2. mother only   10. relatives only (specify)
      3. father only   _____
      4. mother & stepfather   11. other adults
      5. father & stepmother   12. legal foster home
      6. mother & paramour   13. group residence
      7. father & paramour   14. alone
      8. mother & relative   15. other (specify) _____
                                _____
         X. unknown   16. institution
8. Number of siblings living with subject: ☐ 35
   (10 or more code 0; unknown code X)
9. Source of family income: ☐ 36
      1. one parent or guardian working (lives with 2)
      2. one parent or guardian working (lives with only 1)
      3. both parents (guardians) working
      4. public assistance
      5. income from other relatives
      6. other _____
      7. working plus other income (specify) _____
      X. unknown

10. If child has *not always* lived in current
situation, give total number of months
living in current situation: ☐ ☐ ☐ 37–39

11. If child has *not always* lived in current
situation, indicate all former living
situations beginning with most recent
previous one and working back (use same
codes as in 7. above):

    a. from ☐ ☐ ☐ ☐ to ☐ ☐ ☐ ☐ 40–47
        mo. yr.   mo. yr.
    child lived with ☐ ☐   48–49

    b. from ☐ ☐ ☐ ☐ to ☐ ☐ ☐ ☐ 50–57
        mo. yr.   mo. yr.
    child lived with ☐ ☐   58–59

    c. from ☐ ☐ ☐ ☐ to ☐ ☐ ☐ ☐ 60–67
        mo. yr.   mo. yr.
    child lived with ☐ ☐   68–69

    d. from ☐ ☐ ☐ ☐ to ☐ ☐ ☐ ☐ 70–77
        mo. yr.   mo. yr.
    child lived with ☐ ☐   78–79

                    Card ☐2☐ 1
              Case ID No. ☐ ☐ ☐ 2–4

    e. from ☐ ☐ ☐ ☐ to ☐ ☐ ☐ ☐ 5–12
        mo. yr.   mo. yr.
    child lived with ☐ ☐   13–14

    f. applicable but unavailable (X)   ☐ 15

12. Number of addresses in past 10 years: ☐ 16
    (10 or more use code 0; unknown use X)

13. Length of time at current address: ☐ ☐ 17–18
    (99 or more months, code 99)

14. Does the record indicate evidence of neglect
or abuse of the subject?   ☐ 19
    1. yes
    2. no
    X. unknown
    If yes, specify dates, source of evidence, details.

_____

_____

_____

_____

15. Do (did) the parents or significant guardians have any history of the following (1 = definitely; 2 = suggested; 3 = no; X = unknown)?

	Mother	Father	Significant Guardian
Drug abuse	☐ 20	☐ 27	☐ 34
Alcoholism	☐ 21	☐ 28	☐ 35
Mental illness	☐ 22	☐ 29	☐ 36
Criminal behavior	☐ 23	☐ 30	☐ 37
Serious illness	☐ 24	☐ 31	☐ 38
Violent behavior	☐ 25	☐ 32	☐ 39
Other _____	☐ 26	☐ 33	☐ 40

16. How many, if any, of the subject's siblings have ever come before family or juvenile court?
    (10 or more code 0; none leave blank; unknown code X)   ☐ 41

D. *Court/Arrest Record*

1. Age at first arrest   ☐ ☐ 42–43
   Age at first petition   ☐ ☐ 44–45
2. Has the child ever absconded from placement?   ☐ 46
   1. yes   2. no   X. unknown
3. Total number of arrests   ☐ ☐ 47–48
   Total number of petitions ☐ ☐ 49–50
4. Total number of charges:
   Total status offenses   ☐ ☐ 51–52
   Total victimless crimes ☐ ☐ 53–54
   Total property crimes ☐ ☐ 55–56
   Total crimes against persons ☐ ☐ 57–58
      5. Total times found (or pleaded) guilty ☐ ☐ 59–60
      Total times found not guilty   ☐ ☐ 61–62
      Total times dismissed or ACD   ☐ ☐ 63–64
      Total times withdrawn petition   ☐ ☐ 65–66
      Total times adjusted other ways   ☐ ☐ 67–68
6. Total seriousness of crimes (guilties and   ☐ ☐ ☐ 69–71
   adjustments only—see coding instructions)
7. Total number of times on probation ☐ 72
   Total months on probation   ☐ ☐ 73–74
8. Total times in placement   ☐ 75
   Total months in placement   ☐ ☐ 76–77

E. *Current Charge*
    1. Offenses currently charged: Description _____

        _____

        Penal code numbers: _____
        Total number of offenses charged   ☐ 78
          (code 0 if 10 or more)
        Type of most serious offense   ☐ ☐ 79–80
          (see code sheet for codes)

                                  Card ☐3☐ 1
                          Case ID No. ☐ ☐ ☐ 2–4
        Date of current charge   ☐ ☐ ☐ ☐ ☐ ☐ 5–10
                       mo.   day   yr.
    2. Age at target arrest: ☐ ☐ ☐ ☐ 11–14
                               yrs.   mos.
    3. Most significant complainant: ☐ 15
        (codes listed below in order of
        significance)
        1. member of imme- 6. probation officer
          diate family   7. school authority
        2. other relative   8. other (specify) _____
        3. acquaintance   _____
        4. stranger   X. unknown
        5. police
    4. Number of associates (10 or more code 0):   ☐ 16
    5. Give details of case: _____

        _____

        _____

        _____

        _____

        _____

    6. If a personal assault, what was the extent of
       the injury?   ☐ 17
        1. no injury   4. required hospitalization
        2. minor injury   5. fatal
        3. treated by doctor   X. unknown
          and released
    7. Was the subject: 1. released   ☐ 18
                     2. remanded to nonsecure facility
                     3. held in custody
                     4. other (specify) _____
                     X. unknown

If held in custody or remanded to nonsecure facility,
was it: 1. before preliminary hearing
               2. after preliminary hearing   ☐ 19
               3. both

8. Outcome of the charge: _____ ☐ 20

    (see code sheet for code)

                                                          ☐R 21
9. If withdrawn or dismissed, give reason: ☐ 22

    (see code sheet for code)
10. Disposition: _____ ☐ ☐ 23–24
    (see code sheet for code)
11. If refused placement, give reason: ☐ 25

    (see code sheet for code)
    Number of times refused placement: ☐ ☐ 26–27
12. Kind of weapon found on subject: ☐ 28
    1. no weapon
    2. gun
    3. knife
    4. bludgeon, brass knuckles, other instruments
    5. other (specify) _____
    X. unknown
13. If a weapon was found, was it used?   ☐ 29
    1. yes
    2. no
    X. unknown
14. Was force or violence used in the crime?   ☐ 30
    1. no force or violence
    2. unprovoked force or violence
    3. provoked force or violence
    X. unknown
    If the answer was 2 or 3, give details of the violent actions: ____
_____
_____
_____

F. *Five Previous Arrests* (working back from most recent)
a. 1. Date: ☐ ☐ ☐ ☐ ☐ ☐ 31–36
               mo.   day   yr.
    2. Age: ☐ ☐ ☐ ☐ 37–40
            yrs.   mos.

3. Offenses charged: _____

   Penal code numbers: _____

   Most serious offense charged: ☐ ☐ 41–42

     (see code sheet for codes)

4. Most significant complainant: ☐ 43

     (use same codes as in E.3.)

5. Number of associates (10 or more code 0):   ☐ 44

6. If an index crime or assault, give details:

   _____

   _____

   _____

   _____

7. If personal assault, extent of injury: ☐ 45

     (use same codes as in E.6.)

8. Outcome of the charge: _____ ☐ 46

     (see code sheet for code)

   If withdrawn or dismissed, give reason: ☐ 47

   _____

     (see code sheet for code)

9. Disposition: _____ ☐ ☐ 48–49

     (see code sheet for code)

10. If refused placement, give reason: ☐ 50

   _____

     (see code sheet for code)

   Number of times refused placement: ☐ ☐ 51–52

11. Kind of weapon found on subject: ☐ 53

     (use same codes as in E.12.)

12. If a weapon was found, was it used?   ☐ 54

     1. yes

     2. no

     X. unknown

13. Was force or violence used in the crime?   ☐ 55

     1. no force or violence

     2. unprovoked force or violence

     3. provoked force or violence

     X. unknown

   If the answer was 2 or 3, give details of the violent actions: ____

   _____

   _____

   _____

b.   1. Date: ☐ ☐ ☐ ☐ ☐ ☐   56–61

             mo.   day   yr.

2. Age: ☐ ☐ ☐ ☐ 62–65
     yrs.   mos.

3. Offenses charged: _____
   Penal code numbers: _____
   Most serious offense charged: ☐ ☐ 66–67
     (see code sheet for codes)

4. Most significant complainant: ☐ 68
     (use same codes as in E.3)

5. Number of associates (10 or more code 0):   ☐ 69

6. If an index crime or assault, give details:

_____

_____

_____

_____

7. If personal assault, extent of injury: ☐ 70
     (use same codes as in E.6.)

8. Outcome of the charge: _____ ☐ 71
     (see code sheet for code)
   If withdrawn or dismissed, give reason: ☐ 72

_____

     (see code sheet for code)

9. Disposition: _____ ☐ ☐ 73–74
     (see code sheet for code)

10. If refused placement, give reason: ☐ 75

_____

     (see code sheet for code)
   Number of times refused placement: ☐ ☐ 76–77

11. Kind of weapon found on subject: ☐ 78
     (use same codes as in E.12.)

12. If a weapon was found, was it used?   ☐ 79
     1. yes
     2. no
     X. unknown

13. Was force or violence used in the crime?   ☐ 80
     1. no force or violence
     2. unprovoked force or violence
     3. provoked force or violence
     X. unknown
   If the answer was 2 or 3, give details of the violent actions: _____

_____

_____

Card ☑4 1

Case ID No. ☐ ☐ ☐ 2–4

c. 1. Date: ☐ ☐ ☐ ☐ ☐ ☐ 5–10
                mo. day yr.

2. Age: ☐ ☐ ☐ ☐ 11–14
          yrs. mos.

3. Offenses charged: _____

   Penal code numbers: _____

   Most serious offense charged: ☐ ☐ 15–16
     (see code sheet for codes)

4. Most significant complainant: ☐ 17
     (use same codes as in E.3.)

5. Number of associates (10 or more code 0):   ☐ 18

6. If an index crime or assault, give details:

_____

_____

_____

7. If personal assault, extent of injury: ☐ 19
     (use same codes as in E.6.)

8. Outcome of the charge: _____ ☐ 20
     (see code sheet for code)

   If withdrawn or dismissed, give reason: ☐ 21

_____

   (see code sheet for code)

9. Disposition: _____ ☐ ☐ 22–23
     (see code sheet for code)

10. If refused placement, give reason: ☐ 24

_____

   (see code sheet for code)

   Number of times refused placement: ☐ ☐ 25–26

11. Kind of weapon found on subject: ☐ 27
     (use same codes as in E.12.)

12. If a weapon was found, was it used?   ☐ 28
     1. yes
     2. no
     X. unknown

13. Was force or violence used in the crime?   ☐ 29
       1. no force or violence
       2. unprovoked force or violence
       3. provoked force or violence
       X. unknown

If the answer was 2 or 3, give details of violent actions: ____

_____

_____

_____

d. 1. Date: ☐ ☐ ☐ ☐ ☐ ☐ 30–35
              mo. day yr.

    2. Age: ☐ ☐ ☐ ☐ 36–39
             yrs. mos.

    3. Offenses charged: _____
       Penal code numbers: _____
       Most serious offense charged: ☐ ☐ 40–41
         (see code sheet for codes)

    4. Most significant complainant: ☐ 42
       (use same codes as in E.3.)

    5. Number of associates (10 or more code 0): ☐ 43

    6. If an index crime or assault, give details:

_____

_____

_____

    7. If personal assault, extent of injury: ☐ 44
       (use same codes as in E.6.)

    8. Outcome of the charge: _____ ☐ 45
       (see code sheet for codes)
       If withdrawn or dismissed, give reason: ☐ 46

_____

       (see code sheet for codes)

    9. Disposition: _____ ☐ ☐ 47–48
       (see code sheet for codes)

   10. If refused placement, give reason: ☐ 49

_____

       (see code sheet for code)
       Number of times refused placement: ☐ ☐ 50–51

   11. Kind of weapon found on subject: ☐ 52
       (same codes as in E.12.)

   12. If weapon was found, was it used?   ☐ 53
       1. yes
       2. no
       X. unknown

13. Was force or violence used in the crime? ☐ 54
    1. no force or violence
    2. unprovoked force or violence
    3. provoked force or violence
    X. unknown
    If the answer was 2 or 3, give details of violent actions: ____
    _____
    _____
    _____
    _____

e. 1. Date: ☐ ☐ ☐ ☐ ☐ ☐ 55–60
         mo. day yr.
  2. Age: ☐ ☐ ☐ ☐ 61–64
       yrs. mos.
  3. Offenses charged: _____
    Penal code numbers: _____
    Most serious offense charged: ☐ ☐ 65–66
    (see code sheet for code)
  4. Most significant complainant: ☐ 67
    (use same codes as in E.3.)
  5. Number of associates (10 or more code 0): ☐ 68
  6. If an index crime or assault, give details:
    _____
    _____
  7. If personal assault, extent of injury: ☐ 69
    (use same codes as in E.6.)
  8. Outcome of the charge: _____ ☐ 70
    (see code sheet for codes)
    If withdrawn or dismissed, given reason: ☐ 71
    _____
    (see code sheet for code)
  9. Disposition: _____ ☐ ☐ 72–73
    (see code sheet for code)
  10. If refused placement, give reason: ☐ 74
    _____
    (see code sheet for code)
    Number of times refused placement: ☐ ☐ 75–76
  11. Kind of weapon found on subject: ☐ 77
    (use same codes as in E.12.)

12. If a weapon was found, was it used? ☐ 78
   1. yes
   2. no
   X. unknown
13. Was force or violence used in the crime? ☐ 79
   1. no force or violence
   2. unprovoked force or violence
   3. provoked force or violence
   X. unknown
If the answer was 2 or 3, give details of violent actions: _____
_____
_____
_____
_____

Card ⑤ 1
Case ID No. ☐ ☐ ☐ 2–4

G. *Health Record* (source _____)
1. Has the child ever had any major physical
illnesses? ☐ 5
   1. yes
   2. no
   X. unknown
   If yes, give details: _____
_____

2. Is the child currently under regular outpatient care for physical illness? ☐ 6
   1. yes
   2. no
   X. unknown
   If yes, give details: _____
_____

3. Has the child ever been examined by a
psychiatrist or psychologist? ☐ 7
   1. yes
   2. no
   X. unknown
4. If the answer to 3. above was *yes*, list for each
examination, beginning with most recent, the child's
age at examination and the diagnosis (see code
sheet for diagnosis codes):

8–11
a. age ☐ ☐ ☐ ☐ ; diagnosis ☐ ☐ 12–13 _____
    yrs.   mos.
14–17
b. age ☐ ☐ ☐ ☐ ; diagnosis ☐ ☐ 18–19 _____
    yrs.   mos.
20–23
c. age ☐ ☐ ☐ ☐ ; diagnosis ☐ ☐ 24–25 _____
    yrs.   mos.

5. Is the child currently under regular outpatient
care for psychiatric problems?   ☐ 26
    1. yes
    2. no
    X. unknown

                    27–28
If yes, give diagnosis: ☐ ☐ _____

6. Has the child ever been hospitalized for psychiatric
problems?   ☐ 29
    1. yes
    2. no
    X. unknown

If yes, list for each hospitalization the institution, length of stay,
and diagnosis, beginning with most recent:
    a. Institution _____
       from ☐ ☐ ☐ ☐ to ☐ ☐ ☐ ☐ 30–37
          mo. yr.   mo. yr.
       diagnosis ☐ ☐ _____
         38–39
    b. Institution _____
       from ☐ ☐ ☐ ☐ to ☐ ☐ ☐ ☐ 40–47
          mo. yr.   mo. yr.
       diagnosis ☐ ☐ _____
         48–49
    c. Institution _____
       from ☐ ☐ ☐ ☐ to ☐ ☐ ☐ ☐ 50–57
          mo. yr.   mo. yr.
       diagnosis ☐ ☐ _____
         58–59
    d. applicable but unavailable   ☐ (X) 60

7. Is there evidence of brain damage or other neurological impairment?   ☐ 61

1. yes
2. no
X. unknown
If yes, specify: _____

_____

8. Is the child known to use any of the following?:
   1. yes, currently   heroin   ☐ 62
   2. yes, but not currently   cocaine   ☐ 63
   3. no   marijuana   ☐ 64
   X. unknown   pills   ☐ 65
                    glue   ☐ 66
                    hallucinogens   ☐ 67
                    alcohol   ☐ 68
                    other (specify)   ☐ 69

9. Are there statements or other evidence in the
   file that indicate that the subject is   ☐ 70
   1. not a violent person
   2. a violent person
   3. mixed conclusions
         Source _____

H. *School Record* (source _____)
   1. Most recent IQ ☐ ☐ ☐ 71–73
      Date tested ☐ ☐ ☐ ☐ 74–77
               mo.   yr.
      If IQ has changed from former tests, in what
      direction?   ☐ 78
      1. increased slightly
      2. increased significantly
      3. decreased slightly
      4. decreased significantly
   2. Current grade level   ☐ ☐ 79–80
                      Card ☐6☐ 1
                 Case ID No. ☐ ☐ ☐ 2–4
   3. Note any special information about academic performance (e.g.,
      reading and math levels, if available):
      _____
      _____
      _____
      _____

   4. How many times has the subject dropped out of
      school?   ☐ 5

(if never, leave blank; 10 or more code 0)

5. If subject *has* dropped out of school, for each
occasion list grade level and dates out of school:
   a. From ☐ ☐ ☐ ☐ to ☐ ☐ ☐ ☐ ; gr. level ☐ ☐ 6–15
             mo. yr.   mo. yr.
   b. From ☐ ☐ ☐ ☐ to ☐ ☐ ☐ ☐ ; gr. level ☐ ☐ 16–25
             mo. yr.   mo. yr.
   c. From ☐ ☐ ☐ ☐ to ☐ ☐ ☐ ☐ ; gr. level ☐ ☐ 26–35
             mo. yr.   mo. yr.
   d. From ☐ ☐ ☐ ☐ to ☐ ☐ ☐ ☐ ; gr. level ☐ ☐ 36–45
             mo. yr.   mo. yr.
   e. Applicable but unavailable   ☐ (X) 46

6. Has special schooling ever been arranged for the
subject?   ☐ 47
   1. yes
   2. no
   X. unknown

If yes, give dates, descriptions of schooling, and child's grade level
at time schooling was arranged:

_____

_____

_____

7. Have special learning disabilities been diagnosed? ☐ 48
   1. yes
   2. no
   X. unknown
   If yes, describe: _____

   _____

I. *Subjective Appraisal*
   1. Overall, on the basis of the evidence in the file,
      would you regard this individual to be:
      1. violent
      2. not violent   ☐ 49

Appendix C The Sellin-Wolfgang Seriousness Scale

The method of scoring offenses for seriousness used in this study is based on methods developed by Thorsten Sellin and Marvin E. Wolfgang, described in detail in their book *The Measurement of Delinquency* (New York: John Wiley & Sons, 1964).

For offenses involving injury, theft, damage, or a combination of these elements (called index offenses) the basic Sellin-Wolfgang scoring system was applied. A weight was given to each element in the offense, as shown in Table 1-C.

The total score was then computed by summing the weights of each element in the offense and multiplying the result by 100.

For attempts at index offenses (e.g., attempted rape, robbery, burglary), a score for intimidation and premises forcibly entered was computed. Then a score of 1 was added, and the total multiplied by 100. Thus an attempted robbery with a gun would be scored: 4 (intimidation by weapon) + 1 (attempt) = 5 × 100 = 500.

In the case of index offenses for which no details were available in the court and probation records, a score based on the mean seriousness score of the same offense in the Philadelphia cohort study was assigned. Those mean seriousness scores are given in Table 2-C.

Nonindex offense scores (offenses that did not involve injury, theft, damage, or a combination) and nonindex elements of crimes involving both types of illegal behavior were assigned a weighted score developed by Wolfgang and his colleagues at the University of Pennsylvania. The nonindex weights are given in Table 3-C. If the offense charged was not included in the list in Table 3-C, the score of the most similar offense in the list was assigned. (It should be noted that all narcotics offenses

Table 1-C Weights Used in Scoring Seriousness of Index Offenses

Element Scored	Number X Weight		Total
1	2	3	4
I. Number of victims of bodily harm			
(a) receiving minor injuries		1	
(b) treated and discharged		4	
(c) hospitalized		7	
(d) killed		26	
II. Number of victims of forcible sex inter-			
course		10	
(a) Number of such victims intimidated			
by weapon		2	
III. Intimidation (except II above)			
(a) Physical or verbal only		2	
(b) By weapon		4	
IV. Number of premises forcibly entered ...		1	
V. Number of motor vehicles stolen		2	
VI. Value of property stolen, damaged, or			
destroyed (in dollars)			
(a) Under $10		1	
(b) $10–250		2	
(c) $251–2,000		3	
(d) $2,001–9,000		4	
(e) $9,001–30,000		5	
(f) $30,001–80,000		6	
(g) Over $80,000		7	

TOTAL SCORE

SOURCE: Correspondence from Marvin E. Wolfgang.

were assigned the score for possession and sale of heroin in the Philadel-phia scale. The reason for this was that in the scale, developed more than a decade ago on the basis of subjective community evaluations of offense seriousness, heroin possession, use, and sale were considered to be less serious drug offenses than marijuana-related offenses. Because community knowledge and attitudes about the relative importance of heroin and marijuana have certainly changed since then, it was felt that the conservative course was to assign the lower score for all drug offenses.)

Some of the analysis in the Vera study required offenses to be grouped into clusters according to their levels of seriousness. The range of seriousness scores each of the four clusters and the crimes that fell into each range are shown in Table 4-C.

Table 2-C Mean Seriousness Scores by Philadelphia
Crime Code Classification

	Score for Juvenile Offenses	
Crime Classification	X	Standard Deviation
Homicide	2635.7	74.5
Rape	895.7	511.3
Robbery	315.9	188.5
Aggravated Assault	601.4	372.0
Burglary	250.8	95.13
Larceny-Theft	157.6	80.9
Auto Theft	262.0	125.3
Other Assaults	209.0	169.6

SOURCE: Correspondence from Marvin E. Wolfgang.

Table 3-C Nonindex Offenses

Offense	Score
Stolen Property	
Receiver	87
Weapons	
VUFA (illegal possession of a gun)	353
Other Firearms (misuse of gun, etc.)	31
Other Weapons (knife, etc.)	114
Commercial Sex	
Pandering	131
Bawdy House Proprietor	77
Bawdy House Inmate	146
Sodomy with a Prostitute	19
Sodomy/Pros/Solicit (intercourse)	148
Noncommercial Sex	
Incest (father-daughter)	220
Incest (brother-sister)	600
Corrupting	192
Sodomy (consent)	95
Sodomy (solicit)	356
Adultery	36
Fornication	1
Public Indecency	357
Enticing Minors	431
Statutory Rape	1

Table 3-C Nonindex Offenses (cont'd.)

Offense	Score
Narcotics Offenses (See explanation pages 243–244)	
Seller (heroin)	1010
Seller (marijuana)	1643
Possession (heroin)	141
Possession (marijuana)	1061
User (heroin)	113
User (marijuana)	477
Passing a Bad Check	207
Liquor Law	
Illegal Possession	40
Runs House with Sale	149
Drunkenness	
Intoxicated Minors	63
Disorderly Conduct	
Bawdy House Frequenter	48
Corner Lounge	22
Disorderly Conduct	19
Frequents Drinking Place	22
Vagrancy	
Loitering, Prowl, Peep	58
Vagrancy	1
Gambling	
Gambling Highway	74
Gambling House Proprietor	254
Gambling Frequenter	36
Lottery, Numbers	36
Truancy	1
False Alarm	60
Trespassing	1
Incorrigible	122
Runaway	30
Perjury	842
Obscene Phone Calls	33

SOURCE: Correspondence from Marvin E. Wolfgang.

Table 4-C Offenses Included in Each Seriousness Level

Level	Seriousness Score Range	Elements Offense/Included
I	1–99	Status offenses, general (1)
		Trespass (1)
		Disorderly conduct (19)
		Resisting arrest (30)
		Runaway (30)
		Illegal discharge of firearm (31)
		Liquor law violation (40)
		Receiving stolen property (87)
II	100–349	Less than $10 stolen (100)
		Minor injuries inflicted (100)
		Premises entered (100, 200, 300 for 1, 2, or 3)
		Malicious damage or mischief (100)
		Weapons charges, other than gun (114)
		Incorrigibility (122)
		Commercial sex (131)
		Motor vehicle violations (134)[a]
		Possession of drugs (141)
		$10–$250 stolen (200)
		1 motor vehicle stolen (200)
		Nonweapon intimidation (200)
		$251–$2,000 stolen (300)
III	350–699	Possession of dangerous weapons (353)
		Sexual abuse (356)
		Injury, treated and discharged (400)
		Intimidation by weapon (400)
		$2,001–$9,000 stolen (400)
		Debauching morals of a minor (431)
		$9,001–$30,000 stolen (500)
		Incest, brother-sister (600)
		$30,001–$80,000 stolen (600)
IV	700 or greater	Injury, required hospitalization (700)
		Over $80,000 stolen (700)
		Perjury (842)
		Forcible rape (1000)
		Sale of drugs (1010)
		Homicide (2600)

[a] Taken from the average score for the Philadelphia cohort—no equivalent in the scoring system.

Appendix D Three Program Models

Few treatment or prevention programs take in delinquents with histories of violence. Fewer still pay special attention to them. It is customary for violent children to be rejected by one program after another and, between rejections, returned to the streets where they get into further trouble, until finally they are removed to training schools to be temporarily controlled but rarely treated effectively.

In the course of this study, however, a handful of programs were discovered to which this stereotype does not apply. They are willing to take in violent children and have developed methodologies that appear to have some positive effects on their behavior. The examples described below are not the universe of such programs (although a small universe it is), but they are representative of the diversity of approaches that have been tried. Unfortunately, for the most part, formal evaluations of their effects on subsequent violent behavior have not yet been done. No scientifically supportable claims can therefore be made that they "work." Nevertheless, their less rigorously observed results are impressive and deserve, at a minimum, to be studied more carefully in the future and perhaps replicated in other settings.

Downeyside

Downeyside is a placement program that combines a number of desirable attributes: community involvement, continuity of relationships, and group placement. Founded in 1968 in Springfield, Massachusetts by a Catholic priest, Father Paul Engle, Downeyside has sponsored about twenty group homes in ten communities in western Massachusetts, and is considering expanding its work to include Connecticut.

The Downeyside objective, broadly, is to create families for children in trouble—practically from scratch. The process begins with the identification of a community willing to participate in the program. Evidence of community commitment is secured through formation of a local sponsoring group that raises enough money for a down payment on a house within the community. Volunteers contribute time and energy to put the house in order. In the meantime, Downeyside screens and accepts a couple to become foster parents to a group of children. The couple may or may not have children of their own already. Training and orientation in being Downeyside parents are given by others who have already been through the experience.

Children selected for placement in the home have no functioning families of their own and are nearly always referred to the program by state agencies. Many have records of serious delinquency and have failed in other treatment or correctional programs; some have histories of violence. Father Paul says, "On the whole, we do not take severely acting-out youngsters," but the program does welcome children with "noticeable antisocial behavior that has threatened the welfare of others."

The children are placed as a group, all at once, into the new home—up to six children at a time. Most children are 14–16 years old at the time they are enrolled. After a trial period of three months, in which both parents and children can test the viability of the relationship, the children are assured of a place in their new "family" for three years. In practice, Downeyside homes often become the child's family "for life," as contacts are maintained long after the formal relationship ends. Only one "family" is placed with each set of parents; no parents repeat the experience.

Parents are responsible for the care, supervision, and discipline of the children, for assuring that they attend local schools, and for appearing on their behalf in court when necessary. Because it is a demanding task, both members of a couple are paid to be full-time parents during the first year. After that, one may elect to return to an outside job. They receive backup support from other parents, meeting regularly as an "extended family" to share experiences and advice and prop each other up with moral support. Downeyside directors and professional social workers are also available to provide guidance and help.

The costs of maintaining the family groups, including food, clothing, mortgage payments on the house, and other expenses, are covered by foster care grants from the state.

The underlying philosophy of the program is simple. Children need not merely food and shelter, but the security of knowing that they belong someplace and that someone cares for them. Such security is rarely found in the institutional settings to which most severely delinquent children without functioning families are sent. Downeyside believes that the full-time attention of a family can reverse a life of delinquent, antisocial behavior.

As of December 1975, approximately 175 children had been placed in Downeyside homes. "Success" rates are difficult to measure, but staff estimate that 121 of the 175 children have formed "permanent" relationships with their foster families. No data on recidivism of offenders in the program are available.

Father Paul and other Downeyside directors admit that their homes are not appropriate for all children. They screen applications carefully and exclude children with severe psychiatric problems, as well as those who are deemed too uncontrollable to function in the open environment of the family. At the same time, they are willing to take in many children considered too violent for admission to other residential programs. The program thus represents a promising alternative for that portion of violent delinquents who can be treated in community-based programs. Father Paul and others associated with Downeyside see no reason why it could not work in an inner-city environment as well as it has worked in western Massachusetts.

Outward Bound

Outward Bound is a program of severe physical challenge open to adolescents of all backgrounds and from all parts of the country. An adaptation of a British wartime survival training program for merchant seamen, the American version is carried out in six locations, each specializing in its own kind of survival experience: the Colorado School, which features wilderness hiking and camping, rock climbing, and rapelling; the Minnesota School, which focuses on canoeing and camping in the wilderness; the Hurricane Island School in Maine, which concentrates on seamanship and navigation; and three others more recently established.

The essence of the Outward Bound experience lies in meeting a programmed series of physical challenges in a small group setting, designed to improve a youth's self-confidence and ability to cooperate constructively with others. A basic twenty-six-day course involves physical conditioning, technical and safety training, and training in teamwork, capped by a demanding wilderness adventure. The Colorado and Hurricane Island schools put somewhat more emphasis on severe physical challenge, felt danger and excitement than the Minnesota School, which also stresses physical challenge and endurance but is structured to focus more on interpersonal relationships and self-reflection.

Although Outward Bound takes in youths from all backgrounds, a special effort has been made to deal with delinquents; more than 500 have been through the program since it began in 1962. Several states now regularly send delinquent youth to Outward Bound as a treatment alternative. It is the only program among those described here to have been formally evaluated with regard to its impact on delinquency. In 1971, Kelly and Baer[1] reported a study in which sixty delinquent males from Massachusetts were enrolled in one or another of the three existing Outward Bound programs and compared to a matched control group of sixty delinquents given standard dispositions, including institutional placement and probation.

The results showed lower overall recidivism rates for the experimental group (20 percent) than for the control group (42 percent) after one year on parole. The control recidivism rate corresponded to the average for Massachusetts delinquents committed to the Division of Youth Services. Among the three programs, however, the two that stressed danger and excitement showed the best results. Colorado with no recidivism and Hurricane Island with a rate of 11 percent. Minnesota had a 42 percent recidivism rate, the same as the control group.

The interpretation put on these results by the authors is that they "appear to support the belief that delinquent adolescents are action-oriented and respond to programs which challenge them in the sphere of physical activity. . . . On the other hand, programs which call for consistent physical activity and endurance but without periods of high excitement or real danger are not successful in reducing recidivism."[2] The severe physical challenge of Outward Bound appears to fill a delin-

---

[1] Francis J. Kelly and Daniel J. Baer, "Physical Challenge as a Treatment for Delinquency," *Crime and Delinquency* (October 1971); 437–445.
[2] Ibid., pp. 440–441.

quent's need to prove his masculinity, a need grounded, in all probability, in a deep sense of insecurity.

The study also showed that the program works best for those whose first court appearance occurs after the onset of adolescence instead of before; for those who have only one commitment to an institution instead of two or more; for delinquents as contrasted with status offenders; for youths from intact homes instead of broken homes; and, in general for those who are responding to an adolescent crisis instead of to a character defect.[3]

Since the 1971 evaluation, Kelly has completed a five-year follow-up. The results fit a common pattern in delinquency studies: the significant benefits seen in the first year washed out after five. The difference between the recidivism (measured as any subsequent arrest) of the experimental group (38 percent) and the controls (53 percent) is not statistically significant. This underscores the need for additional programming to capitalize on the initial gains from Outward Bound. Even in the absence of additional programming, however, there remained a noticeable qualitative and quantitative difference between the behavior of the experimentals and that of the controls. The subsequent offenses of the Outward Bound group were fewer and less serious than those of the controls and began at a later interval after release. Also, the Outward Bound group spent less subsequent time in detention. Thus, while they may not have been completely "cured" of their delinquent behavior, they did become less of a burden to society than they would otherwise have been.

When the Kelly and Baer study was done, delinquents with crimes of violence against persons were not included in the program. It has since been modified to admit them as well. Other modifications have been developed in an effort to reach the hard-core youth with two or more institutional commitments. Professionals dealing with delinquents, including a psychiatrist in a Massachusetts court clinic and the former director of the New York State Division for Youth, give Outward Bound high marks and consider it to have excellent potential as a treatment alternative for certain types of violence-prone juveniles. The cost of the program ($500–$600 per participant for the standard twenty-six-day course), although high, is well within reason.

Outward Bound is not a panacea. Among its limitations is the fact that it appears to work only if the participant wants the experience. Forced

_____

[3] Ibid., pp. 441–44. Martinson also found benefit in Outward Bound, reporting a study by Miner (1967) that showed the program "did indeed work in reducing recidivism rates." Martinson, op. cit., p. 38.

attendance is generally counterproductive. Thus, it may be impossible to motivate some inner-city youths to take part. Participation is also proscribed for youths with signs of emotional pathology, which leaves out a significant portion of the more seriously violent delinquents. Another problem is that the existing Outward Bound schools have a relatively limited capacity and serve many groups other than the delinquent population, so that the numbers able to benefit are restricted. Perhaps the most significant drawback is that the wilderness experience, although intense, is only a brief exposure. Without follow-up, there is substantial risk that the beneficial impact of the experience will wear off. Consequently, Outward Bound should be used as part of a continuous program that permits participants to incorporate the experience into a changed self-image over a much longer period of time.

In recognition of these limitations, the Colorado and Hurricane Island Schools have developed a capability for extending assistance to other institutions interested in developing Outward Bound–like programs as part of their rehabilitation programs. As a result, in the past five years a number of adaptations of the program, including several aimed solely at inner-city delinquent youth, have been tested with promising results. One worth watching in particular has recently been launched under the sponsorship of the Fund for the City of New York and is aimed at New York City youth committed to the state's most secure training school for violent offenses.

Elan

Among programs willing to take hard-core delinquents with violent records, one stands out for its eagerness to do so—Elan, a milieu therapy program in Maine. It excludes only psychotics and (hedging slightly) the most extreme psychopaths who present an immediate danger to others in the program. It takes many violent, disturbed children, however, including drug addicts, murderers, rapists, potential suicides, children with long assault and robbery records, and even arsonists. Elan staff members pride themselves on giving up on no one. They do not expel residents, and when one runs away, they bring the individual back. (One arsonist who did $4,800 worth of damage to an Elan building was reportedly given a broom, told to clean up the ashes, and then sent back to work in the program.)

Residents live in twenty-five-bed houses located on three "campuses" in rural Maine. Like many milieu therapy programs, its staff consists primarily of paraprofessionals, mostly graduates of the program. However, paraprofessional residential staff are backed up by a professional group that includes a psychiatrist (one of the cofounders), psychologist, medical doctor, registered nurse, and twenty-three teachers (some of whom are also paraprofessionals).

Elan's program consists essentially of work, therapy, and education. The residents, who are almost completely responsible for the management and maintenance of the program, are organized into departments handling business, building maintenance, communications, kitchen service, and medical matters. A variety of individual and group therapy approaches, including primal scream therapy, encounter groups, sensivity groups, and occasionally individual psychotherapeutic counselling are built into the program. Individually tailored educational programs are available to each resident.

The highly stratified organizational structure of the residential units resembles the army's. New residents begin at the bottom of the organization, taking on the more menial maintenance tasks, progressing up the ladder of authority and responsibility as they demonstrate their capacity to handle more demanding assignments. Advanced residents are responsible at all times for supervising and training newcomers in their assignments. "Quality," "pride," and "self-discipline" are the goals of the work program.

Motivation and control are managed by a lavish system of rewards (promotions, recreation time, occasional passes to visit home, and other privileges) and "consequences" (demotions, public denunciations, loss of privileges, controlled encounters in therapeutic groups). Three cardinal rules ban sex, physical violence, and drugs. But when these rules are broken, as they sometimes are, the offender is not banished as he or she might be elsewhere, but is subjected to the negative "consequences" built into the program. The ultimate sanction for physical violence, perhaps the most delicate problem staff must deal with, is called "the ring." In the ring a compulsive, unreconstructed bully is outfitted with sixteen-ounce gloves and headgear, and meets a succession of similarly outfitted house residents, matched for size and strength, in one-minute rounds, "until he (or she) understands that the community will not tolerate physical aggression." More than any other aspect of the program, the ring has stirred controversy among outside evaluators. The staff maintains, however, that the most serious resulting injury has been a bloody nose or a cut lip. And they swear by its effectiveness in ending assaultive behavior.

The approximately 200 residents share one common characteristic:

their failure in other treatment or correctional programs. In other respects they are a diverse group. Approximately 60 percent come from "middle-class" families, with parents who foot the bill. The other 40 percent are wards of the state for one reason or another—usually their delinquent behavior.[4] Referrals come from ten to twelve states. Residents range in age from 14 to about 28.

The usual length of stay is twelve to eighteen months, longer for the toughest cases. To leave the program successfully ("graduation" is a term reserved for a smaller number who pass special tests by an interviewing board), a resident must have progressed sufficiently in school, learned to "work with quality," participated in therapy and, above all, demonstrated a capacity for relationship based on mutuality and respect instead of manipulation and exploitation.

A thorough follow-up of participants has not yet been done. Elan staff claim a retention rate of 90 percent and a recidivism rate (defined as any subsequent contact with "authorities") of 20 percent. If they could be substantiated, these figures would be impressive. The cost of the program is $1,200 per person per month, a rate estimated by the Medical Director to be one-third to one-fifth that of a psychiatric hospital, or "$114 more per month than a Massachusetts foster home costs." The cost covers all living, educational, treatment, and medical expenses.

An official of Connecticut's Department of Children and Youth Services, which placed thirty-two children at Elan between April 1973 and December 1975, says the Department is extremely pleased with the results and, if intake permitted, would "probably have half of our kids up there."

Elan, however, has been embroiled in controversy. A review team from the Illinois Department of Children and Family Services visited Elan in July 1975 to evaluate the program. The team reacted so negatively to what it saw—charging "inhumane" treatment of children, brainwashing, forced labor, and physical abuse—that it immediately removed the eleven Illinois children in the program and took them home.[5] (On the way home, three escaped and ran back to Elan.) The governor of Maine ordered an investigation, and Massachusetts, Connecticut, and Rhode Island sent investigating teams as well. In the end, three of the four states gave their endorsement to the program.

---

[4] Interestingly, private referrals and state referrals tend to be placed in different houses. The staff reports that the reason for this is that, in their experience, the private referrals' rejection of "middle-class" life goals has a demoralizing effect on state wards, who want to believe that such goals are meaningful.

[5] "Evaluation Report: Elan I Corporation," Illinois Department of Children and Family Services, July 22–23, 1975. (Mimeo.)

Massachusetts withheld its endorsement and froze intake pending the working out of "concerns around the use of the boxing ring as a therapeutic tool in the program."[6] Referrals from Massachusetts have not yet been reinstated, by mutual agreement between Elan and Massachusetts. In reports filed at the time, however, the Massachusetts team and the others found no convincing proof for some of the allegations in the Illinois report, reserved judgment on others, and obtained Elan's agreement to terminate use of some disciplinary measures, notably spanking.

The controversy surrounding the Illinois allegations raises some difficult issues. Elan's program offends a number of thoughtful observers concerned about children's rights. More than the other programs described here, Elan comes close to the line that separates treatment from punishment or control. On the other hand, the children it enrolls also come much closer to the line that divides those traditionally regarded as "treatable" from those not so. Staff have arguments to defend each questionable practice, from monitoring phone calls and denying certain kinds of mail, to the ring. In dealing with the highly disturbed, manipulative children, they maintain, the full range of adult rights cannot apply, because total control is crucial to effective therapy for this group in order to screen out reinforcements of negative behavior. Moreover, children who participate in the program also strongly defend the need for the controls and disciplinary measures used. On the other hand, it is at least conceivable that a program placing greater emphasis on respecting civil rights of enrolled children might have the same impact. To know whether that is true or not, Elan's results would have to be matched against those of a similar program that had a stronger civil rights emphasis—a comparison that has not been done.

Elan raises other important questions. With the exception of variations in educational programming and placement of participants who are more violent or more prone to run away in a "secure" house, virtually all participants are subjected to the same treatment. For the most part, applications from parents and state agencies are accepted as there are openings, with an apparent minimum of screening by Elan staff. Certainly, few if any children are rejected because of the seriousness of their records. Psychotics are not accepted, but few diagnostic distinctions beyond that are made. The question arises whether the Elan treatment package is appropriate for all those sent there, or whether some might not be able to benefit from other forms of treatment that are less intrusive and less demanding. Staff cite the failure of most participants

---

[6] Letter from Joseph M. Leavey, Commissioner, Massachusetts Department of Youth Services, to Elan, September 22, 1975.

in other treatment programs before their referral to Elan as proof that nothing else would work with them. Yet, without knowing more about the characteristics of Elan participants and their similarities and differences with participants in other treatment programs, and about the relative response of various kinds of participants to treatment, it is not possible to know for certain whether Elan's brand of milieu therapy is equally effective with all or whether some other approach might not be more effective with some.

A comparative research effort involving Elan or some similar program would be an important step toward answering these and other questions. Although anecdotal evidence, observation, and discussions with program residents leave the strong impression that this is an idea that works for many of the most difficult cases, it will remain just an impression (and one that is frequently disputed) until firmer data are available.

Appendix E Selected Bibliography

Bartollas, Clemens, Stuart J. Miller, and Simon Dimitz. *Juvenile Victimization: The Institutional Paradox.* New York: John Wiley & Sons, 1976.

Block, Herbert, and Gilbert Geis. *Man, Crime, and Society.* New York: Random House, 1962.

Bowman, Paul H. "Effects of a Revised School Program on Potential Delinquents." *Annals of the American Academy of Political and Social Sciences* 322 (1959): 53–61.

Clark, J. P., and E. P. Wenninger. "Socioeconomic Class and Area as Correlates of Illegal Behavior Among Juveniles." *American Sociological Review* 27, no. 6 (December 1962).

Clarke, Stevens H. "Getting 'em Out of Circulation: Does Incarceration of Juvenile Offenders Reduce Crime?" *Journal of Criminal Law and Criminology* 5, no. 4 (1974).

Clarke, Stevens H. "Juvenile Offender Programs and Delinquency Prevention." *Crime and Delinquency Literature* 6, no. 3 (September 1974).

Coates, Robert B., Alden D. Miller, and Lloyd E. Ohlin. "Exploratory Analysis of Recidivism and Cohort Data on the Massachusetts Youth Correctional System." Harvard Law School, Center for Criminal Justice (July 1975).

Cocozza, J. J., and H. J. Steadman. "Some Refinements in the Measurement and Prediction of Dangerous Behavior." *American Journal of Psychiatry* 131, no. 9 (1974).

Curtis, Lynn A. *Criminal Violence.* Lexington, Mass.: D.C. Heath & Co., 1974.

Dershowitz, A. M. "The Law of Dangerousness: Some Fictions about Predictions." *Journal of Legal Education* 23 (1970).

259

Doleschal, Eugene. "Hidden Crime." *Crime and Delinquency Literature* 2, no. 5 (1970).

Doleschal, Eugene, and Nora Klapmuts. "Toward a New Criminology." *Crime and Delinquency Literature* (December 1973).

Elliot, Delbert S., and Harwin L. Voss. *Delinquency and Dropout.* Lexington, Mass.: D.C. Heath & Co., 1974.

Fox, Sanford. "Juvenile Justice Reform: Innovations in Scotland." *American Criminal Law Review* 12, no. 61 (1974).

Fox, Sanford. "The Reform of Juvenile Justice: The Child's Right to Punishment." *Juvenile Justice* 25, no. 402 (August 1974).

Frankel, Marvin. *Criminal Sentences: Law Without Order.* New York: Hill and Wang, 1972.

Glaser, Daniel. *Strategic Criminal Justice Planning.* Center for Studies of Crime and Delinquency, National Institute of Mental Health, 1975.

Gold, Martin. *Delinquent Behavior in an American City.* Belmont, Calif.: Brooks-Cole, 1970.

Gold, Martin. "Undetected Delinquent Behavior." *Journal of Research in Crime and Delinquency* 3, no. 1 (1966).

Gold, Martin, and David J. Reimer. "Changing Patterns of Delinquent Behavior Among Americans 13 through 16 Years Old: 1967–1972." *Crime and Delinquency Literature* 7, no. 4 (December 1975).

Goldstein, Joseph, Alfred Solnit, and Anna Freud. *Beyond the Best Interests of the Child.* New York: Free Press, 1973.

Harper, Mary Jill Robinson. "Courts, Doctors, and Delinquents: An Inquiry into the Uses of Psychiatry in Youth Corrections." *Smith College Studies in Social Work,* 44, no. 3 (June 1974).

Jesinkey, William J., and Jane R. Stein. *Lost Children.* Long Island City, New York: Alternative Solutions for Exceptional Children, Inc., 1974.

King, Charles H. "The Ego and the Integration of Violence in Homicidal Youth." *American Journal of Orthopsychiatry* 45, no. 1 (January 1975).

Klapmuts, Nora. "Community Alternatives to Prison." *Crime and Delinquency Literature* (June 1973).

Kozol, Harry L., Richard J. Boucher, and Ralph Garofalo. "The Diagnosis and Treatment of Dangerousness." *Crime and Delinquency Literature* 18, no. 4 (October 1972).

Lerman, Paul. *Community Treatment and Social Control.* Chicago: University of Chicago Press, 1975.

Levin, Mark M., and Rosemary C. Sarri, *Juvenile Delinquency: A Comparative Analysis of Legal Codes in the U.S.* National Assessment of Juvenile Corrections (June 1974).

Martinson, Robert. "What Works? Questions and Answers about Prison Reform." *The Public Interest* 35 (Spring 1974).

Morris, Norval. "Punishment and Rehabilitation." National Council on Crime and Delinquency, 1965. (Mimeo.)

Morris, Norval. *The Future of Imprisonment*. Chicago: University of Chicago Press, 1974.

Mulvihill, Donald J., Melvin M. Tumin, and Lynn A. Curtis. *Crimes of Violence: A Staff Report Submitted to the National Commission on the Causes and Prevention of Violence*. Washington, D.C.: U.S. Government Printing Office, 1969.

Murray, Charles A. *The Link Between Learning Disabilities and Juvenile Delinquency*. Washington, D.C.: American Institutes for Research, 1976.

National Advisory Commission on Criminal Justice Standards and Goals. *Report on Community Crime Prevention*. Washington, D.C.: U.S. Government Printing Office, 1973.

National Advisory Commission on Criminal Justice Standards and Goals. *Report on Corrections*. Washington D.C.: U.S. Government Printing Office, 1973.

National Council on Crime and Delinquency, Paramus, New Jersey. *Juvenile Justice Confounded: Pretensions and Realities of Treatment Services*. Report of the Committee on Mental Health Services Inside and Outside the Family Court in the City of New York, 1972.

National Institute of Mental Health. "Teenage Delinquency in Small Town America." Research Report no. 4, 1974.

New York State Board of Social Welfare. *Foster Care Needs and Alternatives to Placement: A Projection for 1975–1985*. November 1975.

New York State Division of Criminal Justice Services, Juvenile Justice Institute. "Juvenile Injustice." October 1973.

New York State Office of Court Administration. Office of Children's Services. "Juvenile Injustice," October 1973.

Polk, Kenneth, Dean Frease, and Lynn F. Richmond. "Social Class, School Experience, and Delinquency." *Criminology* 12, no. 1 (1974).

President's Commission on Law Enforcement and the Administration of Justice. Task Force on Juvenile Delinquency. *Task Force Report: Juvenile Delinquency and Youth Crime*. Washington, D.C.: U.S. Government Printing Office, 1967.

Richette, Lisa. *The Throwaway Children*. Philadelphia: J. B. Lippincott Co., 1969.

Robison, James O., and Gerald Smith. "The Effectiveness of Correctional Programs." *Crime and Delinquency Literature* 17, no. 1 (January 1971).

Russell, Donald Hayes. "Juvenile Delinquency." *Psychiatric Annals* 5, no. 1 (January 1975).

Russell, D. H., and G. P. Harper. "Who Are Our Assaultive Juveniles? A Study of 100 Cases." *Journal of Forensic Sciences* 18 (October 1973).

Sarri, Rosemary. *Under Lock and Key*. National Assessment of Juvenile Corrections, 1975.

Sellin, Thorsten, and Marvin E. Wolfgang. *The Measurement of Delinquency*. New York: John Wiley & Sons, 1964.

Statsky, William P. "Community Courts: Decentralizing Juvenile Jurisprudence." *Capital University Law Review* 3, no. 1 (1974): 1–51.

Gilmore, C. P. "The Strange Malady Called Learning Disability." *New York Times Magazine,* March 2, 1975.

Street, David, and Robert Vinter. *Organization for Treatment.* New York: The Free Press, 1966.

U.S. Department of Justice. Law Enforcement Assistance Administration. "Children in Custody: Advance Report on the Juvenile Detention and Correctional Facility Census of 1972–1973."

U.S. Department of Justice. Law Enforcement Assistance Administration. "Children in Custody: A Report on the Juvenile Detention and Correctional Facility Census of 1971."

U.S. Department of Justice, National Criminal Justice Information and Statistics Service. *Criminal Victimization Surveys in 13 American Cities.* Washington, D.C.: U.S. Government Printing Office, 1975.

Vera Institute of Justice. *Felony Arrests: Their Prosecution and Disposition in New York City's Courts.* New York: Vera, 1977.

Vinter, Robert D., George Downs, and John Hall. *Juvenile Corrections in the States: Residential Programs and Deinstitutionalization.* National Assessment of Juvenile Corrections, University of Michigan, November 1975.

Wenk, Ernst, James O. Robison, and Gerald W. Smith. "Can Violence Be Predicted?" *Crime and Delinquency Literature* 18, no. 4 (October 1972).

Wheeler, Stanton, ed. *Controlling Delinquents.* New York: John Wiley & Sons, 1968.

Wilson, James Q. "Lock 'em Up," *New York Times Magazine,* March 9, 1975.

Wilson, James Q. *Thinking About Crime.* New York: Basic Books, Inc., 1975.

Wolfgang, Marvin E. "Crime in a Birth Cohort." *Proceedings of the American Philosophical Society* 117, no. 5 (October 1973).

Wolfgang, Marvin E. "The Culture of Youth," Appendix I of The Task Force Report on Juvenile Delinquency and Youth Crime. The President's Commission on Law Enforcement and the Administration of Justice.

Wolfgang, Marvin E., and Franco Ferracuti. *The Subculture of Violence.* London: Tavistock Publications, 1967.

Wolfgang, Marvin E., Robert M. Figlio, and Thorsten Sellin. *Delinquency in a Birth Cohort.* Chicago: University of Chicago Press, 1972.

Zimring, Franklin E. "Dealing with Youth Crime: National Needs and Federal Priorities." September 1975. (Mimeo.)

Zimring, Franklin E. "Measuring the Import of Pretrial Diversion from the Criminal Justice System." *University of Chicago Law Review* 41 (1974): 224–241.

Index